The Other Veterans of World War II

The Other Veterans

of World War II

Stories from Behind the Front Lines

Rona Simmons

THE KENT STATE UNIVERSITY PRESS

Kent, Ohio

To Bill, Joe, Bob, Eleanor, Bud, Ike, Louis, George,
James, Orin, William, Jack, Howard, Joyce, Frank,
Josephine, Marie, Randy, and Pete

All of the real heroes are not storybook combat fighters. . . .

Every single man in this Army plays a vital role. Don't ever let up.

Don't ever think that your job is unimportant. Every man has a

job to do and he must do it. Every man is a vital link in the great chain.

GEORGE S. PATTON,
General, US Army

Contents

Prologue

My father's story was the first war story I heard, fifty years after he stepped from the cockpit of his P-38 fighter aircraft for the last time. He was one of sixteen million men and women who served in World War II, and like many others of his cohort, he had never shared his experience. The war was long over, the United States had moved on, and so had he. But, at my urging, together we flipped through his photo album and opened his string-tied folder of yellowed rosters to relive each assignment, each raid over North Africa and Italy, each medal earned. Throughout our discussion, he dismissed his service and his deeds as nothing remarkable, but, at the end, he smiled and rose, standing perhaps a hair taller than when we had begun.

Years later, on the cusp of the seventy-fifth anniversary of the end of the war, realizing how many stories like my father's had not been told and would soon be lost, I began searching for veterans who would share their memories. I looked past the popular big-screen panoramas of artillery fire bursting over embattled beaches and dive bombers strafing ships at sea to discover the men and women who had served in noncombat positions, behind the lines. They were the people who had made it possible for my father and the millions of other frontline soldiers, sailors, airmen, and marines to carry out their duties and who helped deliver them safely home. They made up more than half of the US military forces in World War II.

The first story I found was that of Lt. Col. Francis D. Peterson with the army's Graves Registration Service. His moving tale of designing and building cemeteries only hours after a battle—then burying the fallen American, ally, and enemy alike—illustrated for me the enormous gap in my knowledge of the war and of the men and material that compose an army, navy, or air force. I suspected my contemporaries shared that gap in knowledge.

Inspired, I traveled to air shows, attended veterans' meetings, and spoke to authors of military history books and former soldiers who had written their memoirs or were willing to talk about their experience. The yearlong search brought me to nineteen veterans and their sons and daughters, most of whom thought they had nothing to say.

The nineteen veterans whose stories are told here represent a tiny fraction of the sixteen million Americans who served in uniform during World War II. The tellers of these tales did not fly through flak to escort bombers to their targets and then limp back to their base with fuel tank gauges screaming empty like my father did. They did not scramble across mine-strewn beaches, tramp through knife-edged grass in damp jungles, or fire a single shot. Like their counterparts who served on the front lines, however, they, too, rushed to enlist on hearing of the attack on Pearl Harbor. They served just as proudly and proved every bit as instrumental in winning the war, whether they served in Europe, in North Africa, in the Pacific, or at home.

They, too, have stories to tell.

Like George Keating from Cosmopolis, Washington, who expertly wielded crowfoot and spanner wrenches, hammers, and pressure gauges to keep B-17 bombers aloft and saw each of his planes return safely to their base in England. Or like Randy Bostwick from Niles, Ohio, who, while artillery shells flew overhead, loaded cartons of medical supplies into the back of his truck and then delivered them just in time to aid stations and field hospitals. And, like Eleanor Millican Frye from Griffin, Georgia, who, when she wasn't having the time of her life in Charleston or New Orleans, read navigational charts and assigned ships to positions within convoys for their voyages across the Atlantic—positions where she hoped they would be safe from German U-boats.

The stories are told as the veterans remembered them, both with the perspective of time and the flaws introduced by the passing of seven decades. During the interviews, some of the veterans cited dates and times and places without a moment's hesitation, while others struggled to find the words they wanted. Some needed a gentle nudge to rekindle their thoughts or to glance through folders bursting with timeworn records or to touch a keepsake. The mementos of those times lit their faces, and, as they spoke, their words unfroze their arthritic hands and squared their shoulders as if they were fresh faced and twenty-one again.

To plug holes and stitch together fragments, facts, and figures from official military studies, unit histories, celebrated biographies, unpublished memoirs, and veterans' diaries and letters supplement the accounts. These references also reveal little-known but fascinating aspects of the war such as the government's takeover of hundreds of US colleges for military training; the staggering amount of supplies needed to sustain a single soldier for one day; the mountains of trucks, tanks, and jeeps the military left behind; and the fact that after the war there was not one American cemetery in Normandy but 350 scattered across Europe alone.

The stories begin long before the war, when the men and women portrayed here were young boys and girls or teenagers. They went to high school, worked on farms and in factories, and went to college. Some lied about their age to enlist or counted the days to eligibility. Soon, however, they were kissing their mothers, sisters, and wives or sweethearts good-bye, turning to brush a tear from their cheek, and rushing aboard a train or ship, eager, fearless, and naive. After the war, they returned home with the same fervent belief in their country with which they had joined. They married and had families of their own—at last count totaling 210 children, grandchildren, and great-grandchildren—and moved on with their lives.

As it unfolds, this book follows the recruit from induction and training to traveling to their base of operation, to performing their duties during the war, to coming home, experiencing the war as they might have. Along the way, it contemplates the roll of the dice that sent one man to combat and another to noncombat and asks: How did they come to play a noncombat role? How did their service differ from the soldier who saw combat? How, after the war had ended, did they measure their contribution? The veterans answer these questions and more as they tell their stories. But they do much more. They tell their stories for their descendants, the descendants of all Americans, and for readers everywhere, and in doing so they pass on their memories, bits and pieces of history, and their spirit.

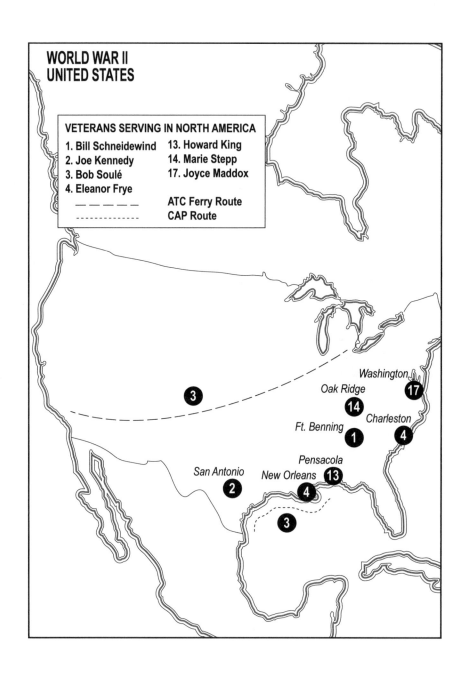

**WORLD WAR II
UNITED STATES**

VETERANS SERVING IN NORTH AMERICA
1. Bill Schneidewind
2. Joe Kennedy
3. Bob Soulé
4. Eleanor Frye

13. Howard King
14. Marie Stepp
17. Joyce Maddox

— — — — — ATC Ferry Route
. . . . CAP Route

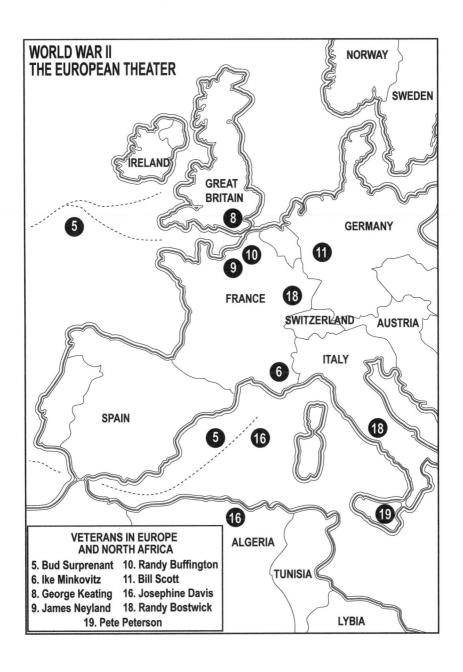

WORLD WAR II
THE EUROPEAN THEATER

NORWAY

SWEDEN

IRELAND

GREAT
BRITAIN

⑧

⑤

GERMANY

⑩

⑪

⑨

FRANCE

⑱

SWITZERLAND

AUSTRIA

ITALY

⑥

SPAIN

⑤

⑯

⑱

⑯

⑲

ALGERIA

TUNISIA

LYBIA

VETERANS IN EUROPE
AND NORTH AFRICA
5. Bud Surprenant   10. Randy Buffington
6. Ike Minkovitz   11. Bill Scott
8. George Keating   16. Josephine Davis
9. James Neyland   18. Randy Bostwick
        19. Pete Peterson

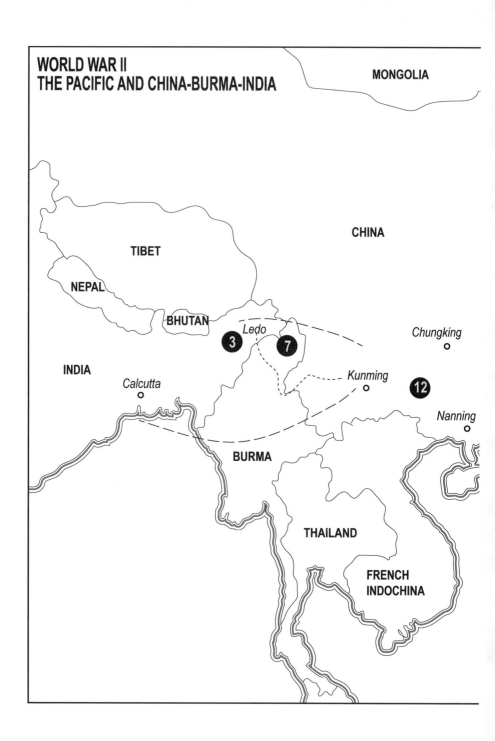

WORLD WAR II
THE PACIFIC AND CHINA-BURMA-INDIA

MONGOLIA

CHINA

TIBET

NEPAL

BHUTAN

Ledo

Chungking

INDIA

Kunming

Calcutta

Nanning

BURMA

THAILAND

FRENCH
INDOCHINA

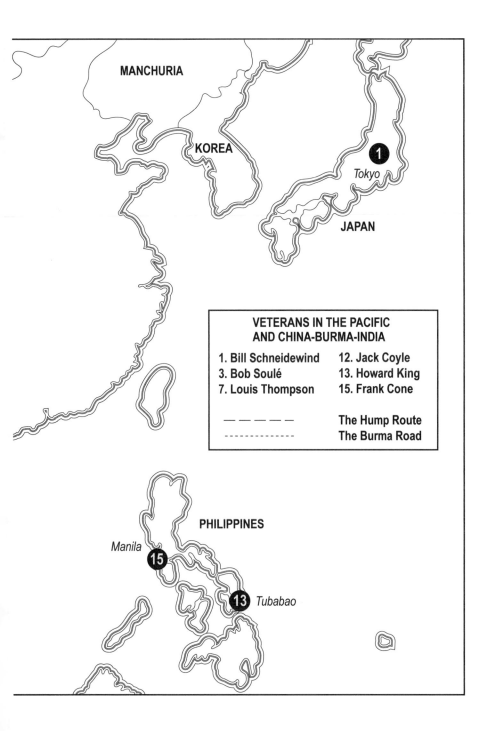

MANCHURIA

KOREA

JAPAN

Tokyo

**VETERANS IN THE PACIFIC
AND CHINA-BURMA-INDIA**

1. Bill Schneidewind   12. Jack Coyle
3. Bob Soulé   13. Howard King
7. Louis Thompson   15. Frank Cone

— — — — —   The Hump Route
- - - - - - - - - - - - -   The Burma Road

PHILIPPINES

Manila

Tubabao

PART I

The Army Knows Best

*This is no time for "fancy dans" who won't hit the line with
all they have on every play, unless they can call the signals.*

OMAR N. BRADLEY,
General, US Army

By the summer of 1940, the borders within Europe and Asia had been redrawn. Japan occupied large swaths of China and Indochina while Nazi Germany controlled Europe from the Pyrenees Mountains to the Russian frontier. The United States could no longer maintain its decadelong stance on isolationism or its pretense at neutrality. The country could no longer sit on the sidelines.

The United States, however, was grossly unprepared for war. Regular army, navy, and marine forces stood at five hundred thousand, a fraction of the size of the German and Japanese forces.[1] Germany boasted a military of 4.5 million men with quality and efficiency in firepower and armed forces far exceeding any of its rivals, and the Japanese claimed a fighting force of nearly two million.[2]

Thus, on September 16, 1940, President Franklin Delano Roosevelt, recognizing the need to prepare the country for war, signed the Selective Training and Service Act, creating the country's first peacetime draft. It was that stroke of his pen, not the surprise attack on Pearl Harbor a year later, that started the war for families across the United States. The law required the country's twenty million male citizens and residents aged twenty-one to thirty-five to register with their local draft board. There, the civilian staff classified registrants as either available (class I) or deferred (classes II through IV) and further by subcategories for each class. Men assigned a designation of I-A were deemed fit for general military service and issued a draft card and a draft number.[3]

The first draft was held a month later on October 29 in a public ceremony infused with Americana. Nine thousand opaque capsules containing draft numbers were placed in the same glass bowl used for the First World War. The capsules were stirred with a wooden spoon made from a beam of Independence Hall, and a strip of cloth from a chair used at the signing of the Declaration of Independence served as a blindfold for Secretary of War Henry Stimson. As reporters' flashbulbs popped, Stimson withdrew a capsule and handed the slip of paper it contained to the president. Roosevelt read the first number to the assembled crowd and to the millions listening by radio: "Serial number 158." With that announcement, some six thousand men with cards bearing the number 158 would soon receive an induction letter in their mailboxes, inviting them to report to their local induction center.[4]

Of the sixteen million people who served in uniform during the war, ten million (60 percent) entered through the draft and six million (40 percent) volunteered. The military had naively expected the volunteers, who had the advantage of being able to choose their branch of service, to enlist without regard to branch of service. Ninety-five percent of the volunteers, however, selected the navy, marines, or air corps. Only 5 percent chose to serve in the army. They had heard their fathers and uncles tell of the horrors of fighting as doughboys in the trenches during World War I. They had only to walk around town to see their maimed and blinded neighbors, veterans whose lives would never be the same.[5]

To make up for the imbalance, the vast majority of the draftees were funneled to the army—at least the vast majority of white draftees. Although, by law, the Selective Training and Service Act prohibited racial discrimination, prejudices and assumptions about black men's abilities and the viability of a mixed-race military meant the draft boards bypassed most black registrants. As the war dragged on and the need for replacements grew more acute, whites protested the lopsided practices; blacks, eager to serve, argued for inclusion; and attitudes changed. Draft boards, as a result, sent more blacks through to induction centers and training camps and more blacks joined voluntarily. By the end of the war, of the seven million men and women in the military, blacks totaled seven hundred thousand, roughly equal to their representation in the general population—Congress's goal from the start. For the most part, however, black men continued to be assigned to all-black units and predominantly to noncombat units.[6]

Although women had served in the Army Nurse Corps and the Navy Nurse Corps since the turn of the century, they were excluded from the draft and prohibited from enlisting in the armed services in 1940. Two years later, over the objections from Representative Hampton Fulman of South Carolina who stated, "[A] woman's place is in the home," Congress passed legislation allowing women to enlist in auxiliary units, including the Women's Army Auxiliary Corps and later the Women's Naval Reserve, the Coast Guard Women's Reserve, and the Marine Corps Women's Reserve. Three hundred thousand women would serve in uniform during the war.[7]

Washington's proclamations and local draft board quotas aside, the armed forces head count barely rose. The selective service was partly to blame. The local boards turned away scores of candidates; some were too young or too old, others too short or too tall. They rejected nearly half the registrants because they could not read or write or for a variety of medical issues, including flat feet, or defective or too few teeth.[8]

The situation changed after the attack on Pearl Harbor in December 1941. Men of all ages, some as young as fourteen and lying about their age, flooded the understaffed recruiting offices. With neat parts etched in their Brylcreem-slicked hair and wearing their best suit of clothes, the fresh-faced volunteers stood cheek to jowl in block-long lines, ready to serve in whatever capacity the country needed. The prevailing attitude among the recruits was, "Let's win this damn thing and get on with our lives."

While the process evolved over the course of the war, generally, once selected for service, whether draftee or volunteer, the recruits reported to induction centers and reception centers for further evaluation. The staff assessed each man's physical condition, mental health and acuity (based on Army General Classification Test scores), and made note of their family status (whether single or married and how many children they had) and prewar occupation.

Those who survived the initial scrutiny were assigned to specific jobs within their chosen or designated branch of service. For this, the centers consulted the military's tables of organization listing more than five hundred jobs in each branch of service and the number of recruits needed for each position. They tried to match registrants with military jobs most closely resembling their occupation before entering the military: boilermakers, bricklayers, riveters, steelworkers, and miners to the Corps of Engineers; longshoremen to the Quartermaster Corps; and detectives to the military police. Thus, in theory, the army could maintain morale, reduce training time, and produce a higher-functioning force more quickly.

The dilemma came in selecting men for combat jobs. Except for recruits who might have listed handling firearms or hunting, no civilian occupational equivalents existed to fill rifleman, artillery specialist, or tank gunner positions. As a result, men who lacked specific trade skills found themselves in line for combat positions.[9]

Those who objected to serving in combat or serving at all because of religious belief could apply for status as "conscientious objectors" (CO). By law, registrants could not be forced to undergo combat training. Forty-five thousand physically able men claimed CO status. About half the conscientious objectors entered the military, not in a noncombat role, but as noncombatants; the remainder, except for those imprisoned for refusing to serve in any capacity, served on the home front in civilian public service camps.[10]

At best, assignment was a haphazard effort, complicated by the military's complex tables, imprecise occupational matches, the questionable validity of the army's classification test scores, and the prejudices of individuals serving on the local boards. Induction or replacement training centers might receive a recruit the draft board assigned to one role but then reassign him according to the center's needs or preference. Or they might make no assignment at all and simply send the recruit onward.

As the war proceeded, the flaws in the classification approach resulted in a noticeable lack of infantrymen with physical stamina and leadership skills. In a near about-face, in 1943, the military revamped the approach, placing more emphasis on physical classification than prewar occupation for combat roles and test scores.[11]

Wearing their newly issued uniforms, sporting identical short haircuts, and holding their papers in hand, however, did not make the young men soldiers, sailors, marines, airmen, or coast guardsmen. For that, the recruits boarded a bus or train to one of the military training centers that had sprung up overnight across the country. There, the recruits stood in more lines, filled out more forms, and took more batteries of medical and intelligence tests. They held and shot their first weapons and learned to salute and march.

Later, even after weeks of training, few recruits knew where they would serve, what they would do, or whether they would be home in weeks, months, or never again. Two young men, William Schneidewind and Joseph Kennedy, stood among them. Committed to the ideals of democracy and freedom, and willing to fight for their country, both had volunteered. William registered at his recruiting center in Verona, New Jersey, and waited on pins and needles to hear if he'd be leading an army platoon as he hoped. Joseph registered in Richmond, Virginia, and drew an assignment with the air corps. He imagined himself in the cockpit of a P-38 Lightning, dogfighting a German Focke-Wulf in the skies over France.

William and Joseph were fortunate to receive assignments to their preferred branch of service and had moved on to training in their desired fields. They were about to have their hopes dashed.

So how and why did William and Joseph and men like them find themselves far from combat, William standing with chalk in hand at the front of a classroom blackboard in Columbus, Georgia, and Joseph on a Marianna, Florida, airstrip training a crew of eager cadets? It was the first lesson the new recruits learned: the military was in the driver's seat. The second lesson: the military changes its mind. Often. And with little notice.

In the following chapters, William and Joseph share their stories of finding their place in the military—even if not the place they expected. Both became instructors and were among the first military men whom recruits encountered, and both helped make soldiers of the recruits.

CHAPTER ONE

A Platoon of Students

William H. Schneidewind

✷ ✷ ✷

You make your luck, you don't wait for luck to come to you.

WILLIAM H. SCHNEIDEWIND,
First Lieutenant, US Army

Bill Schneidewind was thirteen, far too young to enlist, when the United States entered the Second World War. Still, all he wanted was to join the military, all he could think about was the war. At breakfast, he scoured the local papers for every tiny scrap of war news. Then, he watched as his neighbors put on uniforms and headed off to war. Even his father, an ambulance driver in France during World War I, wore a uniform—if only that of a Verona, New Jersey, air raid guard. Nights were no better. He dreamed about the war and prayed for it to continue.

Finally, in the spring of 1945, the dark-haired young man with perfect posture that made his six-foot frame appear even taller, graduated from high school. With his parents' support and their signature on his application, he reported to the army's local recruiting office and enlisted. He posted high scores on the Army General Classification Test, qualifying him to join an innovative and ambitious government education effort: the Army Specialized Training Program (ASTP). To Bill, the ASTP offered the best of all worlds: he could get a college education, become an officer in the army, and eventually lead a platoon into battle—if the war would just last long enough.

The ASTP was created to develop technically and professionally trained officers on an accelerated timeline. But the army lacked adequate training facilities, and so it turned to 350 colleges and universities across the country to execute its plan. As the army envisioned the program unfolding, ASTP students would share the civilian students' curriculum but study under a discipline more typical of a military post. They had reveille at 6:15 A.M. and taps at 10:00 P.M., marched to and from classes in uniform, and slept in sparsely furnished rooms.[1]

The program was intended to be a win-win-win situation: the army would fill its ranks with college-educated officers; colleges and universities whose enrollments had plummeted during the war would see an influx of students; and the program's young men would receive college degrees and complete a modified version of basic military training by the end of the eighteen-month program.[2]

Despite its promise, the ASTP had its critics, notably, Gen. Lesley McNair. As commander of the Army Ground Forces, among his many duties, McNair was responsible for troop mobilization and training. He argued the army was already understaffed and the proposed ASTP, with its officer-candidate school-like program, would rob the enlisted ranks of the more intelligent and better qualified candidates. While the army wrestled and tinkered with the program's design, a year passed. And when the ASTP finally launched in 1942, its focus had shifted and narrowed from preparing officers to developing specialists—men with science, engineering, medical, and foreign language skills.[3]

Over time the ASTP became well regarded and was reputed to be more difficult than West Point or the Naval Academy. Graduates included such notable figures as the future secretary of state Henry Kissinger, New York City mayor Ed Koch, Idaho senator Frank Church, and author Kurt Vonnegut.[4]

Then, in early 1944, with the invasion of Europe looming, the program suffered a nearly fatal blow. The army slashed the ASTP's goal of training 150,000 men and reneged on its promises, pulling four-fifths of the already enrolled ASTP men from their college campuses and sending them to basic training or into active army platoons.[5]

The turmoil had, for the most part, settled when Bill arrived at the Rutgers, New Jersey, campus in 1945 along with three hundred other recruits. By entering the program at seventeen, Bill fell under the auspices of an offshoot of the ASTP: the Army Specialized Training Program Reserve (ASTPR). On paper, at least, the ASTPR protected Bill and others his age from the army pulling them into service before the end of their studies and military training.[6]

As Bill soon learned, the army preferred ASTP students to pursue technical degrees. "But mathematics was not my strong suit," Bill said, so he took courses in social studies, a degree he thought suited him best. Nevertheless, before he finished his first year at Rutgers, the war ended. Soldiers returned en masse to civilian life and the need for officers plummeted. Despite the supposed protection of the ASTPR program, the army pulled Bill from school and sent him to basic training at Fort McClellan, Alabama. Luck was not on his side. But, as Bill believed, "You make your luck, you don't wait for luck to come to you," a belief shared by Gen. Douglas MacArthur who said, "The best luck of all is the luck you make yourself." And, luckily, the army still needed men. They needed men to manage the war's aftermath.

First, though, Bill had to complete basic training, which he described as tough and aggressive. The program was nothing like the stereotypical drill-sergeant hazing routines depicted in the movies. "They expected more from us," Bill said.

And he planned to give the best he had. After completing sixteen weeks of basic training, Bill was singled out to attend the Officer Candidate School (OCS) at Fort Benning, Georgia, the home of the army's infantry school. Over two hundred future World War II generals, including George Marshall, Omar Bradley, George Patton, and Dwight Eisenhower and his chief of staff W. Bedell Smith, trained, taught, or otherwise enhanced their résumés by spending time at Fort Benning, contributing to Benning's cachet and the school's reputation as the military's premier school.[7]

Half of Bill's OCS class failed to graduate. Bill, however, did, achieving his dream—or at least part of his dream. He received his commission as a second lieutenant, but he didn't have a college degree or a war to fight.

Because of the outstanding abilities he demonstrated during basic training and OCS, the army made Bill a social services discussion leader at Fort Benning. The role, no different than that of the wartime instructors who preceded him, was part education, part public relations, and part propaganda. Despite sounding mind-numbingly dull and hardly like a top job, Bill thought it a "plum." As he saw it, in this role, he had the opportunity to shape the minds of the young men in his charge. He had a chance to give the group of mostly high school graduates a much-needed perspective on world events and the American way of life. War had changed the world, and the United States faced new challenges, chief among them Soviet expansionism and the spread of communism. The Cold War had begun. It was a war Bill was equipped to fight—a war of words on political and economic fronts.

Fort Benning instructors had outlines to follow, but they did much of their own preparation for teaching the courses. "Teaching about communism and other threats," Bill said, "was a responsibility you grew into." Bill pored over notes from his college-level social studies courses well into the night and then did hours more research on current events.

He taught at Fort Benning for a year, and then in late 1947, Bill received orders to transfer to Japan as part of the army of occupation. As conquerors and occupiers, Americans considered it their duty to indoctrinate the Japanese people into the American way of life and influence the reestablishment of Japan's political, economic, social, and educational systems along the lines of their American counterparts.

Like the leader of any platoon, Bill had to adapt to the battlefield—or in his case the classroom. During the year he taught from the army's offices in the center of Tokyo, his discussion topics shifted. The troops in Japan worried less about the spread of communism and more about how best to oversee a country with unfamiliar customs and values. Conversely, "The Japanese," Bill said, "were very willing to take orders from the occupying forces." The not-so-subtle symbolism of Gen. Yoshijiro Umezu surrendering to Gen. Douglas MacArthur and Gen. Richard Sutherland aboard the US flagship *Missouri* was not lost on the Japanese. It was as clear an order as if Emperor Hirohito had issued an edict to the Japanese people to accept the country's defeat and US occupation.

Their acceptance proved as true in cities like Tokyo as it did in the countryside, something Bill witnessed firsthand. As often as he could, Bill toured the country, visiting large cities and small villages, traveling by jeep and accompanied by a driver and translator. Although he suspected venturing too far from US bases could be dangerous, he never encountered hostility or suffered mishaps.

Bill stayed in local hotels with primitive conditions by US standards. Often without running water, he made do by washing and shaving from basins. He slept according to Japanese custom on floor mats and ate traditional Japanese meals. "More than once, I can remember wondering what I was eating," Bill said. "Thankfully, I carried army rations as a backup."

Despite the general atmosphere of acquiescence across the island nation, the army insisted on making an occasional show of force, like the time Bill and a group of his men stood guard at a voting precinct to deter ballot tampering or other voting irregularities. Bill also inspected schools in the prefectures under his unit's command. Working with their US overseers, the Japanese Ministry of Education abolished military training in schools and encouraged teaching representative government, international peace, and freedoms of assembly, speech, and religion. Bill's role included reviewing the ministry's personnel appointments and monitoring compliance with the new curricula.[8]

Of all his memories, the visits he made to Hiroshima and Nagasaki stand apart from the rest. Although the United States understood little about the danger of radiation exposure, early reports claimed ground contamination from radioactive materials measured well below hazardous limits. Troops moved into Nagasaki as early as forty-five days after the bombing, and Bill wanted to see the aftermath. The army offered no objection but, as a precaution, suggested he wear protective clothing.

In Nagasaki, Bill found signs of devastation everywhere he looked. Open basements yawned before him, the floors above disintegrated and blown away, and crumbled remains of walls marked where homes and offices once stood. "The city was flattened. Battered and dusty vehicles lay toppled over and shoved to the side," he said. Yet he saw signs of progress too. US troops and Japanese citizens had cleared mountains of debris from the cities and countryside with the United

States supplying and operating the heavy equipment and Japan providing the laborers. "Overall, the conditions were not as bad as I had imagined," Bill said.

During one memorable visit, he toured a hospital ward of survivors of the bomb's impact and of exposure to radiation. The experience drove home the ravages of war as nothing else could. "Their injuries were horrific," Bill said, "but it was gratifying to see the United States treating the injured. The patients had every right to show their anger and hostility, yet they accepted us into the wards and to their bedsides." And, although time has clouded his memory of the conversations he had, Bill remembered apologizing to one survivor for what transpired and in the same breath explaining what necessitated the bomb. Only someone with Bill's background and skill with words could have conducted that conversation.

Toward the end of his tour of duty, in recognition of his service to Japan, the army awarded Bill the Army of Occupation Medal and a Bronze Star and recommended him for a Silver Star. Bill returned to Fort Benning and shortly afterward, while still in the military, he returned to Rutgers to complete his studies. He proved himself as much a leader on campus as he had been at Fort Benning and in Japan—becoming president of his fraternity, a member of the glee club, and head cheerleader for the Rutgers Scarlet Knights.

At a campus pep rally in the fall of 1950, Bill, dressed in his scarlet sweater with a gray R on the front, met Barbara MacWhinney. Barbara, or "Bobbie" as she was known, was a student at Douglass, a college in the Rutgers University system. Bill and Bobbie became engaged soon afterward and set a wedding date for the spring of 1951. When the big day finally arrived, Bill, still a soldier in the army, found he had no leave and had to go AWOL for the ceremony. Fortunately, his absence went unnoticed—at roll call a sympathetic army chaplain answered for Bill.

One month shy of receiving his degree, the army intervened, again, calling Bill back to active duty for the Korean War. While waiting for his orders to come through, Bill spent a few weeks instructing at Fort Benning where luck intervened—luck that, as always, Bill had a hand in making. In May 1951, the New York Times had commissioned an article on troop information and education and sent a reporter to Fort Benning to interview students and their instructors. The students generally described the "I and E" programs as boring and meaningless and, as the reporter wrote, "wholly inadequate to give men and women in uniform the facts necessary to understand their responsibilities as soldiers and citizens." To gain a better perspective, the reporter attended one of the program's lectures, given by none other than Lt. William Schneidewind. The reporter discovered, as he wrote, how one man, the right man, could make a difference. "Before we got him [Schneidewind]," one recruit said to the reporter, "It was dull as dishwater."[9]

"I love this work," the reporter quoted Bill as saying in explaining the key to his success. "There's nothing I like better."

The lecture was his last, but the *New York Times* article may have helped Bill escape a combat role in Korea. The army assigned him not to Korea but to Japan to resume his role in information and education and to instruct troops deploying to Korea from Japan.

Fifty men boarded the plane that carried Bill across the Pacific. When it touched down in Tokyo, Bill and another man disembarked. Later Bill learned that most of the forty-eight who continued on to Korea perished at one point or another during the war. The incident left its mark on Bill. Had luck not intervened, he would most likely have served in Korea. In a combat position or not, he might have been one of the forty-eight.

Bill was thankful for his appointment to his noncombat role in Japan for personal reasons as well. Bobbie was pregnant. Bill had a family to consider. One year later, with his Korean War service complete, Bill and Bobbie relocated, making a last move to New Jersey. Bill graduated from Rutgers in 1953 and then left the military to pursue a career in insurance sales, first in New Jersey, where he and Bobbie raised their two children, then in Boston. After he retired, the couple moved again, this time to Atlanta. Bill's ever-erect posture attests to his athletic youth and years in the military. His gray hair frames his face and adds to his distinguished appearance. Whether he greets a stranger or an old friend, he rises and offers a firm handshake—the mark of a man who spent years engaging successfully with the public.

Today with the perspective of his years of experience, Bill realizes how foolish his teenage dreams of fighting were, and he is convinced that everyone who contributed, regardless of the role they played, helped win the war. His background in social studies helped him understand the nation's purpose for going back to war. His role in information and education allowed him to teach soldiers bound for the front lines the purpose of fighting and to be better equipped for battle. And, in a sense, he led not one platoon but many, in class after class.

Bill Schneidewind died on January 31, 2019, three weeks after celebrating his ninety-first birthday. He and his wife, Bobbie, spent sixty-seven years together, many of which were in their spacious Atlanta apartment surrounded by memorabilia from their life and travels abroad, often to Japan. He is survived by Bobbie, their son, daughter, nine grandchildren, and one great-grandson.

CHAPTER TWO

The Man Who Wanted to Fly

Joseph A. Kennedy

* * *

I just took to flying. I think I could have beat anyone.

JOSEPH A. KENNEDY,
Lieutenant Colonel, US Air Force

Word spread quickly around the small town of North Attleboro, Massachusetts. A crop duster had landed at the Wilkins family farm, and the pilot was offering rides. The young boys of North Attleboro could think of nothing better than soaring high above the earth. One of those boys was ten-year-old Joe Kennedy (no relation to Joseph P. Kennedy Jr. who flew for the navy in World War II). Joe and two friends grabbed their bicycles and rode, as Joe remembers it, "up and over the hill and down the other side," racing four miles to the farm outside town.

At the far end of Wilkins's field, the single-engine biplane sat with its engine humming—the open cockpit, canvas-covered wings, and wooden propeller holding all the dreams Joe could imagine. The boys dug deep in their pockets. With three dollars and twenty cents from his newspaper sales and a handful of nickels and dimes from his friends, Joe approached the pilot. They were a few pennies short, but the pilot, knowing what was going through the boys' minds and hearts, strapped the three boys into the front seat and took them up.

"Good Lord, what a feeling," Joe said. "You could hear the wind blowing as we sailed high over the farmland. It was just wonderful. I was hooked."

A second event, seven years later in 1938, sealed Joe's fate. A North Attleboro High School friend returned home from the military sporting knife-edge pleats on his olive drab uniform and a gleaming set of wings pinned over his heart. Joe, a senior, could not take his eyes off the wings. He knew in an instant what he wanted to do. He wanted to fly. At the time, Joe had no way of knowing he would fly, in one capacity or another, for thirty years in service to his country. His route to flying, however, like his career, took many twists and turns.

Before graduating from high school, Joe spent part of two summers at one of the country's Citizens' Military Training Camps (CMTC) to improve his chances of becoming an officer and to gain a little worldly experience. The government had opened fifty of the camps across the country to prepare men for military service and speed the production of officers. Actually, for the chance at a commission as a second lieutenant, the men needed to attend for four consecutive years, completing the basic, red, white, and blue increments. The program fell far short of expectations. Six hundred thousand men attended at least one summer of training, but the army commissioned only five thousand.[1]

Although two future presidents, Harry Truman and Ronald Reagan, had participated in CMTC programs, Joe says his camp experience did little to advance his career or make him an officer. He said, "The training was mostly learning to salute, make a bed, and peel potatoes."

Then, on graduating from high school, Joe decided before enlisting in the military he would put a little money in his pocket and see something of the world. He signed on as an AT&T lineman's apprentice, laying telephone cable in Virginia. The dollar an hour he earned wasn't much money nor was Virginia much of the world, but Joe figured the military and the war could wait. The wings, however, were never far from his thoughts, and one day in September 1942 in Richmond, he passed a recruiting office. Posters on the side of the building caught his eye—aircraft flying in formation in high white clouds, the stars and stripes, a group of young men all smiles in olive drab, and those silver wings.

Joe drew up his five-foot ten-inch lanky frame, put on his easy smile, and walked through the front door. He looked every bit the part and easily passed the US Army Air Forces' written entrance test. The physical exam, however, revealed a double hernia. Joe had to undergo surgery before he could attend aviation school.

In the meantime, with his papers noting his work experience and his CMTC participation, the military made Joe a sergeant. "I was only twenty-one, but I had work experience that the other men didn't," he said. He considered the sergeant duty as a temporary distraction and underwent surgery while the war raged on unabated. Finally, in 1943, he felt well enough to reapply for aviation school. Joe retook and passed his physical and made it to Lakeland, Florida, for primary training at the Lodwick School of Aeronautics, one of the many private enterprises under contract with the army to train military pilots.[2]

Putting a young man in the seat of a fighter plane in the early 1940s required close to a year of training, with aviation cadets progressing from flying a small, low-powered aircraft to a heavier plane with more complex controls, and only then to more powerful aircraft.[3] With the attack on Pearl Harbor, the military toyed with speeding the process and eventually shaved three weeks off each of the twelve-week training segments: primary, basic, and advanced.

In primary, Joe trained in a Stearman PT-13, a biplane with a reputation for being rugged and thus expected to withstand the stresses and strains of a novice flyer. Joe never forgot the first time he saw a Stearman. The Boeing aircraft, a primitive plane by twenty-first-century standards, had wooden wings covered with fabric, a canvas-covered cockpit, and a 215-horsepower engine capable of flying 135 miles per hour.[4]

"The instructor climbed in," Joe said, "and I watched as he lifted the elevators and then the ailerons. I was absolutely thrilled to death and could not wait to fly."

Weeks later, when he reached basic flight training at the army's airfield in Bainbridge, Georgia, Joe flew the all-metal BT-13 made by Vultee Aircraft. With a 450-horsepower engine, the BT-13 boasted more power than the Stearman and could fly 50 miles per hour faster.[5] Joe and his fellow cadets referred to the Vultee by its nickname, the Vultee Vibrator. "At high speeds," Joe said, "the engine vibrated so much it made the whole plane shake. You thought it was going to fall apart."

One day, the BT-13 almost did and nearly brought Joe's flying career to a halt. His instructor, seated in the back at the controls of the two-seater, wanted to impress Joe and the other students and instructors in the squadron. The instructor nudged his plane toward a BT-13 on his left to lay his airspeed indicator (a needle-like object protruding from the aircraft's left wing) on the right wing of the adjacent plane. "Well," Joe said, "the indicator hit the wing and broke off. We hurried back to the airfield and landed, but we didn't leave the plane right away. The instructor told me to say I had been flying when the accident occurred. I worried I'd lose my chance to fly, but the instructor said nothing would happen." Nothing did. Joe completed basic without further incident, soloing after only six hours of flight time—most cadets took eight to ten.

In the final stage of training, advanced single-engine instruction at Marianna, Florida, Joe and his fellow cadets flew the North American T-6 Texan. The T-6 represented a transition between basic trainers and first-line tactical aircraft. A low-cost monoplane with the characteristics of a high-speed fighter, the 600-horse-power T-6 could reach 210 miles per hour. Pilots around the world trained in the aircraft, learning tactics from ground strafing to bombardment to acrobatics.[6] Aloft in the T-6, Joe also learned the finer points of flying, including flying at night; by instruments; in formation with three, six, or more planes; and across the country.[7]

"I just took to it," Joe said. With the requisite cockiness of aviators, he adds, "I think I could have beat anyone in the skies."

On graduating from advanced training in March 1944, Joe received his coveted wings and bars and became one of the army air forces' nearly two hundred thousand pilots.[8] But, apparently, Joe's commanding officers thought as highly of Joe as Joe did. Rather than send him to Europe, they kept him in Marianna to train future cadets. "They said I was too good to waste in combat." All Joe wanted was to go to Europe to fight, but he had learned more than how to fly during training—he had learned not to argue with his superiors.

Over the next four months, for seven days a week, Joe taught cadets what he had learned in his own months of flight training. Meticulous, he did whatever he could to give the young men the skills they needed. "By the time I finished with them, they were all," in Joe's words, "very, very good pilots."

Good pilots learn to keep calm during trying situations. In combat, with so much happening at high speeds, a lot can go wrong, and a pilot's split-second decisions can have dire consequences. Instructors like Joe had to set an example. He remembered flying with a student pilot, practicing takeoffs and landings on a short field. After making several loops, the two turned and headed around for another circuit when their engine caught fire. From the backseat, Joe looked up to see the student unbuckling his harness, preparing to eject. Cool as a cucumber, Joe said, "Sit tight." He took the controls and landed the aircraft, smoke billowing from the engine and fire trucks screaming in pursuit.

Sometimes, however, things don't go as planned. Even for instructors. Once Joe flew a Curtiss P-40 Warhawk—one of the primary fighter aircraft used by the Allies in the war and made famous by the Flying Tigers who flew the Warhawk in China. "It was a real hot aircraft and a thrill to fly," Joe said.

The military had parked several P-40 Warhawks at the edge of the airfield near where he worked. In the midst of the war, with the authorities busy elsewhere and the rules about flying outside combat lax, the Warhawks proved too much of a temptation. Joe climbed into the cockpit of one, eager to see how fast the P-40 could go. Once he reached a decent altitude, he leveled off and started a steep descent. The needle on the airspeed indicator ticked from 350 miles per hour, the designated maximum speed, toward the redline at 480 miles per hour.[9] Joe held the descent, and kept going down, down, down—the seconds ticking away, and blue sky and clouds flying by outside.

Boom!

He had no idea what had happened, but the P-40 kept flying. Joe leveled off, turned, and landed. Only then, as he took stock of his surroundings, did he notice that a section of the cockpit's plexiglass canopy had blown out, leaving a gaping hole.

Despite the mishap, Joe continued to impress his superiors. "I must have been one of the best of the best," he said, because in July 1944, the army air forces transferred him and a select group of pilot instructors from Marianna, Florida, to San Antonio, Texas. There, at the Randolph Army Air Forces Central Instructor

School (CIS), the group trained pilots returning from combat to become flight instructors. "It was another step up in my career," Joe said.

"Combat flying was not precise or coordinated. It's more . . . you go like hell, get that guy, get out of the way, slip this way, go that way, get back in formation with your unit, and go back to the field. These men had developed a lot of bad flying habits, which we needed to eliminate. When they left me, they were very special people." Joe, too, became a better pilot through training these men. "You can learn a lot from the mistakes others make," he said.

In his spare time, Joe took part in public flight demonstrations, doing acrobatics such as flying inverted and doing loops and barrel rolls to the crowd's delight. "We ended with a maneuver we invented, the 'bomb burst,'" he said, referring to a popular airshow finale during which three or four aircraft fly in unison as close to vertical as possible and then, at a designated altitude, separate and spread across the sky.

Joe stayed at Randolph, training pool after pool of pilots until the number of pilots coming to CIS dwindled. On August 22, 1945, with the war near its end, Col. Benjamin W. Armstrong, Air Corps, Command, wrote a letter of commendation to the CIS instructors: "The accomplishments of the school are a matter of record and remain a source of much satisfaction to the AAF Training Command. Not only did we fulfill their requirements for an abundance of qualified flying instructors when they were urgently needed, but progressively raised the caliber and uniformity of instruction. . . . It has been a rare privilege to serve with you and I can say without qualification that no finer group of officers, better pilots or more qualified instructors exists anywhere."[10]

Armstrong also addressed a subject on many of the instructors' minds: their not having served in combat. He added, "I ask you to compare, impartially, any contribution you may have made overseas to the immeasurable advancement that has been effected in flying training by you and your fellow officers."[11]

Armstrong's words did not satisfy Joe, but the sentiment would have to do—for now.

Joe left Texas, returned home, and signed up with the reserves, but he didn't leave flying. Back in Massachusetts, he opted not to go back to AT&T although the company kept the doors open for returning soldiers. Instead, Joe took advantage of the GI Bill to go to a civilian flight school for advanced ratings—obtaining his flight instructors rating, then commercial pilot and instrument ratings. To make ends meet, he drove a truck for W. H. Riley & Son, a Massachusetts family-owned fuel oil company, making just over one dollar an hour.

Whether it was fate or luck, the two brothers who ran the oil company raised and raced horses and needed a pilot to take them to horse racing events. Joe found himself back in the pilot's seat, flying the brothers to races across New England.

Five short years later, the United States was going to war again, this time to help South Korea defend itself against a North Korean invasion. The US military called up the reserves, and Joe returned to active duty. In Stockton, California, while waiting to board a steamship for deployment in the Pacific, Joe caught wind of a nearby dance for officers. He told a friend waiting with him, "There'll be dollies we can dance with there."

That evening, while strains of Glenn Miller and Duke Ellington tunes wafted through the dance hall, the "dollies" sat on a bench against the wall. Never the shy one, Joe approached a young woman and asked her to dance. "She said she didn't dance the jitterbug, but the girl at the end of the bench did," Joe said. He walked to the end of the bench and asked the girl seated there to dance. The future Mrs. Kennedy, Virginia Bogolea, took his hand and joined Joe on the dance floor. "She was a good dancer," he said with a smile. Joe and Ginny dated a few times before he packed his bags for Korea.

Joe never made it to Korea. The US Air Force (now independent of the US Army and renamed) plucked five men from the roster destined for the peninsula and diverted them to Okinawa. Joe was one of the five. He became an aircraft controller with the 623rd Aircraft Control and Warning Squadron, supporting B-29 bombers making bombing runs into North Korea.

Joe kept up a steady correspondence with Ginny, but he was lonely. "Everyone else had someone with them," Joe said. "Wives. Children. Everyone but me. So, I told Ginny to come to Okinawa. There were plenty of jobs out there." One week later, Ginny Bogolea arrived in Okinawa. Soon after, while out with another couple and in the backseat of his friend's car, Joe asked Ginny to marry him. She said no.

Surprised and very disappointed, Joe told a few friends about Ginny's refusal. "That's what they all say the first time," one advised. "Ask her again," another suggested. Joe did, and this time Ginny said yes. They married six months later on Valentine's Day 1953.

In the Okinawa Ground Control Intercept Station, Joe and his fellow aircraft controllers monitored aircraft activity coming into and out of Korean airspace. Radar picked up aircraft signals, displaying them as blips on a controller's scope. Monitoring the scopes required great patience and alertness through hours and hours of tedium and minutes of intense anxiety. In between the tense moments, the men found time to relax. Joe, who also oversaw the officers' club, took that responsibility as seriously as he did his duty at the scopes—once donning a gorilla suit for the club's revelers during an event he dubbed "The Week of the Circus." From that point forward, his well-deserved reputation for creating a fun-filled environment followed him from post to post.

Often in charge of festivities, Joe never lost a chance, even at a party, to conduct a bit of business. At one of the many officers' club parties he attended in Okinawa, Joe found a way to see combat. Over drinks Joe mentioned to a B-29 officer that he'd not seen combat during World War II. "Can you see what you can do to let me go on a bombing mission?" Joe asked. The next day, the B-29 captain called. "Friday morning. Five A.M. Have your suit on."

When Friday finally arrived, Joe suited up, the crew checked him out, and he hopped aboard. "Bombers don't have passenger seats, so I had to sit on a cover over the emergency exit just behind the two pilots. We headed to our first target, a bridge in North Korea, but the radar failed so we diverted to a secondary target, a marshaling yard." On the way, antiaircraft fire, or flak, exploded around them in puffs of black smoke and flames.

"You see that, Joe?" the pilot asked.

"Hell, yes, I see it."

What concerned Joe more, however, was what the pilot said next. "If it gets bad and we have to parachute out, you have to move."

Beneath Joe's improvised seat a small ladder led down and out the aircraft. "I had my good shoes on under the flight suit boots. And all I could think about was if the boots came off when I pulled the parachute cord, I'd have to land in a rice paddy in my good shoes."

Later during the flight, the pilot said, "Get on up here, Kennedy. Earn your money."

Joe obliged. From the copilot's seat, he took the controls of the huge beast of an aircraft. "It was nothing like flying a fighter. More like riding a bucking bronco. I could hear those four engines growling away as we climbed out of eight thousand feet." Joe grinned. He was flying in combat, at last, even though in a bomber, not a fighter. Nevertheless, the experience of that single flight assured the older and wiser man he had become that combat was not something to wish for.

Another B-29 incident became the highlight of Joe's military career, earning him a Bronze Star. On a late-night shift in the ground control station, the pilots of a B-29 radioed they were lost somewhere over the East China Sea. Joe took the call. When the pilot repeated his message, Joe could hear the concern in the pilot's voice. The timing could not have been worse: a power outage had knocked out everything on the island—the airfield, the runway lights, everything. Everything but Joe's scope.

Drawing on all he had learned as a pilot and as a controller and his years of experience, Joe asked the B-29 crew for the details he needed: how far from the runway and how high a B-29 needed to be to begin its descent. Then he picked up a grease pencil and marked a course from the bomber's blip at sea to the runway on his scope. Joe talked the pilot through the route, calling out adjustments and coaxing them down in the darkness. While his words remained measured and calm, as he watched the blip on his screen tick closer his nerves twisted and turned into a bundle of knots.

"Got the runway in sight," the pilot radioed finally and gratefully.

"It's all yours," Joe radioed, handing the responsibility back to the pilots. Moments later, the bomber's landing lights guided them to a safe landing.

Almost seventy years after the event, Joe's eyes teared at the memory. Without someone with Joe's skills and clear head, the men might have suffered a very different outcome. Joe never spoke to or heard from the crew, but he guessed they reported the incident to their chain of command. A week later, the commanding officer called Joe to the station headquarters and awarded him the Bronze Star Medal for outstanding performance and for bringing "credit to him, his organization, and the United States Air Force."

Joe's son, Michael Kennedy, saved the letter of commendation that accompanied the award. It reads, in part: "In July 1952, while working on the night shift, Lieutenant Kennedy distinguished himself by alert, quick thinking in effecting the save of an aircraft. A bomber returning from Korea radioed they were low on fuel and off course. Lieutenant Kennedy by his personal alertness and perseverance, vectored the aircraft on a proper heading and by dead reckoning, maintained a steady stream of chatter to the pilot to instill confidence, and finally brought the aircraft, together with its crew, to Kadena for a safe landing."[12]

The citation also mentions an incident during a typhoon in 1952 when Joe remained on duty over a twenty-four-hour period without relief and contributed to the "proper issuance of warnings which resulted in the safety of all personnel on Okinawa."

After the Korean War's end, Joe stayed with the air defense command, seeing duty at and traveling with his wife and three children to far-flung stations from New Mexico to Canada, back to Korea, and to Alaska, with other stops along the way. In New Mexico, he protected the airspace surrounding Los Alamos—the site of America's national laboratory for atomic weapons. At Sioux Lookout in Ontario, along the Pinetree Line—the southernmost of three early-warning radio networks strung across Canada—Joe watched for and sent intercepts to Russian planes coming over the North Pole. Mostly, he said, they chased bush pilots who strayed into the zone. Joe received promotions to captain, major, and then lieutenant colonel. As he climbed the military career ladder, his duties became more staff oriented and less about events in the field and what he knew best. So, in 1971, with twenty-nine years behind him, Joe retired and settled in Aurora, Colorado.

In his newfound leisure time, Joe took up painting. He'd always had a steady hand and a good eye but no time to pursue the craft. With a group of fellow artists, he traveled to art shows across the country, returning at the end of each sojourn to Ginny and their home in Aurora. His splendid paintings grace his home and his children's homes and homes of people across the country who know nothing of the artist's past.

"You did a swell job" were the closing words in Col. Benjamin Armstrong's 1945 letter of commendation to Joe Kennedy. They are a fitting tribute to the man's career and his life, but it might be Joe's own words from the summer of 2018 that say it best: "I ain't finished yet." He wasn't and was looking forward to his ninety-seventh birthday in 2018. On October 14 of that year, however, after returning home from a World War II Pilots Association Convention in Dayton, Ohio, Joe passed away. He is survived by his son and two daughters and their families.

PART II

Across the Sea and
over the Hump

If this war has demonstrated anything, it has shown that our efforts to launch attacks on the enemy have, in every case, been governed by logistics—transportation and supply.

BREHON B. SOMERVELL,
General, US Army

During the Second World War, one of the largest migrations in history took place. In the United States, sixteen million people traveled from their homes and workplaces to military training camps set up across the country. After weeks of training, the twelve million destined for service overseas convened in marshaling yards near seaports for the final leg of their journey. From there, they traveled by land, sea, and air—blacks and whites, men and women, generals and privates, combat and noncombat personnel.

Initial supplies of uniforms, arms and ammunition, tents, food, pots, pans, forks, and knives—everything the men needed while camped in the field—accompanied the soldiers to their destinations. By the time the war ended, the military had transported 132 million tons of cargo, including an astounding 1.5 million motor vehicles, 85,000 aircraft, 8,000 mules, 2,000 locomotives, and 1,900 war dogs.[1] The undertaking was a logistical exercise of unprecedented proportion.

Allied and Axis armies alike understood the importance of logistics and of the role of an army's quartermasters, a noncombat unit charged with handling logistics. German field marshal Erwin Rommel claimed, "The battle is fought and decided by the Quartermasters before the shooting begins."[2]

Fortunately, America's military, including its quartermasters, came to understand what was at stake and acted with determination. It wasn't always so. For the first six months of the war, a confusing and often overlapping patchwork of bureaucracies in the Quartermaster Corps and Corps of Engineers handled the army's transportation services. And to complicate matters, the navy maintained a separate transportation organization. Multiple attempts to broker a common transportation authority failed as neither branch of the military wanted to be subject to the command of the other or a third party. Eventually, the two branches would agree to coordinate operations when possible or necessary, for the most part, in joint use of ships.[3]

In the meantime, to streamline its own transportation services, in July 1942, the US Army formed the Transportation Corps under the Army Support Forces

(ASF), the army's umbrella administrative arm. The new corps sat alongside the Army Medical Department, Chemical Warfare Services, Corps of Chaplains, Corps of Engineers, Ordnance Department, Quartermaster Corps, Signal Corps, and Special Services groups.[4]

Despite the transportation mandate given to the Transportation Corps, high-ranking army officers often interfered, demanding supervision of the movement of their men and matériel when critical to an operation. Gen. George Patton, for example, railed at attempts to control logistics—particularly fuel supplies—where his troops were concerned. "My men can eat their belts, but my tanks have gotta have gas," he said.[5]

TRANSPORT BY LAND

Oceans apart and in ranks far below the admirals and generals in the theaters of war, stateside Transportation Corps clerks managed the details of moving men and matériel from their homes to theaters of operation. These clerks had the authority to decide what items moved in what manner, whether by road, rail, air, or sea.

While the corps moved much of the military motor vehicle fleet under its own power on public roads, for transporting the bulk of military personnel and supplies, it turned to the nation's network of railroads.[6] It was a highly complex effort and required close cooperation between the military and the railroad. To deploy even a single army division, Transportation Corps clerks first estimated the space needed for the troops' supplies and equipment. From the estimate of supplies, they calculated the number and types of railcars needed, including baggage cars, kitchen cars, and Pullman cars. From the number, type, dimension, and weight of the accompanying tanks, half-tracks, motorcycles, and other vehicles, the clerks determined the number of flatbed railcars, the number of blocks, the lengths of heavy-gauge wire needed to secure the vehicles, and the precise manner of loading.[7]

In days long before computer software programs became available, the clerks made the calculations by hand or at best with simple adding machines. Then, after loading the railcars and sending them on their way, corps personnel telephoned ahead to railroad stations along the planned route, giving the order to "clear the tracks." As military transport trains proceeded, passenger and nonmilitary cargo trains shuttled to vacant railroad sidings to allow the military transport to pass. During the early years of the war, the clerks repeated the same complex planning exercise for each division waiting for transport, twenty-four hours a day, each day of the year.[8]

The process was captured in a 1940s military-commissioned film, although it represents a highly idealized glimpse of troop transport by rail. In the film, men dressed in freshly laundered and starched uniforms march in formation from their barracks to a rail station and a line of waiting railcars. They smile and walk empty-handed, as if they are taking a short trip across town. As they climb aboard, a military band plays "Auld Lang Syne." The scene switches to one of the congenial soldiers passing time playing cards, rolling dice, reading, and speculating about their destinations. Meanwhile, in the train's kitchen car, another smiling crew busily peels potatoes and prepares meals. Later, the soldiers prepare for bed in bunk-lined sleeper cars. Two men sleep in each lower bunk, one in each upper. In an idyllic scene at one stop along the route, the men disembark, engage in calisthenics, and then shower beneath a raised railway water barrel. In minutes, they climb back aboard, all still wearing their broad smiles.[9]

The movie version bears little resemblance to what the veterans here experienced on their six-day, two-thousand-mile journey across the country, east to west or west to east. They heard no band playing when they departed. They had no breaks for calisthenics or group showers. They sat, read, wrote letters home, played cards and dice, stared out the window, wondered exactly where they were headed, and worried about what lay in store.

Many men did not discover their destinations until their train pulled to a stop and orders came to disembark in one of the many hastily built tent camps near East or West Coast seaports. There, the troops faced anywhere from a few days to a few weeks of waiting, while army or navy embarkation camp personnel handled final preparations. These included issuing additional equipment and conducting last-minute training for troops bound for jungles, deserts, and other less familiar environments. The men waited, doing what they had grown accustomed to by now, playing more card games, reading more books, and writing more letters home.[10]

TRANSPORT BY SEA

When at last their orders arrived, often with little warning, the men scrambled from their quarters, shouldered their duffel bags, and sped to waiting troop transport ships for the next leg of their journey. For many, the voyage was their first aboard a ship. Although novices, the men were well aware of the dangers.

Seasickness and the likelihood of encountering rough seas, particularly on a winter crossing of the North Atlantic, were fleeting and unpleasant thoughts. What weighed heavily in their minds was the possibility of an attack by German submarines or aircraft, both common threats to troop transports and supply ships. Whether a soldier held a combat or a noncombat position meant nothing. All aboard were at risk of being bombed or torpedoed, each man playing a role in his own Battle of the Atlantic or the Pacific.

Germany's infamous submarines, or U-boats, derived from the German word *Unterseeboot,* or undersea boat, began wreaking havoc off America's Eastern Seaboard and the Gulf of Mexico within days of Germany declaring war on the United States. The government tried to keep the losses from becoming general knowledge, but many of the ships carrying supplies went down in plain sight of sunbathers, and detritus from shipwrecks and the bodies of merchant mariners littered beaches along the coast.[11] Eventually, despite the government's censorship efforts, some stories found their way into American newspapers.[12]

It took a civilian-led group, the Civil Air Patrol (CAP), to take the threat seriously and launch countermeasures against the U-boats. Veteran Robert Gara Soulé and hundreds of other experienced commercial pilots, crop dusters, and barnstormers volunteered to serve with CAP, flying their own planes up and down the coast. In total, they flew over twenty-four million miles on routes hugging the coast from Maine to the Panama Canal. They spotted over 170 U-boats, and with their relatively light weaponry sank two.[13]

Nevertheless, out at sea, far from CAP's reach, U-boats and enemy air raids continued. Fifteen hundred US merchant supply ships and seven hundred navy vessels were lost and hundreds more damaged while crossing the Atlantic.[14] For merchant mariners like Bud Surprenant who crossed and recrossed the Atlantic and sailed into the Mediterranean Sea, the danger was particularly acute. Their ships, traveling alone, unarmed, and unprotected, were vulnerable from the moment they left their port until they docked at their destination.[15]

In March 1942, with mounting public pressure over the loss of ships, lives, and goods, the United States took a more proactive stance. First, the government ordered cities along the country's coasts to dim their waterfront lights, reducing the chance of a ship being silhouetted against the bright lights. While many municipalities balked at the orders, for fear of discouraging tourism at amusement parks along the shore, they complied. Even New York City's Times Square went black after sundown. Then, by summer, the military began using ship convoys, adding armed escorts, and arming transport vessels.[16] Casualties dropped dramatically.

Eleanor Millican, one of the first US Navy WAVES (Women Accepted for Volunteer Emergency Service), played a hand in protecting the ships. Instead of navigating the waters of Rhode Island aboard her beau Gus Frye's sailboat, Eleanor was hard at work at the Charleston, South Carolina, seaport in 1943. As part of her job, she assisted troop and cargo ships' captains in forming convoys and consulting the navy's classified navigational charts for their Atlantic crossings.

TRANSPORT BY AIR

Before the United States entered the war, the country's use of air transportation was limited largely to delivering American-made aircraft from Lockheed, Boeing, and Ford Motor Company to Britain, France, and Russia, countries already at war. American civilian pilots, under contract to one of the purchasing nations, delivered, or ferried, the planes to modification centers for wartime outfitting. Secondary factories, often located near the Canadian border, added performance upgrades, armament, and communications equipment. There, after modification, Canadian civilian pilots took over, flying the planes across the Atlantic to their final destinations.[17]

The first trans-Atlantic flights to the United Kingdom were across the North Atlantic, which often required refueling stops in Newfoundland and Scotland. During the winter months, because of the treacherous North Atlantic storms along the route, the ferrying command established a second route through the southern Atlantic. This route originated in Miami, traveled across the Caribbean to British Guiana, Brazil, and then to Ascension Island in the mid-Atlantic, before arriving on the west coast of Africa. Aircraft destined for Russia went by a third route across the country or up the West Coast to Alaska, where Soviet pilots took over and ferried the planes for the final leg. All the routes were hazardous, but with its limited communications capabilities and the extreme weather, the Alaska route was the most severe.[18]

By early 1941, the United States realized its own military pilots could benefit from the experience of flying the long-range routes and mastering the skills needed to fly the newer aircraft being shipped abroad. The military established the US Air Corps Ferrying Command in May 1941 for that purpose and employed US military combat pilots for ferrying duties. The first ferrying command delivery occurred on June 7, 1941, at the US-Canada border. Neutrality laws prohibited the United States from flying planes from America to any nation at war. To preserve the image of neutrality, if not the fact, a crew towed the aircraft across the border.[19]

The arrangement between the ferrying command and the military lasted until Pearl Harbor, after which the military recalled their pilots. At that point, the command turned to a combination of civilian pilots, the manufacturer's own pilots, and a few of the available newly trained military pilots to continue the domestic ferrying service.[20]

By June 1942, with the United States ferrying its own planes and increasingly using air transport for American men and matériel, the military combined the Air Corps Ferrying Command and Troop Carrier Command under the umbrella organization the Air Transport Command (ATC). The ATC was responsible for all War Department air transportation, including all aircraft ferrying and transport of critical personnel and supplies not suited for the longer sea-based voyages to Europe, North Africa, and the Pacific.

As the war ramped up, the ATC found it increasingly difficult to recruit pilots for ferrying services. It relaxed its standards and allowed men like former CAP pilot Robert Gara Soulé, who wore glasses, to become ferry pilots. Some military pilots scoffed at the pilots and other Air Transport Command personnel, claiming the initials ATC stood for "allergic to combat." The ATC's mission was in fact designated as a noncombat mission, delivering aircraft, personnel, and supplies to rear areas of operation. Most ATC routes, however, entered or traversed hostile areas, and one in particular classified as a combat route. That route, known as "the Hump," charted its way from India through the valleys of the high Himalayas and the mountains of Burma and deep into China's interior.[21]

When the ATC exhausted the new source of pilots, it asked for permission to hire women, despite the relatively small number of females licensed as pilots at the time. In the summer of 1942, the War Department approved the request, and twenty-five women, each boasting over one thousand hours of flying time, became members of the ATC's Women's Auxiliary Ferrying Squadron (WAFS). Shortly afterward a second group of women entered the military as pilots in the Women's Flying Training Detachment under the Army Air Force Flying Training Detachment. In mid-1943 the two groups combined as the Women Airforce Service Pilots organization with a total of just over a thousand women serving as military pilots.[22]

Although the women flew only domestic, noncombat routes, they filled critical vacancies during the war, 141 of them serving as ferry pilots. In 1944, when the number of returning combat pilots sufficed for the military's needs, the army disbanded the women's group.[23]

In total, from 1940 to 1945, the army air forces moved over two hundred thousand new aircraft from their factories of origin to their places of service in the war. Of those flown under their own power, the ferrying command and later the ATC ferried approximately two-thirds of the aircraft. The remainder, particularly smaller fighter aircraft, crossed by sea as cargo.[24]

SUPPLY MANAGEMENT

The terrain and thus the transport and supply challenges differed in each theater. The war in Europe and North Africa was essentially a ground war with the army air forces and navy providing support. In the Pacific, the war was a naval war with ground and air support. While soldiers in Europe and North Africa billeted at and fought from land bases and outposts, in the Pacific the navy and marines had to maintain men on both land and sea.

Keeping track of the millions of moving parts was not a small job and not one learned on the job. Fortunately, men like Ike Minkovitz, a retail business manager who managed inventory for his family's business in southeast Georgia, brought his knowledge and skill to the Fifteenth Air Force on the shores of Italy. He ordered and managed delivery and distribution of everything from uniforms to bombs along a supply line stretching from factories in America across four thousand miles of ocean and to the front lines in Europe.

Finally, one other veteran in a support role talked of their duty spent delivering supplies to the troops. Louis Thompson, like Ike Minkovitz, was a volunteer, though half a world away in the China-Burma-India theater, and high in the mountains of northern India, helping build roads into the sides of jungle-enveloped hills, paving the way for supplies. After raising his hand for the chance to escape the mud, rain, and insects on the ground, he found himself flying high above those roads, over uncharted jungle to deliver supplies. He served for sixteen months, flying more than a thousand missions during his tour of duty. The work took its toll on his body and nerves, but not on his pride or his satisfaction for having done his duty.

In the following chapters, Robert, Bud, Eleanor, Ike, and Louis share their stories, telling about the small but interconnected parts each played in moving men and matériel to the war front.

CHAPTER THREE

Jack of All Trades

Robert Gara Soulé

*I asked my mother what I was supposed to list at school for my
father's occupation. "Just write Jack of All Trades," she said.*

LETIA SOULÉ HENSON
about Robert Gara Soulé,
Flight Officer, US Army Air Forces

Robert "Bob" Gara Soulé came by his reputation honestly. At various times he owned a flying school; raced and repaired hydroplanes; and worked as a used car salesman, a realtor, a boat broker, a shrimper, a Taylorcraft Aircraft dealer, and an Indian Motorcycle distributor. For a while, he tried working behind a desk in his family's business, the Soulé Steam Feed Works, but the tedious desk job was short lived. Bob preferred working with his hands, taking engines apart and putting them back together better than before. He also preferred soaring high above the ground, viewing the world from the cockpit of an airplane. Any airplane would do.

Bob's aptitude for anything mechanical was his birthright. His father, George Wilberforce "G.W." Soulé, an inventor and industrialist, founded Soulé Steam Feed Works in 1892 in Meridian, Mississippi. He owned over twenty-five patents, mostly in industrial applications for the lumber industry's sawmills, but also one for the Success Cotton Seed Huller.[1]

As alike as the two were, Bob barely knew his father. G.W. had many demands on his time—the business foremost—and the strains of a large and growing family. The Soulé family patriarch had five children by his first wife, Olivia Sherman Soulé, and four by his second, Constance Gara Soulé. In 1907, when G.W. and Constance married, Constance was thirty-two years his junior and five years younger than G.W.'s oldest living child, Clyde.

Bob Soulé, the youngest and the last of G.W.'s children, was born in December 1914 in Camp Walton, the site of a Civil War camp on the Gulf of Mexico, near present-day Fort Walton Beach, Florida. He was Constance's favorite, a fact not lost on Bob, and could get away with just about anything. While in elementary school in Meridian, Bob would skip school for days at a time. He'd spend the hours, not idly as a typical young boy might, but reading at the library. After one long period of truancy, the teacher reported Bob's absence to his mother. Constance punished her son by making him return to class, but she never mentioned Bob's transgressions to his father.

G.W. might have seen the merit in allowing his young son to explore the world on his own through books. Unfortunately, he died in 1922 when Bob was eight. After his death, Constance took four of her children, Eda, George Halbert, and Bob, to live in West Palm Beach, Florida, near her family.

There, as a teenager in the waning days of Prohibition, Bob had his first encounter with an aircraft. The plane, loaded with contraband alcohol, had crashed into Lake Worth near Palm Beach and lay submerged beneath the clear water. Standing beside the local police eyeing the wreckage, Bob asked one of the authorities, "What are you going to do with it?"

The answer was music to Bob's ears: "You're welcome to it if you want it."

Bob wanted it. He dragged the wreckage from the lake and carted it to his mother's garage where he took apart the engine and carefully dried and reassembled the parts. Constance watched with mixed emotions. While she wanted Bob to follow his passion, she had no intention of seeing him fly the plane. Shortly, a fire of dubious origin erupted in the garage, destroying the plane and, with it, Bob's dreams. At least for the moment.

While attending Rollins College in Florida, Eda, Bob's sister, met and married Ernst Zoeller and then moved with him to New York. Bob, now out of high school and looking for new opportunities, followed. In White Plains, Bob enrolled in a technical school to refine his mechanical skills. Soon, however, he stumbled on another aircraft wreckage. Bob started over, this time far from his mother and her cache of matches. After rebuilding the small aircraft and then learning to fly, Bob traded the plane for a larger and more advanced model.

Things did not work out as either Eda or Bob planned. Within a couple of years, both the brother and sister found themselves back in Meridian. Eda's marriage had failed, and Bob needed a paying job. Bob went to work at the Steam Feed Works but still found time to perfect his flying skills.

The young man was not alone in his passion for flying. Brothers Al and Fred Key were a Meridian institution, famous for their daring flight demonstrations and the flight school they operated at Bonita Field, a few miles outside Meridian. Unfortunately, it was the height of the Great Depression and the city of Meridian, strapped for cash, was considering shutting its municipal airport. Al and Fred devised a scheme to save the airport and thereby their school. They would attempt to break the twenty-three-day world record for flight endurance and raise enough funds from selling tickets to spectators to keep the airport open. The two bought and customized a small-engine Curtiss Robin aircraft named *Ole Miss* and added extra fuel tanks and a catwalk from which they could do in-flight maintenance.[2]

While testing their Rube Goldberg–like apparatus, the Key brothers encountered several problems. On a test flight, the hose between the *Ole Miss* and the fuel-resupplying aircraft disconnected prematurely and spilled fuel over the aircraft. The Soulé family business, with a reputation for encouraging innovation, came to the rescue. A Soulé Steam Feed Works employee, A. D. Hunter, invented an automatic shutoff valve to prevent the hose from spilling fuel. Years later the US Air Force adopted the shutoff valve design (which is still used in modern-day refueling procedures) and honored Meridian with the privilege of housing the Air Force's 186th Refueling Wing.[3]

Satisfied with the shutoff valve, the brothers lifted off from Meridian in late June 1935. While they flew figure eights in the *Ole Miss,* Jim Keeton, one of the brothers' star students, flew the refueling aircraft. The stunt was a success, with the record-breaking twenty-seven-day flight encompassing a distance of 52,000 miles, twice around the earth.[4]

Bob and his sister, Eda, joined the crowd of thirty-five thousand people who came to watch the stunt. Shortly before her divorce, Eda met Jim Keeton when he and Bob made a trip to New York. Eda was single now, and so was Jim. Two years after the Meridian stunt, Eda and Jim married.

Romance filled the air for Bob too. In the summer of 1939, he met Loletia Mae Cooper while on a double date. Loletia was not his date, but Bob, at the wheel of the car, engineered the sequence of drop-offs so Loletia was last to go home. One thing led to another and, after a whirlwind courtship, the two married.

Flying, however, remained Bob's first love. He opened his own flying school at Bonita Field near the Key brothers' school. When the war broke out, Bob, hoping to fly, approached the army recruiting office. The army was happy for Bob to enlist, but because he wore glasses, he was told he could not serve as a pilot. Bob looked elsewhere, and his search brought him to the Civil Air Patrol (CAP).

The idea of hiring civilian pilots to patrol and defend the American coastline had been tossed around since 1936. The War Department finally gave CAP its approval on December 1, 1941, just days before Pearl Harbor. It was a timely decision. Four days after Pearl Harbor, Germany declared war on the United States and, within another week, the first wave of U-boats headed for the American coast.[5]

Bob signed on with CAP, becoming one of the all-volunteer force of pilots who flew a ragtag fleet of yellow-and-red aircraft from a variety of manufacturers. In very short order, he and the other CAP pilots were put to good use.

During the first six months of 1942, German U-boats harassed US ships at will. Without military ships or aircraft available to intervene, they attacked seventy ships—fourteen alone coming under fire in the Gulf of Mexico.[6] CAP pilots began flying in pairs as far as sixty miles offshore, searching for enemy submarines from the tip of Maine down the East Coast and along the Gulf Coast. Bob's route followed the Texas, Louisiana, and Mississippi coastlines.[7]

Unarmed, they could do little more than note and report sightings. Then in May 1942, CAP upped the stakes, arming their pilots' planes with demolition bombs or depth charges, depending on the aircraft's carrying capacity. By mid-year 1942, CAP's efforts together with other US military defensive measures—using convoys, adding armed escorts, and arming transport ships—diminished the U-boat threat.[8]

The CAP coastal patrol operation ceased in August 1942 when the army agreed to transfer all antisubmarine operations to the navy. Still, CAP had filled a vital mission for the unprepared US military at the war's outbreak. To recognize its contribution, President Roosevelt transferred CAP from the Civil Defense Department to the War Department in 1943.[9]

During its nearly two years of independent operation, one hundred thousand men and women served in CAP. They located and sighted almost two hundred submarines, attacked fifty-seven submarines, dropped eighty-two bombs, and sank two U-boats. In the line of duty, CAP lost ninety planes and twenty-six CAP volunteers were killed.[10]

With his CAP days behind him, Bob started searching for other opportunities to fly. Months later, strapped for new pilots, the army air forces relaxed its standards, allowing men with correctable vision to fly. Bob switched uniforms and jumped back in the cockpit, this time flying for the army air forces as a flight officer in the former US Air Corps Ferrying Command, now the Air Transport Command.

In his new role, Bob picked up aircraft rolling off West Coast factory assembly lines and flew the planes across the country to modification centers, such as Ford Motor Company's Willow Run facility in Detroit, Michigan. The war-service modifications varied by the demands of the plane's final destination; for example, the modification centers added pontoons with retractable wheels to planes that needed to operate on ice, snow, water, or land.[11] Once the modifications were complete, the pilots ferried the planes to their debarkation point for overseas service. The pilots then returned by rail or deadheaded with other ferry pilots to the West Coast to pick up another aircraft. During his service, Bob again proved himself to be a "jack of all trades," flying a wide variety of models, including bombers (B-17, B-24, and B-25), cargo planes (C-46 and C-47), and pursuit or fighter aircraft (including the P-51 Mustang, arguably the best fighter of the war).

The Sixth Ferrying Group's yearbook pays tribute to the ferry pilots' abilities in multiple aircraft. A dedication reads: "Trainers, fighters, medium bombers, heavy bombers, transports: Ferry pilots of the Sixth Ferrying Group fly 'anything, anywhere, anytime.' Their 'Qualification Cards' read like a roster of American military aircraft. Versatility is their goal and their pride."[12]

The ATC also opened its ferrying operations to women and Bob flew several routes with them at the controls of aircraft in his group. Although the women boasted hundreds of hours of experience, part of Bob's duty called for him to take the lead position and guide the female pilots to their destination. During their cross-country flights, if any problems developed or if they needed to refuel, the aircraft convoy could stop at one of several designated support stations. Later, when they reached their final destination, Bob circled the field and, ever the southern gentleman, he watched as each woman in his convoy landed. Only after the women were safely on the ground did he bring his own aircraft down. They became a close-knit group, and Bob made lifelong friends with a few of the women.

While the military restricted the female ferry pilots to domestic routes, male pilots had no such restrictions and could fly any of the ferry routes around the globe. Bob flew bomber aircraft to the war's North Africa theater of operation, taking the southern route—flying from Alabama to Brazil and then across the ocean to Ghana. The ten-thousand-mile flight to Africa was three times longer than the nearly three-thousand-mile Maine-to-Britain route. The southern route, however, enjoyed far better weather, particularly in winter.[13]

For his last tour of duty, Bob transferred to Burma and flew aircraft across the notorious air route, known as the Hump, running from the Assam Valley in northeast India through the winding valleys of the Himalayan mountains into China. One afternoon in India, while Bob was peering through his eyeglasses at the paperwork spread across his desk, a new commander walked past. Staring at Bob, the commander announced, "I'm not going to have any 'four eyes' flying my planes." The commander grounded Bob, appointing him the executive officer for the army air forces' local military police, a cadre of black men. Later, Bob claimed he'd been given the particular duty because he came from the South. "They thought I would be more knowledgeable than the other officers about working with blacks," he explained. The transfer was a bitter disappointment. Bob had flown across oceans and along the treacherous Hump route only to find himself relegated to picking up soldiers from the local jail after a weekend of revelry. Still, Bob completed his service and then after the war returned home to Mississippi. He refused to give up flying and rented a hangar in Gulfport where he opened yet another flying school. Although he knew almost everything there was to know about flying, he knew little about politics. When his hangar's lease came up for renewal, he discovered the city's mayor had given the lease to someone else, likely someone who promised more political favors.

Bob went back to work at the Soulé Steam Feed Works where, after Clyde died in 1949, his half brother Hal had taken the helm. Shut in an office day after day and working under Hal's scrutiny proved untenable. In 1953, after three years at the Steam Feed Works, Bob moved back to Gulfport and began flying again. He found a position at Keesler Air Force Base in Biloxi teaching flying.

Loletia, Bob's wife, wanted to learn to fly and kept after Bob. "You teach all these other people to fly," she said. "Why not me?"

"All these other people are not my wife," Bob said.

Loletia would not give up. She convinced Red Cleveland, another teacher at Keesler, to teach her to fly. Soon Loletia made her first solo flight with Bob watching and cheering from the flight line at Gulfport.

Bob also taught foreign students how to fly. Emblematic of how quickly both the United States and Japan had put the war behind them, some of his students came from Japan, America's World War II adversary. Letia and Bo, Bob's children, remember many of the young foreigners who, after flying with their father, visited the Soulé home for dinners and enjoyed their mother's southern hospitality.

As in his early years, Bob was not content to focus on any one thing. He worked as a corporate pilot and for a time owned the Goldcrest 51 Beer distributorship. He studied artificial insemination to raise cattle on a farm he purchased east of Meridian. Once, he became involved with a get-rich-quick scheme for a miracle ointment containing zinc. "We had a garage filled with boxes of 'Z Ointment,'" Letia remembered. "Dad had big ideas but was not so good at following up."

Letia and Bo grew up with a natural curiosity about their father's service, but like other veterans, their father said little to them. He did, however, share his stories with adult friends, sometimes at meetings at the local Veterans of Foreign Wars post or with the OX5 Aviation Pioneers, a group of aviation enthusiasts. Whenever Bo came within hearing range, he listened intently and captured Bob's memories to preserve them for the family.

Bob passed away at the age of eighty-eight in 2003, leaving behind three children, seven grandchildren, and two great grandchildren. He died more than a decade before Congress awarded the Civil Air Patrol the Congressional Gold Medal—the country's highest civilian honor. Congress delivered the medal, which bears the likeness of a male in a garrison hat, a female in a soft flying helmet, and the text "Honor Civilian Volunteers Who Flew Armed & Humanitarian Missions," to the Smithsonian Institution in 2014 for permanent display. Unfortunately, fewer than one hundred of the hundred thousand World War II–era CAP members lived to hear of or see the award.[14]

CHAPTER FOUR

Dressed in Mainbocher

Eleanor Millican Frye

✷ ✷ ✷

I can't really explain to anyone living today why I joined.
It was a different time back then. People had a different mind-set.
Everyone did anything they could to support the country.

ELEANOR MILLICAN,
Lieutenant, US Naval Reserve (Women's Reserve)

Eleanor Millican joined the navy as a member of the first class of Women Accepted for Volunteer Emergency Service, or WAVES, and became an officer of the US Naval Reserve (Women's Reserve). At one hundred years old, she said her memory of the war was foggy. Still, she spoke with a firm, honey-toned voice, hinting of her mannered, southern upbringing, and threaded her story with a large dose of dry wit.

She was born Eleanor Jefferson Millican in Atlanta, Georgia, to Earle and Lillie Millican on July 30, 1918. Shortly afterward, the Millicans moved to Griffin, Georgia, a small town just south of Atlanta. Eleanor spent a happy childhood there and became good friends with Augustus "Gus" Frye, a young boy who lived on the same street. She lost touch with Gus when he left Griffin for prep school, but fate intervened. The two met again at the University of Georgia. Although the future Mrs. Frye claims Gus was busy "attending to half the women on campus," she snared a handful of dates with him. The July 15 entry in her 1937 datebook reads, "Gus Frye. Date. Picnic."

While at the university, Eleanor studied journalism and landscape architecture, imagining herself "writing wonderful articles for the pages of *House & Garden* or *House Beautiful*." It was a glamorous image, full of comfortable, cushioned chairs set on wide verandas, vases overflowing with flowers, and glasses of sweet tea on a nearby table. An image well suited for a proper southern lady. But Eleanor found she was not fond of writing. In her honest, plain-speaking manner, she confessed that a good friend and fellow student who wrote for the university's newspaper also wrote a few articles in her name for an occasional journalism assignment. The young man was eager to help, no doubt smitten by the slim, dark-haired coed, but Eleanor had set her sights on Gus.

In 1939 she and Gus graduated, but their future together appeared doubtful. Gus, who was planning to attend medical school, was facing years of intense study. Two years later, with the United States on the brink of war, Gus joined the army. Although she had not given up hope, Eleanor realized separation was inevitable and marriage out of the question, at least for now. As she would discover later, marrying Gus proved equally difficult after the war.

With journalism off the table and Gus out of the picture, Eleanor pondered her next step. She took a room with several other young, career-minded women at a boardinghouse in Atlanta. There, she modeled fashions for the respected J. P. Allen department store and then went to work at the "telephone company," as she said everyone referred to AT&T.

She also made connections. Eleanor audited a night course at the Georgia Institute of Technology taught by US Navy Lt. Paul Ellis, a friend from Griffin. Ellis later introduced Eleanor to another naval officer, Cdr. J. M. Sweeney, a native of Albany, New York, and, at the time, the highest-ranking naval officer in Atlanta. Eleanor became good friends with the commander and his wife, spending many nights at the Sweeney home. And, although he was happily married, Eleanor admitted to having a schoolgirl crush on the handsome navy officer. In an interview Eleanor granted to a Charleston newspaper after the war had started, she explained, "It was merely a case of hero-worship."[1]

Ellis and Sweeney, both graduates of the US Naval Academy at Annapolis, influenced Eleanor's next step as did the military's very active program to recruit women. Radio programs, recruiting posters, and magazine advertisements popularized the idea of women serving in the military with slogans like, "Have you got what it takes to do a job like this?" and, "Bring him home sooner." The promotional images featured attractive women with big smiles and smart uniforms. By serving in the armed forces, Madison Avenue asserted, women could free more male officers for combat duty.[2]

Eleanor was eager to enlist and, due to Sweeney's influence, her heart was set on joining the navy. Earle and Lillie, her parents, gave her their full support. They had little choice. When Eleanor made up her mind, nothing stood in her way.

"I can't really explain to anyone living today why I joined. It was a different time back then. People had a different mind-set," she said and tried to describe how families at home made great sacrifices on behalf of the troops. Rationing was one of her most vivid memories. From just after the war started until 1946, the US government limited access to food, gas, and clothing to divert resources and production capacity to wartime needs. Every household—the wealthy and the less fortunate—received a book of coupons for the restricted items.

"No one complained, that was just the way it was," Eleanor said. "We didn't see butter for years." Instead, a substance resembling white grease graced the family's dinner table. "It came with a little packet of yellow dust. If you wanted the grease to look like butter, you mixed the two together. And a steak? Well, a steak was just a lovely memory."

Eleanor continued, "We believed we were doing the right thing and helping the troops get what they needed." In her case, the "troops" included a number of her male friends—and one soldier in particular, Gus Frye.

In an irony not lost on Eleanor, on July 30, 1942, twenty-four years to the day after she was born, President Roosevelt signed Public Law 689, allowing women to enlist in the newly formed women's units. Eleanor lost no time in applying.

At the time, the US Navy's entry requirements for women more closely resembled those for a finishing school. Applicants needed to demonstrate "good character" and supply three letters of recommendation. They needed to exhibit the appearance, manner, bearing, and capacity of leadership; stand at least five feet tall; and weigh at least ninety-five pounds, with weight in proportion to their general body build. They also needed a minimum of eighteen sound teeth with four opposing front teeth.[3] Further, women who wanted to be officers needed a college degree. In 1940, with less than 5 percent of the female population over twenty-five holding a college degree, they were a relatively rare commodity.[4]

Eleanor breezed through the application, easily marking off where she met or exceeded the requirements. She sealed the envelope, dropped it through the mail slot at the post office, and went back to work. Separately, Lieutenant Ellis and Commander Sweeney wrote letters of recommendation for their young friend Eleanor. Although she never read or saw their letters, in a rare moment of modesty, Eleanor credited the gross exaggerations she imagined they contained with convincing the navy to accept her into the ranks.

On enlisting, Eleanor became one of what would be nearly 300,000 women serving in the military by the end of the war. Over 150,000 served with the Women's Army Corps (WAC), 100,000 in the US Naval Reserve under the WAVES, 23,000 in the US Marine Corps Women's Reserve, 10,000 in the US Coast Guard Women's Reserve (SPAR, for *Semper Paratus*—Always Ready), and 1,100 with the Women Airforce Service Pilots (WASP).[5]

In August 1942, the navy welcomed its first female recruits. With a group of other like-minded young women, Eleanor traveled from Atlanta to the US Navy's training school at Smith College in Northampton, Massachusetts. Already near capacity with traditional students attending the 1942 fall semester, the school's dormitories could not accommodate the additional nine hundred military women.[6] The navy assigned some women, including Eleanor, to rooms at the nearby Hotel Northampton, a refined establishment, famous for its Colonial Revival design, museum quality antiques, and fine dining.[7]

The rest of the country might endure rationing, but the WAVES at the Hotel Northampton dined on steak, scallops, and shrimp and, Eleanor said, buttered their dinner rolls with real butter. To the women's dismay, however, the hotel had removed the sumptuous antique furnishings for safekeeping until after the war. In their place, they found each of the large rooms furnished with eight navy-issued bunk beds, four chests of drawers, and a handful of waste bins. And, as the women quickly learned, according to military rules, beds served a single purpose. They were for sleeping, not for lounging, resting, or sitting. So, when at liberty in their rooms, the women upended the bins and took turns sitting on the improvised chairs. In later years, conditions at Smith improved, as Eleanor presumed they did at the other colleges as well. She scoffed at the thought, describing the women who followed her pioneering class at Smith as sissies. "They were pampered with desks and chairs."

The accelerated program at Smith began with an indoctrination into naval etiquette, teaching the women, now apprentice seamen, about navy life and military procedures. Like their male counterparts, however, the women also learned to march at a time when learning to drill was deemed "a particular challenge for mature women."[8]

Challenge or not, Eleanor shivered as she recalled marching across the Smith athletic fields in the depths of winter. "It was," she said, "the coldest December Northampton had seen since 1875. And I'd never been north of Virginia in my life." She remembered the snow blanketing the campus in drifts. "It was very, very deep. I was so angry."[9]

On one bone-chilling march, Eleanor fainted. She picked herself up, dusted the snow off her uniform, and stepped back in line, but the instructor suggested she return to the barracks with an escort. With a bit of quick thinking, Eleanor—a woman practiced in the art of displaying on cue the fragility of southern femininity—suggested two escorts might be better. The instructor acquiesced. Eleanor had spared a second woman from marching in knee-deep snow that afternoon. Despite the snowy mishap, Eleanor's platoon became the best-performing group and was photographed marching two abreast "down a gentle hill" for a 1943 *Life Magazine* article. The pioneering WAVES, in their smart dark uniforms, were a curiosity across the country but also in Northampton where townspeople often took time to watch the women drill.[10]

After their first thirty days, the women became midshipmen and entered another monthlong period of training. The advanced training in this phase covered all three navy jobs open to women: radio communications, bookkeeping, and secretarial work.[11]

Eleanor dreaded the thought of secretarial work. She had never mastered the art of typing—nor, as she recalled, the similar finger dexterity needed to play the piano. When she was a child, her piano instructor counseled Earle and Lillie not to waste their money or the teacher's time on piano lessons for the young girl. The navy reached the same conclusion and assigned Eleanor to a job in communications.

Then, after a final eight weeks of specialized training, she graduated, earned a promotion to ensign, and donned her new uniform. "Mainbocher," Eleanor said and sighed, remembering the blue tailored jackets and gored skirts the famous designer created for the navy. "We thought they were pretty cool."

None of the WAVES had any idea where their first assignment would take them. After her one Massachusetts winter, however, Eleanor hoped hers would be in a warmer climate. Two factors mentioned on her application influenced her destiny. First were the night courses she audited at Georgia Tech. As it so happens, they covered celestial navigation and nautical astronomy. Eleanor also had claimed practical familiarity with navigation and navigational charts, drawing on her experience from summers spent sailing with Gus. "My background—or luck—must have worked. The navy sent me to Charleston." At the Sixth Naval District Headquarters in Charleston, South Carolina, Eleanor served as the assistant to the routing officer in the port director's office. "It was just the duty I wanted."

From a navy-commandeered suite of hotel rooms on Charleston's Battery, Eleanor and the rest of a team headed by a lieutenant commander communicated shipping routes to merchant marine vessels traveling the coast. As the ships' captains called at their offices, Lt. Cdr. Cornelis Johannis Hitz and Eleanor turned over orders, pulling as needed navigational charts depicting routes and ports of call from file cabinets lining the walls.

"Thank God, none of us had to make the actual decisions," Eleanor said, knowing the dangers the men faced. Unarmed and unarmored, the merchant marine vessels were the most vulnerable to attack from German U-boats. The team at the port director's office did what it could to slot the vessels to the better-protected center of a convoy for their voyages.

The director's office was photographed for an article the navy commissioned for the *Charleston News and Courier*. In the photograph, Eleanor stands between Lieutenant Commander Hitz and an unnamed merchant marine ship's captain. The trio appears to pore over a navigational chart spread on the desk before them. Eleanor remembered being horrified as they staged the shot. Someone had pulled the captain's actual chart from a file cabinet to use as the central prop. No one else seemed to notice. Eleanor swallowed hard and pointed out the indiscretion. Seconds later, an innocuous, generic map covered the desk for the photograph.

The first WAVES became a close-knit group, and Eleanor made several good female friends both in Charleston and later, when she was stationed in New Orleans. Rosemary Nelson, who the team in Charleston nicknamed "Admiral Nelson" after the famous British Admiral Horatio Lord Nelson, worked one door away from Eleanor in the Charleston hotel. Although good friends for the year or more they spent in South Carolina, the two had never discussed their work.

Everyone was tight-lipped during the war years. Besides the ever-present and well-known caution "loose lips sink ships," Eleanor recalled a sign at a favorite Charleston bar that read, "What you see here, what you say here, let it stay here." Eleanor and Rosemary heeded the advice. Not until they met years after the war did Eleanor ask Rosemary what her duties had been and discover the two had performed similar functions.

There was, however, another less appealing aspect of being one of the WAVES—the flip side of the navy's idea that women who joined "freed men to fight." To this day, Eleanor worries about the man she replaced and likely sent to sea. "There's a woman somewhere who hated me," she said.

But while they shouldered their responsibility and took their work seriously, the WAVES also found ample time to enjoy themselves. In New Orleans, the women made the rounds of local restaurants, dining at Antoine's, Galatoire's, Court of Two Sisters, and other of the city's finer dining establishments. Often, she said, heads turned when the uniformed women walked through the door. It was not uncommon for the waiter to come to their table after dinner and inform the women a patron had paid for their meal.

Their singular position, and no doubt their attractiveness, opened other doors and opportunities. Doris Blackwell, a friend, fellow member in the WAVES, and daughter of the then secretary of state of South Carolina, invited Eleanor to attend a national meeting of secretaries of state. The venue for the glamorous event was the rotunda of Louisiana's state capitol. While ogling their opulent surroundings and the cadre of handsome, and eligible, young politicians, the women paid little attention to the clock. Toward the end of the evening, Eleanor and Doris found themselves short on time to return to New Orleans. With a word from Doris's father, the highway patrol brought a car to the front door and whisked the women away. Giddy with delight, the girls sped the ninety-mile-long trip to New Orleans with sirens blaring and lights flashing. Eleanor paused in the middle of telling her story and stepped from the room. She returned with a prized souvenir—the menu from the Baton Rouge evening, a fine meal that started with a martini sec, followed by hors d'oeuvres, crevettes lafitte, and on and on to bifteck grillé with sauce d'Orléans, and ending with fraises à la mode.

The hard work and tough duty, as Eleanor described her assignments, ended as the war wound down. She received a promotion to lieutenant, and, after her honorable discharge in 1946, she returned home to Griffin.

Two years later, in 1948, Congress passed the Women's Armed Services Integration Act, allowing women to serve in all military branches. The Women's Reserve unit became obsolete, and the WAVES transferred to the regular navy and the naval reserve.[12]

Approaching the ripe old age of thirty, Eleanor began to think seriously about her future and, she said, "To try to catch Gus." But Gus had other plans. As a successful practicing surgeon gaining national renown, he was devoted to his work. He was not going to marry. "I'm just not the marrying type," Eleanor recalled Gus saying. One day in July 1950, however, Gus called the Millican home in Griffin from a favorite vacation spot in Maine, a place Gus and Eleanor had enjoyed together the previous year. He asked to speak with Eleanor's father, Earle.

Gus's annual trip to Maine had proved less enjoyable without Eleanor. The man who said he would never marry changed his mind. For the second time in her life, Eleanor asked for and received her parents' blessing. The next morning, she packed a bag, drove to Atlanta, and purchased a wedding dress and "a collection of negligees" from the fashionable Leon Frohsin's shop. With a level of service unheard of in modern times, Frohsin's altered the dress in a few hours. Eleanor, dress in hand, departed for Maine a day later.

The wedding was a simple, private ceremony on July 15, 1950—thirteen years to the day after Eleanor and Gus had picnicked at the University of Georgia. The bride, as the *Portland News* reported, wore a street-length marquisette gown fashioned with lace sleeves and carried a colonial bouquet of white delphiniums.[13] Gus and Eleanor idled away the next few weeks sailing together on Gus's boat, *Our Joy.*

After sixty-one years of true joy as a couple, Gus passed away in 2011. Eleanor treasures her memories of her lifelong partner and of the years she spent serving her country. At the century mark, Eleanor sleeps late, spends her time in the couple's home in Tennessee, and enjoys her extensive mountaintop garden. The Frohsin's marquisette gown still hangs in her closet.

CHAPTER FIVE

An Athlete on the High Seas

Francis Rae Surprenant

✳ ✳ ✳

Everyone loved us. We had all the supplies.

<small>Francis Rae Surprenant,</small>
Able Seaman, US Merchant Marine

On Maritime Day 1942, President Roosevelt commended the officers and men of the US Merchant Marine for their contribution to the war effort. "During these dangerous days and nights on the sea lanes of the world," he said, "with danger lurking above, below, and on the surface, they do not falter in the performance of their duty. Hundreds of them render service far beyond the call of duty."[1] Roosevelt's recognition was one of the few the members received then and for decades after the war.

Despite its name, the US Merchant Marine was not a branch of the military but an association of privately owned shipping companies sailing under the American flag. In wartime they played a vital role, delivering supplies and war matériel from US ports to the field of battle, whether across the Atlantic or the Pacific.[2]

In 1943, at seventeen years old, Francis Rae "Bud" Surprenant stood six feet tall and weighed a lean 180 pounds. A high school photo captured his broad smile and jet-black hair—boyish good looks that combined with the congenial manner his son, Roland Surprenant, remembered made Bud popular among his peers at Glens Falls High. He was also a talented athlete, captain of the Glens Falls, New York, high school track team, cocaptain of the football team, and a member of the ice hockey team.

With the Second World War in full swing, Bud was anxious to finish high school so he could enlist and serve his country. Then, months before graduation, Jackie MacDougall, Bud's football team cocaptain, threw caution to the wind and joined the merchant marine. Bud hadn't given much thought to how he wanted to serve, but having spent his youth around New York's Lake George, he loved the water and considered serving at sea far preferable to the prospect of trudging across a battlefield and dying in a foxhole. He followed Jackie into the merchant marine.

With their fellow mariners, Jackie and Bud trained for ninety days at Sheepshead Bay, New York, where the new US Maritime Training Service Station had opened in September 1942. After completing a six-week period of general training, the men underwent another six weeks of training in their choice of deck, engine, or steward duties.[3] Bud elected deck service, completed his training, and became certified as an ordinary seaman by the US Department of Commerce on May 19, 1943. A month later, he deployed aboard the SS *Mariposa*, a former luxury liner requisitioned for military service after Pearl Harbor.

The papers Roland Surprenant preserved list Bud's position aboard the *Mariposa* as porter. In that entry-level deckhand position, Bud performed many of the crew's most tedious duties, including loading and unloading cargo and washing, scraping, and painting deck surfaces. But starting at the lowest rung and working their way up the ranks was a common practice, referred to as "coming up through the hawsepipe" (hawsepipe is the pipe in the bow through which the anchor's chain passes). Later, Bud was assigned to lifeboat operations. His certificate for this role cites his familiarity with all operations connected with launching and handling lifeboats and the use of oars.

After two months aboard the *Mariposa*, Bud deployed aboard the SS *Edwin Markham* where he served for five months with the rating of an ordinary seaman acting able seaman, a position just below able seaman.

The *Markham* was one of the 2,700 mass-produced Liberty ships, designed and constructed specifically for service during World War II. The ships had a simple design and were built using assembly-line techniques, prefabricated sections, and welding rather than riveting to reduce construction time. The first Liberty ship, the *Patrick Henry,* was built in 245 days, and the average in thirty days. As a demonstration of peak performance, however, the *Robert E. Peary* was completed in fewer than five days after the keel was laid.[4]

When President Roosevelt saw the initial ship blueprints, he mused, "I think this ship will do us very well. She'll carry a good load. She isn't much to look at, though, is she? A real ugly duckling." The name stuck, and the Liberty ships became known as Ugly Ducklings.[5] On September 27, 1941, when the United States was ready to launch the first fourteen Liberty ships, in his speech Roosevelt said, "They have caught the true spirit with which all this nation must be imbued if Hitler and other aggressors of his ilk are to be prevented from crushing us." Aware the *Patrick Henry* was among the boats to be launched, Roosevelt invoked the words of the patriot for which the ship was named, saying it renewed the demand to "Give me liberty or give me death."[6]

Roosevelt's gamble to direct so much of the country's resources to the production of Liberty ships and later the faster and larger Victory ships proved instrumental in America's success. Capable of carrying close to five hundred men and over one hundred vehicles and delivering troops and their supplies—food and clothing, as well as trucks, tanks, aircraft and aircraft fuel, ammunition, bombs, and raw material to make bombs and airplanes—the ships provided critical logistical support to the theaters of war in both the Atlantic and the Pacific.[7]

After receiving a promotion to able seaman in February 1944, Bud transferred to another Liberty ship, the SS *Josiah Nelson Cushing,* where he served for eleven months. As he recounted in his letters home, Bud's days aboard the *Cushing* kept him busy. For security reasons, the men could say little about their actual duties or their ship's location, so Bud wrote of trips he made to England, Ireland, and Scotland; of the forts and castles he toured; and later of North Africa. He wrote of trying to buy souvenirs but finding little available because of rationing. Instead he bought, among other items, a sweater in Ireland and a pair of handmade leather shoes in Scotland—sending some purchases home to his mother or father or to his brother, Joe. The voyage provided Bud and his fellow seamen, many like Bud in their late teens, an eye-opening experience. In his letters, Bud described the sights as "very interesting, but [he'd] take the good ole US any day." And he admitted, "The more I write this letter the more homesick I get."[8]

Homesick and, once, very seasick. On a three-week voyage in the rough North Atlantic, Roland said, Bud claims he was "sick as a dog." He might have even questioned his choice of service, but he persevered.

To give his parents a better sense of his duty, Bud wrote about his daily activities and his living conditions. At sea, he said, he stood a wheel watch and served as a lookout from eight in the morning until noon and then again from eight at night until midnight. At anchor, he stood a bridge watch at night. He described the mess hall where he sat while one fellow read, two others played checkers, and a second pair played chess. Others chatted or listened to the radio, a favorite pastime for most of the men. "Programs from home sure boost our morale," the homesick able seaman wrote. He confessed, "If there was anything I wanted it was to be back home for the football season and fall weather."[9]

Whether to spare his family worry or to avoid censorship, Bud did not elaborate on the dangers he faced. Men of the merchant marine suffered some of the highest casualty ratios of any branch of service. One of every twenty-six men serving aboard merchant marine ships perished, and two hundred Liberty ships fell victim to attacks by wolf packs of German submarines, surface vessels, or aircraft, or they were sunk after hitting mines.[10]

Bud had joined the merchant marine largely ignorant of what he had signed up for. He had simply followed in the footsteps of his high school friend. And, although Bud soon understood the dangers, his fate was sealed. Good luck kept him from encounters with the German U-boats during his many ocean crossings, but, still, he faced other perils.

In the opening days of June 1944, after weeks of roaming the waters around Britain to prevent the Germans from detecting a concentration of ships, the *Cushing* and hundreds of other merchant ships headed for the beaches on the French coast. On June 6, D-Day, Bud found himself in the middle of the Normandy invasion. As a supply ship during the invasion, the *Cushing* dropped its cargo at Omaha Beach in France and then returned to Britain to begin a multiday shuttle service between the two countries.[11]

The carefree tone of his earlier correspondence changed. Bud apologized for not writing more, explaining he was in the middle of a run between France and England. His shore liberty amounted to five hours, and he said, "That's not much . . . besides working seventy-two hours regularly with but a few hours of sleep and just when you get to sleep to be awoken by air raid alert or sub alert or shell fire from shore." With a touch of sarcasm, he added, "So folks, it's not as much of a picnic over here as you read about in the daily papers."[12]

Bud's handwritten itinerary of his ship's ten-month voyage, from the time he boarded on March 6, 1944, until the end of December the same year, indicates he made not one expedition in support of D-Day but crossed the English Channel eight times. After the invasion, Bud wrote that as the "Mighty *Cushing*" sat off the shore of France, he had been swimming despite water temperatures of fifty-five to sixty degrees. He said, too, he had watched every day as hundreds of planes flew overhead to Germany to "give those morons more hell. They asked for it and now they're getting it!"[13]

Roland, Bud's son, recalled that his father, like many of his generation, spoke little of his war experience. One of his rare tales concerned a fellow mariner killed while carrying ammunition across the ship's deck. And, later, while on leave at home, Bud recounted for his hometown newspaper, the *Glens Falls Post Star*, a particularly harrowing event toward the end of his service. While unloading supplies in the harbor at Naples, Italy, the *Cushing* came under attack by Nazi warplanes. When ordered to take cover, Bud said, "Believe you me, we didn't waste any time taking shelter." Another attack occurred the next day, this time by planes carrying torpedoes. The *Cushing* narrowly escaped being hit by a torpedo as it sped past and struck a nearby merchant ship. Luck stayed with the *Cushing*. Another swarm of fighters strafed the convoy with machine-gun fire, resulting in several casualties, but none aboard the *Cushing*.[14]

As proof, Bud showed Frank Garcin, the *Post Star* reporter, several small bomb splinters he had carried home. By then, Bud had an impressive trove of souvenirs, including, according to the newspaper report, a pair of handmade Arabian slippers, handkerchiefs, scarves, a Moroccan hand-tooled wallet, and numerous photos of life in North Africa.[15]

During his last few months of duty, Bud held the rating able seaman on any waters—a designation licensing him to sail both on the ocean and on inland waters such as the Great Lakes. In that capacity, he spent two months aboard the SS *Louis Bamberger* and then two months aboard the coast guard ship SS *Robert H. Harrison*. He was discharged from the merchant marine in May 1945.

For his service, Bud was awarded the Merchant Marine Service Emblem, a Combat Bar with Silver Stars (the stars indicated a seaman had been forced to evacuate or abandon a ship after attack), the World War II Victory Medal, the Atlantic War Zone Bar, the Mediterranean-Middle East War Zone Bar, and an Honorable Service Button. He also received a Presidential Testimonial Letter from President Truman, extending the heartfelt thanks of a nation for perform-ing a "most severe task—one which called for courage and fortitude."[16]

Decommissioned after the war, hundreds of Liberty ships were "mothballed." For years, many sat anchored side by side in a miles-long line along the Bruns-wick River near Wilmington, North Carolina, waiting to be scrapped or sold. Only two of the 2,700 survived as operational ships—the *John W. Brown* in Baltimore and the *Jeremiah O'Brien* in San Francisco. Both, although mothballed for three decades, bear fresh coats of battleship gray paint. Restored to their wartime operating conditions, the two serve as museums dedicated to all those who built the ships or sailed with the merchant marine in World War II.

Congenial and outgoing, Bud made a number of lasting friends during his war years, including Tom Stanfield, whom he met in Europe and saw again after the war in Glens Falls. Tom, a former businessman and PhD candidate in history turned merchant mariner, was a decade older and far more experienced than Bud. Stanfield wrote to Bud in February 1946, encouraging Bud to return to school and get a high school diploma. Sage advice fills Stanfield's letter, some disparaging, including remarks about how little Bud would learn in school and how it would seem like "a lot of adolescent crap" after what Bud had seen of the real world. Still, Stanfield wrote, without a degree, "every son of a b. and his brother will be slamming the door in your face."[17]

Bud followed Stanfield's advice and returned to school. He earned his high school diploma and then won a football scholarship to Ithaca College. In November

1948, however, before he could finish his first course at Ithaca, Bud received a Korean War draft notice in the mail. Still, Bud thought he was safe. Three years earlier, the War Shipping Administration (WSA), with oversight of the merchant marine, matched the military's stipulations for draft eligibility. The WSA allowed merchant mariners a deferment if they had served thirty-two months of "substantially continuous service."[18]

Bud qualified for the deferment, but despite a frantic search and calls home to his mother, he could not locate his service records. Fearing he would be drafted, he enlisted in the air force. Bud spent the next three and a half years as a US Air Force recruiter in Florida, where he met his future wife, Myrna Burke.

In August 1952, Bud left the military for the second and last time. He returned home and went to work with his father, who owned an office equipment and supply company. The elder Surprenant managed the company and sales while Bud oversaw operations, including managing crews who installed office partitions.

Today, many former merchant mariners still talk of being considered "second class" or members of the forgotten service. Bud, too, held a grudge against the government for not recognizing the men of the merchant marine as veterans until the 1980s. Ever the pragmatist, however, Bud recognized life was not going to go the way he or anyone else wanted and, Roland said, his father looked back on his time in the merchant marine fondly.

The negative image once popularly attributed to men of the merchant marine, in actuality, had less to do with their reputation as fiercely independent, "beholden to alcohol," and engaging in "criminal mischief" than their status as members of the National Maritime Union at a time when radical unionism was spreading across the country.[19] One evening, decades after the war, father and son sat together and watched actor Nick Nolte play a rough-and-tumble merchant marine in a television adaptation of Irwin Shaw's *Rich Man, Poor Man.* As that image played in his head and on the screen, Roland asked his father if, as a young seaman, he had been in fistfights or run into trouble. With a crooked smile on his face, Bud dodged the question. He replied, "Everyone loved us. We had all the supplies."

Bud Surprenant enjoyed years of good times following his service in the merchant marine. His family grew to include eight children, ten grandchildren, and eleven great-grandchildren. Since his death in 1995, his son, Roland, tirelessly carries on his father's aspirations for recognition of the merchant marine, honored today with its own section at the National World War II Museum in New Orleans, Louisiana.

CHAPTER SIX

Talking Logistics

Ike Minkovitz
(with Kay Minkovitz)

*You know what a stickler I am anyway for
wanting everything functioning just so.*

IKE MINKOVITZ,
Staff Sergeant, US Army Air Forces

In 1926 Ike Minkovitz graduated from high school in Sylvania, Georgia. Despite the fact that he was only sixteen and hailed from a rural community in the flat, coastal plains of central Georgia, Ike had big ambitions. Without wasting a minute, he enrolled at the University of Georgia, graduating cum laude four years later. For Ike, achieving his degree, even a degree with distinction as one of the youngest in his class, was nothing. As a Minkovitz, it was expected.

The Minkovitz family history reads like a classic Horatio Alger tale. So the story goes, as a teenager in the early 1900s, Ike's father, Hyman Minkovitz, fled the family home in Dokshitsy, Belarus, to escape the Russian pogroms against Jews. With nothing but his parents' meager savings in his pocket, Hyman rode concealed beneath sacks of hay in a horse-drawn cart and ran, walked, and sometimes crawled to make his way across the Russian border to Hamburg, Germany. There, he exchanged the last of his rubles for space aboard the steamship *Prager,* arriving at Ellis Island in 1905.

Hyman didn't venture far from his point of entry to America. He settled in New York City like the hundreds of thousands of immigrant Jews before him.[1] Those early immigrants brought their old-country skills with them and helped establish New York's garment industry. In that close-knit community Hyman found work, and in 1908 he met Gussie Goldie Mason, also a garment industry worker and also from Belarus. The two married and two years later their first child, Ike, was born.

Following the tentacles of the garment industry, which by the early twentieth century reached across the country, Hyman and Gussie moved to Brooklet, Georgia. There, with dreams of a prosperous future, Hyman opened a dry goods store.

The business evolved and expanded. Hyman added sewing supplies, ready-to-wear clothing, household essentials, and sundry items to the inventory. Soon, he opened a second store twenty-five miles north of Brooklet in the town of Sylvania, where he also relocated his family.

By 1919, the family included two more boys, Harry and Solomon, and a girl, Emma. When old enough, Ike and his brothers joined Hyman at the store, and, to reflect its growth and the boys' involvement, Hyman renamed the store "H. Minkovitz & Sons: Department and Five and Dime Store." Emma, too, went to work at the store. She did more than ring up purchases at the register and wrap packages; Emma attracted customers. Years later, the dark-haired beauty would become Miss Georgia 1939. In keeping with the times, however, despite her contribution, the sign over the front door remained H. Minkovitz & Sons.

On returning home to Sylvania from college, Ike hung his diploma on the wall and picked up where he had left off at Minkovitz & Sons. Shortly afterward, Hyman expanded the enterprise once again, purchasing a store in nearby Statesboro, Georgia. Ike moved to Statesboro to manage the store. As a young bachelor, Ike often took his meals at Statesboro's Teapot Grill, where he met Elizabeth Clayton DeLoach. Ike began a seven-year courtship of Elizabeth—or perhaps it was the other way around, said Ike's daughter Donna Minkovitz Darracott. Elizabeth developed an endless list of excuses to shop at Ike's store, buying a new dress one day and then returning to purchase a pair of shoes or gloves, or a hat the next. However the relationship unfolded, after Elizabeth converted to Judaism in 1941, the two finally married.

When World War II broke out, Ike's brother-in-law Morton Friedman and Ike's youngest brother, Solomon, joined the army. Both became officers. Ike was eager to follow, but besides having a new wife, Hyman needed him at home to help manage the business. And as Ike knew, what Hyman wanted Hyman got. Ike fulfilled his obligations to his father and to the business but never stopped thinking of joining the army, becoming an officer, defending his country, and standing up for what at this juncture in the war was known at home only as persecution of the Jews in Europe and a refugee problem for the United States.

In April 1943, although far from over, the war's tide was turning. Fearing his chance was slipping away and that he would be drafted soon, Ike persuaded Hyman to let him go. He sped to Fort McPherson, Georgia, to inquire about enlisting in the army and earning an officer's commission. The army declined Ike's request to attend Officer Candidate School, so he turned to the army air forces. Rebuffed again, Ike surrendered—at least temporarily—and joined the army air forces as a private. While Ike was now at least able to do his part, he refused to give up trying to become an officer. In a letter Ike wrote eight months after he enlisted, he said, "It has been practically an impossibility to get into Officers Candidate School. . . . The situation seems to be that the Air Force and other branches of the Army have about as many officers as they need. This, however, still doesn't keep me from wanting to get a commission."[2]

With his thirteen years of experience in store management where he did everything from purchasing goods to taking inventories to promoting sales, Ike was the perfect candidate for a role in military logistics. In the next few months, he'd become even more qualified. After basic training in Miami Beach, Florida, and weeks of technical training first in Colorado and then in Utah, Ike acquired a dizzying array of new skills in operations, maintenance, and logistics. Then, along with sixty other enlisted men, Ike traveled to Davis-Monthan Army Air Field in Tucson, Arizona, to handle logistics for the headquarters group of the newly formed 459th Bombardment Group, part of the Fifteenth Air Force's 304th Bombardment Wing. The three-thousand-person-strong group comprised four squadrons of B-24 Liberators Ike described as "those heavy bomber jobs, four-motored B-24s."[3] The logistics men in the group, like Ike, managed the large and ever-growing stock of the Bombardment Wing's supplies. Despite his experience and training, with the number of stock items approaching five hundred thousand, Ike had his hands full.[4]

Although the military desperately needed men and matériel, Ike faced endless delays before going overseas. His future station was a military complex near Foggia in southern Italy. The station had several advantages over England-based operations, including a milder climate. Further, as the army saw it, bombers departing Giulia and the other airfields clustered around Foggia would have easier access to strategic bombing targets in Europe, including enemy military, industrial (oil refineries, aircraft factories, and airfields), transportation, and communications centers across the continent. Italy's proximity to France also meant the group could support the invasion of southern Europe and provide a second front to attack the German Army.[5]

Foggia's airfield, however, had been badly damaged while under German occupation. As soon as the Allies successfully invaded Italy and forced the Germans north, repairs began. Ike and his unit waited stateside, spending much of the fall and winter of 1943 in Massachusetts practicing what they had learned during training and preparing for overseas duty. Finally, in January 1944, the 459th's bombers took to the skies to cross the Atlantic. Their flight proved a perilous journey with the group losing five bombers in transit. Two disappeared without a trace over the Atlantic, another crash-landed in Puerto Rico, and two were destroyed in an airfield accident in British Guiana (now Guyana).[6]

Meanwhile, the 459th's troops crossed by sea aboard a converted cruise ship outfitted to carry men packed in bunks stacked six high. Although the ship made it safely across the Atlantic with a convoy and armed escorts to discourage attack by the infamous German U-boats, the voyage was not without its hazards. Germans attacked the ship from the air in the Mediterranean and then after the men disembarked in Taranto, Italy, a cargo truck plowed into a group of soldiers, sending eight to the hospital. Fortunately, Ike escaped both incidents unharmed.[7] In fact, he said nothing of them and claimed in a letter home to Elizabeth the crossing was "the longest month I ever spent in my life . . . too much time for thought I suppose."[8]

By the time Ike arrived in Giulia, the military emblem on his sleeve sported two new stripes and a rocker—the upward curving bar worn below the chevron-shaped stripes. He was now a staff sergeant with the 459th. Along with the higher rank came more responsibility. Ike supervised ten enlisted men in engineering, supply, ordnance, and armament sections. The job fell far short of what he imagined he would be doing. Ike tried again to seek a commission, submitting his application in early 1944 for Warrant Officer, Junior Grade. Perhaps trying to temper his own desire and his wife's expectations, he wrote, "Fellows with longer service overseas will probably get preference." He followed with a nonchalant, "I'm not very excited about it. If I make the grade and get accepted, all well and good. If not, I won't be disappointed. It's . . . nothing to rave about," but he quickly added, "I'm praying that it comes through."[9]

The promotion did not come through and Ike went back to work and to corresponding with Elizabeth. Donna saved the trove of over 250 letters her parents exchanged during Ike's eighteen-month absence. Each is filled with stories of friends and family, particularly news of his firstborn daughter, Kay (Donna's older sister), updates on his wife's pregnancy, and censored words of the war's progress. Elizabeth often enclosed comic strips clipped from the local paper, including Chic Young's *Blondie* and Al Capp's *Li'l Abner*. "It's funny about the comics," Ike wrote. "The boys can hardly wait for me to finish them."

Ike's letters home reveal he was at times excited and optimistic about the war and his role. The job required diligence and care, qualities Ike had in abundance. As he wrote to Elizabeth in March 1944, "You know what a stickler I am anyway for wanting everything functioning just so." At other times, Ike was bored and frustrated. In August that year, he wrote, "Naturally things get monotonous at times but guess it would take a guy with iron nerves who didn't get fed up with life in Italy and army routine occasionally.[10]

Without a doubt, logistics personnel, by and large, escaped the dangers and excitement their frontline counterparts saw, but they played an important and often-overlooked role in the war. The amount of supplies (whether food, fuel, water, clothing, or other war matériel) needed to support a single bombardment group staggers the imagination. To put one 36-plane heavy bomb group into the air for a single mission, for example, required 96,000 gallons of gasoline, 300 bombs, and 190,000 rounds of .50-caliber ammunition.[11]

As impressive and critical to success as the United States' ability to ramp up manufacturing for the war was—diverting resources such as rubber, tin, and nylon to wartime needs and turning factories over to war-related production—producing the matériel was not enough. Ammunition, guns, bombs, airplanes, trucks, and tanks as well as food, clothing, blankets, and tents needed to arrive at the right place at the right time. That was the job of the men and women in logistics, and it was more art than science. The supply lines stretched from factories in the United States to Ike's air base in Giulia, Italy, as well as airfields and stations across the globe: in England, North Africa, New Guinea, and China, wherever Allied planes operated.

By modern standards, World War II logistics planning was primitive. Ike and his men made requisitions and reports by hand, often based on inadequate and outdated information from the field. When the requests arrived stateside, supply clerks faced the difficult task of balancing the requests from American fighting units with those from the British, Free French, Russians, and Chinese, and the very different needs of very different wars in Europe and the Pacific. Further, layer upon layer of military jurisdictions and never-ending organizational infighting complicated matters. The army air forces recognized the difficulties and, in 1944, took steps to streamline air base services. Duplication persisted, however, with logistics personnel both at the group level (where Ike worked) and at the squadron level. At least one factor made Ike's job easier: heavy bombers needed more extensive and bulkier support equipment, and so their depots and bombardment group personnel generally remained fixed at their bases for the duration of the war. Other strategic forces had to consider unit mobility in their logistics planning.[12]

The men had downtime, too, and they made the most of it. The USO and Special Services group brought numerous shows to the troops at their bases throughout Europe. In his letters, Ike mentions having seen everything from Jascha Heifetz, the renowned violinist, to an Arabian performance complete with a female dancer. Of the dancer, he said, "I have never seen any female that could even come close to her in the art of shaking the hips," but he claims the troop gave both acts large ovations.[13] And, there were card games in which Ike won enough poker hands to amass a tidy sum. A slip of paper Ike saved lists debts of ten, twenty, and even fifty dollars from men named Murdock, Butcher,

Shaw, Water, Baria, and Paris. Ike sent the winnings home to Elizabeth for what he hoped would be the down payment on a new house.

Ike's duty came to a relatively sudden end during the winter of 1944, one of the coldest and wettest on record. "Ike wasn't known for being handy," his daughter said, "but somehow, as he told the story years later, he and his tentmates pieced together a stove from metal drums and other items scavenged from the airfield. They bought coal from one of the villagers and burned it to heat their tent." But Ike couldn't stay indoors forever. One day, after riding for hours in an open truck, he contracted pneumonia. When he couldn't shake the effects, the military sent Ike to the hospital in Cerignola in the Foggia area and then to the army air forces' rest camp on the Isle of Capri. The island, long a favorite Italian getaway with its abundant sunshine, clear blue waters, and quaint villages with whitewashed buildings lining the narrow streets, offered a bit of home and a taste of the world the soldiers had left behind. While Ike rested and tried to regain his strength, thousands of other men arrived for their own much-needed, seven-day rest periods. On landing, each soldier received a passbook. Inside it read: "This rest camp program is designed to provide you the maximum pleasure, rest and relaxation. And to make this your most pleasant overseas experience. All functions are controlled for your benefit primarily. Therefore, admissions to messes and theaters and boats are made only by attached tickets. Keep this book, do not lose it. Fill out the spaces in the book, NOW."

The military also encouraged the men to contribute a dollar for each night of their stay to help defray costs. The passbook noted, further: "Refunds will be made to any man who is not entirely satisfied that he has received the greatest dollar value anywhere obtainable."[14]

Capri was a restful place, but as another soldier who stayed on the island said at the end of his seven days, "Capri was okay—Chicago would be better."[15] Ike likely felt the same. In the summer of 1945, still weak from his bout with pneumonia, Ike left Capri and returned to the United States to continue his recovery.

For his service, the army air forces awarded Ike several commendations, including a European-African-Middle Eastern Campaign Medal, seven Bronze Battle Stars for battles the 459th Bombardment Group took part in (Rome-Arno, Rhineland, southern France, northern France, Balkans, Po Valley, and the North Apennines), a Distinguished Unit Citation Badge for support of a raid on the Bad Voslau airfield and assembly plant in Austria, a Good Conduct Medal, and a Bronze Star. The award citation accompanying the Bronze Star reads, "for meritorious achievement in support of aerial operations." The citation also commends his outstanding work in "maintaining a smooth flow of vital supplies needed to support the combat operation of his unit against the enemy in over 240 missions to hostile territory."[16]

Another of Ike's keepsakes was a letter Field Marshal Harold R. Alexander, supreme allied commander for the Mediterranean theater, wrote to the troops on May 2, 1945. Addressed to "Soldiers, Sailors and Airmen of the Allied Forces in the Mediterranean Theatre," the letter reads:

> After nearly two years of hard and continuous fighting which started early in the summer of 1943, you stand today the victors of the Italian campaign. You have won a victory which has ended in the complete and utter rout of the German armed forces in the Mediterranean. By clearing Italy of the last of the aggressor you have liberated a country of over 40,000,000 people. You may well be proud of this great and victorious campaign which will long live in history as one of the greatest and most successful ever waged. . . . No praise is high enough for you sailors, soldiers, airmen and workers of the United Forces in Italy for your magnificent triumph. My gratitude to you and my admiration is unbounded and only equaled by the pride which is mine in being your Commander in Chief.[17]

The letter did not distinguish between combat and noncombat personnel. And, although Ike likely carried home his "dented pride" for not having earned a commission, the letter also did not single out officers from enlisted men.

While his dreams of being an officer were never fulfilled, after seeing a clipping from his hometown newspaper that Elizabeth sent him in 1944, Ike wrote: "They really make it sound good, almost makes me believe that I'm something like the eighth wonder. Guess on occasions, I am contributing some infinitesimal part to the war effort."[18]

Ike Minkovitz died at the age of eighty-three on July 6, 1993. With Ike's children having moved on to other careers, H. Minkovitz & Sons, the business Ike worked hard to grow and prosper, was liquidated and closed. He is survived by three children and five grandchildren. Ike and Elizabeth's wartime correspondence, a few of his medals, his letters of commendation, photographs, and newspaper clippings sit in a dust-covered box in Donna Minkovitz Darracott's attic today. But downstairs a Bronze Star, a testament to her father's service, hangs on the wall for everyone to see.

CHAPTER SEVEN

Around the World

Louis C. Thompson

✯ ✯ ✯

This is as far as the road goes.

Louis C. Thompson,
Corporal, US Army

By his eighteenth birthday, Louis Thompson had crossed the country twice. The first transit occurred during the Great Depression after his father, Clifford Thompson, lost his job. When Clifford heard work was plentiful in California, he bundled his three boys, James and twins Louis and Harold, and his wife, Christobel, into the family's 1932 Chrysler and drove from Chicago to San Diego. But the Depression followed in their tracks, and soon San Diego succumbed to hard times. Two years later, however, Clifford received news of an inheritance—the Thompson family home in Washington, DC, was his. Clifford, Christobel, and their now four children piled back in the car and drove east. Clifford found work in the nation's capital only to lose his job once again.

"Save your pennies," Louis remembered Christobel saying. "Save your pennies so you can go to college." Louis did and amassed enough by the time he finished high school to pay for his education at the University of Miami in Ohio. Louis's future looked bright, even if war threatened to disrupt his plans. But while working as a clerk typist with the War Department in Washington and waiting for the university's reply to his application, Louis received a different letter in the mail. This one came August 14, 1942, the day after he turned twenty-one. Decades later, he paraphrased the letter in a somewhat mocking tone, "Your friends and neighbors have selected you to join the army." He had been drafted.

The military swept up Louis's brothers, James and Harold, too. James, working as a skip tracer for a private concern, thought his position an unlikely skill for the army. But the army decided they could use him to track men in default on debts to army exchanges and other military vendors. Louis's twin, Harold, imagined he would have better luck. As a member of the National Guard, Harold presumed he could serve out the war at home. He was wrong. The military called up the National Guard.

Louis put his college plans on hold and headed for basic training at Fort Lee in central Virginia. After going through standard military training for infantrymen, he attended Fort Lee's Quartermaster School and took courses in supply management. Still, he said, "We were never told where we would be going or what we would be doing. But we were putting supplies together to go overseas, so we knew that much."

For his next round of training, Louis transferred to Camp Sutton, a training site for both the Corps of Engineers and the Quartermaster Corps near Monroe, North Carolina. When his orders came, Louis gathered his military-issued gear and boarded a troop train for a six-day, cross-country journey to Camp Anza, a staging area for the Los Angeles port of embarkation. After a few days at Camp Anza, Louis and hundreds if not thousands of other soldiers put out to sea aboard a former Italian ocean liner refurbished and outfitted for troop transport.

The ship took the men on a journey from Los Angeles to New Zealand; then to Sydney, Melbourne, and Perth, Australia. Finally, loaded with new supplies and accompanied by an American destroyer to discourage attack by Japanese submarines, the ship steamed across the Southern and Indian Oceans to Bombay (now Mumbai), India. "It was just 'full steam ahead,'" Louis said. He had traveled twenty thousand miles and had at least a general idea where he was going, if not what he would be doing.

After a week in a British military camp in Bombay, Louis was on the move again. His company boarded a train for a ten-day, two-thousand-mile, coast-to-coast journey across India to Calcutta. No wider than an American streetcar, the Indian railcars had hard wooden seats and windows without panes of glass in second class, where Louis traveled. Officers traveled in first class, but both found the ride long and uncomfortable. At top speed, Louis said the train made thirty-five miles per hour, and, he added tongue in cheek, "When it wasn't moving, it wasn't going very fast at all." To make matters worse, in his first days in India, Louis contracted amoebic dysentery and suffered severe abdominal pains, but he made it to Calcutta and steeled himself for the next leg of the journey.

This time, the group of six hundred or so soldiers traveled aboard a shallow-draft paddle wheeler to northern India. With the arrival of the monsoon season, conditions deteriorated over the four-day journey. To escape the relentless seasonal wind and rain, the men congregated on the lee side of the riverboat, only to cause the boat to list perilously. Military police ordered half the men back to the opposite side, into the elements. Their misery deepened—when night came, the men discovered there were not enough bunks or hammocks to go around. They slept wherever they could find a flat, empty surface, whether on the deck, in the hallways, or beneath the stairs. Louis commandeered one of the few bathrooms on the ship and stretched—or rather stuffed—his six-foot one-inch frame into the tub to sleep.

Finally, the boat docked at Dibrugarh in Assam, India, near the country's northern border with China and eastern border with Burma (now Myanmar). The men disembarked and hopped aboard several trucks for the road trip to Ledo—Louis's home for the next many months. The Ledo camp sat in a valley six hundred feet above sea level, surrounded by ridges 3,500 feet tall and carpeted in a jungle of virgin timber. "Here it is," someone said, when they rounded the last curve into the camp. "This is as far as the road goes."

Everywhere they looked, men—American soldiers and a throng of Indian and Chinese laborers—hacked at the ground and loaded the scrabble of rocks and debris onto trucks. At last, the men learned why they had come so far. It was to restore the vital supply line to China. Their immediate task, however, was to join the mass of arms, legs, and torsos bent over the ground or, if they were lucky, to take a command of one of the trucks or other pieces of heavy equipment.

Years earlier, during the Second Sino-Japanese War, Japan invaded China and blockaded its seaports, denying the country access to supplies from the sea. Goods destined for China traveled a longer and more circuitous route to alternative seaports such as Rangoon in Burma. From there the goods traveled overland by train to Lashio in northern Burma and then by road—the Burma Road—from Lashio to Kunming in southwest China. By the start of the Second World War, however, Japan had taken control of most of Burma, severing the ground-based supply line from Lashio. Undaunted, China and its British and American allies began constructing a new road to bring supplies through India. From Ledo, India, where Louis stood in 1943, the planned road headed eastward across northern Burma to a section of the original Burma Road still under Chinese control and from there to Kunming.[1]

Fortunately, by the time Louis and his company arrived, much of the fighting between the Japanese and the Allies in the area had ceased, with the Japanese withdrawing to other parts of the region. Other than an occasional artillery bombardment, the soldiers working on the road encountered little to no resistance.[2]

After a quick scan of the wet, muddy landscape, someone near Louis asked, "Where are the tents?" The reply could not have been worse news. "Tents? There are no tents. They haven't gotten here." Instead of tents, Indian laborers sat busily weaving bamboo shelters, or *bashas,* for the new arrivals. The process fascinated Louis. He watched as the natives stripped leaves from bamboo stalks, beat the stalks into shreds, and then wove the shreds into mats for the shelter's walls. Next, the Indians took softened bamboo leaves from a water-filled tub, where the leaves had soaked for a week, and wove them into a thatch for a roof.

Louis and the other soldiers stowed their gear, picked up shovels, picks, and axes, and joined the men clearing the jungle. Over the next several weeks, each day blending with the one before and the one after, Louis helped clear large stands of bamboo, drove a truck, and did any other job needed. The men worked side by side with bulldozers larger than India's elephants, carving the way through the passes and zigzagging up the steep hills. With the terrain muddy from rain, the fifteen-ton behemoths sometimes became mired in the mud. "I saw one tumble end over end down the mountain until it came to rest," Louis said. "Another bulldozer had to pull it out."

When they reached the top of one ridge, the work didn't stop. The army set up a new camp and established the next goal fifty or sixty miles to the east toward Shingbwiyang. At designated intervals along the road, the soldiers constructed warehouses to hold supplies destined for the Chinese Army's 38th Division.

Although he had little time to take in his surroundings, either on his trip to Ledo or in the camp, Louis said, "We saw a lot of strange things, things you never see here in the United States."

One was during the Bengal famine that blanketed the area in 1943. In Bombay and Calcutta, Louis saw people starving. "They would lie down in the street to die," he remembered. "The next day, the Indian military would sweep through the streets and pick up the bodies. We had rations, corned beef and hard tack in cans left over from World War I. We tried to share the meals with the natives, but they refused. 'No, no,' the starving men would say as they shook their heads." Adhering to their Hindu beliefs, they could not eat the beef.

Another was his encounter with the Nagas, indigenous people who lived at the top of the mountains around Ledo. Periodically, the Nagas came down the jungle trails from their villages to trade rice for matches, flour, and other basic supplies. Naga women carried the rice in large baskets tied by headbands to their heads. "They were good-looking women," Louis said, then added, "but our men got the message," as he recalled the spear-wielding men at the head and the rear of the convoy of women.

With the less than sanitary conditions and the hours of hard, sweaty work, Louis suffered another round of dysentery and caught malaria. When his condition worsened, the army sent him to the camp's hospital, a tent-housed facility. For ten to twelve days, Louis stayed in the hospital and battled a high fever. Attendants poured alcohol over his skin and then fanned him to bring down his fever. While the treatment cooled his skin, it gave Louis violent shakes. The mantra, however, was "back to duty." Soon Louis returned to the road.

In late 1944, the camp commander came looking for volunteers to return to Ledo. Louis was well aware of the risks of volunteering in the army. However, considering the alternative—more days trudging through the mud, more nights in a *basha,* more days battling snakes, monkeys, leeches, and flies—Louis said, "Put me down." He couldn't wait for his first night in a real tent.

When he arrived back in Ledo, Louis learned he had joined the army's air supply group, ferrying supplies to Allied ground troops fighting in the Burmese jungle. The group, dubbed Flying Quartermasters, delivered not only standard cargoes of ammunition and food but everything from clothing and medical supplies to instruments, blood plasma, typewriters, radios and radio parts, lights, generators, tank and truck parts, and mail.[3]

As a "kicker" with the group, Louis and two other men flew in the back of a C-47 from which the cargo doors had been removed, and when the plane reached the predesignated drop point coming in low over the terrain, the men pushed and kicked out the supplies. Louis quickly learned the reason the army needed volunteers. Scores of men and planes had been lost delivering supplies. On the way to and from the drop zones, the C-47s often flew at dangerously high altitudes and crossed and recrossed routes where a very active Japanese Army encamped.

On a typical day, Louis took off at five in the morning, flew one hundred miles down the Malay peninsula, dropped supplies while circling a drop zone for fifteen or twenty minutes, then returned to his base, an average round-trip of up to three hours. Louis made three or four flights every day, seven days a week, totaling over one thousand flights during his sixteen months of duty.

Close to the end of his tour of duty, as Louis returned from a mission to south Burma, a radio call diverted the crew to Myitkyina, Burma. There, the Japanese had pinned down a group of Merrill's Marauders, a special operations jungle warfare unit of the US Army led by Frank Merrill. With a high cliff overlooking a river at their backs, the American soldiers had nowhere to go, and they were running out of ammunition. A colonel at the time, Merrill offered his personal aircraft, loaded it with ammo, and summoned a crew—Louis's crew, as it so happened. "You, you, and you, hurry up. Get aboard," Louis remembered Merrill saying. One of the men Merrill had pointed to was Louis. As the men scrambled aboard the C-47, Louis learned Merrill had malaria and was suffering a bout with dysentery but was going along anyway. "Those were his boys," Louis said.

Their target was a drop zone that measured less than half the size of a football field. And, it was "hot." To unload the thousand pounds of ammunition, Merrill's plane made not one drop but eight. As they approached the drop zone for the final pass, enemy fire struck one of the C-47's engines and its landing gear. The pilot flew to safer territory and then crash-landed, skidding Merrill's formerly spotless C-47, now with a ruptured oil line and damaged hydraulics, into a rice paddy.

The crew survived, but the trauma of the event stayed with Louis. "When we returned to our base, everyone asked, 'What happened? What happened?' I couldn't answer," Louis said. "I was so scared I could hardly walk or talk. I couldn't make my mouth talk. I was in shock."

A firsthand account from two of Merrill's Marauders on the ground in Burma, although during a different battle, tells of their desperate need for supplies and the Flying Quartermasters who brought relief.

> We were trapped for fourteen days, cut off from all supplies—even water. The village was on top of a hill, an area of only about one hundred square yards. Japs were on all sides of the hill and we held the top. For all of those fourteen days we were supplied entirely by air. The area was so small that the planes had to come down to about seventy-five feet of the ground to drop supplies. . . . There wasn't any airstrip or cleared area. They just had to drop the equipment right among our foxholes while we crouched down to avoid getting hit.[4]

Two days after his crash landing, Louis developed a severe stomach ache. "I felt so bad I stayed in bed, until someone put me in an ambulance and took me to the hospital in Ledo. They called the doctor in the middle of the night." After a quick operation with nothing more than a local anesthetic, the doctor removed Louis's appendix. While he recuperated in the hospital, one of the company's men came to see him. "He had packed my things. My papers were in, he said. Those were the magic words."

Louis returned home the long way, completing his circumnavigation of the globe, a fitting end for someone who'd crossed the United States three times, sailed across the Pacific Ocean, traveled across India, and flown thousands of miles across the Himalayas and up and down the Malay Peninsula. From Ledo, he flew to Karachi, Pakistan, where a sandstorm sidelined him for ten days. Then he continued to Cairo, Egypt, and was on one of his last flights over the Mediterranean and headed for the Atlantic Ocean when he learned of the surrender of Germany. Later, while in Washington, DC, he heard the Japanese had surrendered. The war had ended and Louis was discharged on September 25, 1945. For his service, the army awarded him not one Distinguished Flying Cross but four, not one Air Medal but five, and two Bronze Stars.

When Louis stepped off the train in Florida where his parents had settled, no brass bands played, no flags waved, but his mother and father could not have been happier to have their son home. Eventually, the yellow skin he'd developed from taking atabrine tablets to combat malaria faded, but the internal damage took much longer. Louis suffered from shell shock, World War II's version of post-traumatic stress disorder. For several years, Louis suffered severe anxiety attacks, preventing him from finishing school or working. But he persevered.

In 1952, while in Washington, DC, Louis's roommate introduced him to, in Louis's words, "a beautiful young woman" named Evelyn King. Louis wasted no time in courting Evelyn, seeing her the next day and for days afterward. They married that same year and later had two daughters and a son, who Louis said are the treasures of his life. Then, in 1957, he fulfilled his stepmother's dream. He graduated from the University of Florida with a degree in engineering.

Completed in January 1945, the Ledo road ran 1,079 miles from Ledo, India, to Myitkyina and to Bhamo in Burma, and then to the junction with the original Burma Road and into Yunnan, China. The road was named the Stilwell Road in honor of Maj. Gen. Joseph W. Stilwell, better known as "Vinegar Joe," chief of staff in the China-Burma-India theater. With his no-nonsense persona, tough guy reputation, and short temper, Stilwell proved to have the perfect temperament to overcome the harsh conditions and see the road through.[5]

Eventually the airlift of supplies over the Hump into China and the restoration of the oil pipeline to Kunming overshadowed the road. After the war, the road, pipeline, and Hump operations ended. Supplies bound for China once again traveled directly into the Chinese port at Shanghai.[6]

Despite the road's ultimate demise, the supply services in the China-Burma-India theater represent one of the military's finest hours. David Hogan, writing of the India-Burma campaign for the US Army, mentions the "tremendous distances, the difficult terrain, the inefficiencies in transport, and the complications of Indian politics that presented formidable obstacles to efficient logistics." He goes on to say the road represented a tremendous feat of engineering and deserves considerable applause.[7]

Louis's postwar civilian career spanned thirty years, most of it as an engineer at the National Aeronautic Space Administration in Huntsville, Alabama. After retiring, Louis settled near his daughters outside Atlanta, Georgia, safe from snakes, monkeys, leeches, and malaria-carrying flies and, on the right occasions, sporting his medals. In 2019 he was recognized as one of the most decorated living World War II veterans in the state of Georgia and invited to participate in the inauguration of the state's newly elected governor.

PART III

Keep 'Em Rolling and Flying

*This is not a war of ammunition, tanks, guns, and trucks alone.
It is as much a war of replenishing spare parts to keep them
in combat as it is a war of major equipment.*

ERNIE PYLE,
Pulitzer Prize–winning US war correspondent

In Part III, six veterans stand in for the millions of men and women behind the battle lines who kept the fighters and bombers flying, the ships at sea, tanks and trucks rolling, lines of communication open, soldiers clothed and armed, and everyone's bellies full. They include the soldiers and sailors who served in Europe, North Africa, the Pacific, and the most distant and sometimes solitary posts in the China-Burma-India theater. They include those who served in the air, on the seas, and on the ground.

Flying had come a long way since Orville and Wilbur Wright made their first flight in 1903, but it was still in its infancy on the cusp of World War II. And just as the United States was undermanned at the time, it was also woefully unprepared to wage war in the skies. In 1939 the country's military could boast of a mere two thousand obsolete aircraft and three thousand mechanics—well below the number the peacetime fleet needed. Further, with the added complexity of the newer aircraft coming on line, pilots could no longer look after their own planes as they had in World War I. Instead of a pilot and a set of wrenches, a cadre of aircraft technicians was needed.[1]

The military began a massive recruiting and training program in 1941 with a goal to train a hundred thousand technicians each year, including not only airplane mechanics but also sheet metal workers, welders, and machinists. After Pearl Harbor the goal mushroomed to six hundred thousand per year.[2]

Military, civilian, and factory schools opened their doors, operating in multiple shifts six days a week, with classrooms and laboratories open around the clock. But training a mechanic did not happen overnight. Because of the different specialties and skills required and the very different needs of cargo planes, light bombers, medium bombers, heavy bombers, and fighters, mechanics needed nearly half a year to complete their training programs.[3]

Each trainee received a thick repair manual filled with images and diagrams with keys to numbered parts. The five-hundred-page manual for the seventy-four-foot-long, four-engine B-17 heavy bomber, for example, covered the aircraft's landing gear, propeller, wing flaps, tail (stabilizers, elevators, rudders), instruments and instrument panels, hydraulic systems, electrical systems, heating, oxygen, and bombing and gunnery equipment. Bold-print warnings on nearly every page reminded the crews of the importance of their work. They were not just putting a plane back in the sky; they were sending ten men back into action.

The airplane mechanic's job was far more difficult than maintaining commercial planes for flights across the country. One of their planes might return from a mission and need only to refuel and rearm before taking off again, all within minutes. Another might limp back to its base where ground crews would spin into action, clambering over the aircraft to fix bullet holes and flak tears in the sheet metal, bent propellers, damaged engines, and failed instruments, and to replace any defective part of the thousands the planes needed to fly.

Complete overhauls and more difficult repairs, such as replacement of sheet metal, took place in depots serving multiple types of aircraft. In the European theater, the depots were located in England and North Africa and, later, were scattered across the Allies' large and growing territory on the continent as the Germans retreated.[4]

In the Pacific, because aircraft operated largely from carriers, repairs took place in hangar bays below the flight deck. For aircraft not able to return to the carrier and instead forced to land on remote islands without resources, the army air forces launched a classified joint military repair operation known as Ivory Soap. The operation consisted of six Liberty ships and eighteen auxiliary ships that carried repair parts, equipment, and aircraft technicians. From a short distance offshore, they airlifted men and matériel by Sikorsky helicopters—a new and barely more than experimental aircraft—or ferried them on amphibious trucks to the downed planes. Ivory Soap was one of the little-known but highly successful logistical operations in the Pacific, responsible for saving and returning hundreds of American aircraft to service.[5]

Repairing carriers and other ships in the fleet while at sea was limited to "rerouting pipes, installing spare parts, and drying and restoring flooded equipment, as well as making other minor repairs within the crew's capacity." For ships with severe damage, the crews did what they could to make the craft seaworthy and then had the ship towed or sailed it under its own power to the nearest shipyard, whether in occupied territory or back in the United States.[6]

George Keating, James Neyland, and Randy Buffington, who tell their stories here, were three of the army of mechanics the military needed to sustain its air operations. These men saw duty at flight lines and in depots, working tirelessly to oversee or make repairs to the army air forces' B-17 bombers and P-38 and P-47 fighters, respectively. To call these men and the thousands like them "mechanics" is a disservice. They were all highly trained specialists who spent months in military training schools before deploying overseas.

Crew chiefs—noncommissioned officers like Randy and George—headed a team of enlisted men, all of whom had also trained as mechanics. Each team was attached to a particular aircraft. They lived and worked near their aircraft, and often, when missions took place around the clock, they slept next to the flight line.

Teamwork was a must among the ground crews. And while some ground crews developed lifelong bonds with the flight crews of their planes, many did not. George remembered his pilots returning white faced and silent, in no frame of mind to mingle with the curious crew. Still, years after the war, as veterans from squadrons or divisions gathered in reunions across the country, a number of flight crew members expressed regret at not getting to better know their crew, especially their crew chiefs. The former pilots and their fellow aircrew members understood how their lives depended on the skill of their airplane's mechanics. Long before the war, Col. Bush B. Lincoln, chief of the plans section, recognized the interdependence of the two teams. "All failures in the air can be directly or indirectly traced to failures on the ground," he wrote in a 1937 memo to the chief of the air corps.[7]

Despite how similar, routine, and monotonous we imagine their roles and responsibilities, George, James, and Randy had very different stories to tell. And the three had their share of excitement. Not one mentioned becoming bored or feeling their jobs were unimportant.

Communications served another vital, behind-the-scenes role in the war, requiring another set of specialists. Today we take for granted the ability to communicate with a family member, friend, or complete stranger across town, the country, or the world. Our military leverages the latest technologies, many of them top secret, to speak with soldiers on the battlefield and to observe military actions from the safety of a command center half a world away. World War II battlefields offered no such advantages.

Although communications technology was advancing at a speed unimaginable only a decade or two earlier, communicating basic information critical to executing maneuvers during the Second World War was problematic. Weather, the terrain, power interruptions, or enemy action easily hampered communications with troops on the ground.

Two veterans from theaters of operation oceans apart share their stories on very different aspects of communications. William Alexander Scott III was a reconnaissance sergeant, photographer, and historian for the 183rd Engineer Combat Battalion and followed George Patton's Third Army through France and into Germany. There, Scott was told to "go see" the Buchenwald concentration camp. He did more than see—he bore witness, his photographs a lasting testimony to the horrors of the Holocaust.

For his part, Jack Coyle did the unthinkable. Knowing full well it was unwise to volunteer for anything, he raised his hand when a call came for volunteers for a secret mission. His assignment changed overnight. Jack crossed the country and the Pacific to reach his post far behind the lines, manning a radio station in China. From his post he gathered weather and intelligence about the Japanese occupiers and radioed messages to the Pacific fleet. He and three thousand men like him became members of the Sino-American Cooperative Organization (SACO) Navy—a little-known outfit at the time and for decades after the war.

Howard King closes out the group with his tales of one other invaluable service provided to all who served, whether sailor, soldier, or marine. The young navy messman, who thought he could improve his career prospects by transferring, came close to leaving the safety of his home in Pensacola, Florida, to serve deep below the surface of the Pacific on a submarine. His superior asked if Howard could think of anything more important than the job he was doing at the time, delivering food to the troops. Howard gave the question a moment's consideration and then went back to work. He couldn't think of anything more important. Besides, with stocks of Coca-Colas, fresh meat, eggs, cigarettes, and beer, he was everyone's favorite.

CHAPTER EIGHT

The Man with a Perfect Record

George H. Keating

✯ ✯ ✯

My service was routine. It was nothing exceptional,
but I did my job and did it well.

GEORGE H. KEATING,
Technical Sergeant, US Army Air Forces

Charles Lindbergh soared over the Oregon landscape in September 1927 during one leg of his forty-eight-state tour to promote aeronautics and to celebrate his May 1927 record-breaking solo flight across the Atlantic in the *Spirit of St. Louis.* "Everyone came out to watch," George Keating said in a video of his memories recorded in 2013.[1] "Lucky Lindy was our hero. As kids, we all wore hats with flaps over our ears, and we made airplanes out of apple boxes." And George had had a very brief taste of what it was like to fly. Once in the late 1930s, he and his sister Wilma rode on a fabric-covered trimotor aircraft. "It was wonderful. I was hooked." He added, "Like everyone in my age group, I wanted to fly."

He thought he would get his chance too. In late 1941 George checked with his draft board and discovered 8239, his number, was the third drawn in the recently enacted draft. He knew he would not receive a deferment because of his age (George was twenty-one years old) or his occupation (he was working as a grocer, helping his father manage Keating's Market, the family business in Eugene, Oregon). He was healthy and single without dependents. George was certain the army would classify him 1-A, fit for military service, and equally certain he was headed for the infantry.

Although today at the age of ninety-seven, George confessed his memory was fading, he recalled clearly that he had had no desire to serve in the infantry—what he feared was a death sentence. So he pursued his dream and enlisted in the army air forces. During the routine physical examination, however, George failed the eye test. He was color blind. The door to his becoming a pilot closed, but although he couldn't fly, he could fill another role for the army air force. He became a crew chief, "the next best thing to flying," George said, describing the duty as "the top of the line."

Even better, with the military's massive pilot and technician training program in high gear, some maintenance recruits like George were hurried through the program. He skipped boot camp altogether, attended a few weeks of indoctrination in Salt Lake City, Utah, and then did a short stint in Saint Louis, Missouri, before transferring to the Chanute Field Air Corps Technical School in Rantoul, Illinois, just south of Chicago. To his surprise, on his first day at Chanute, George was asked if he would stay on as an instructor. He didn't hesitate or mince words. "Hell, yes," he said.

To keep up with the flood of recruits coming through the school's doors, the military desperately needed instructors. In the 1938–39 prewar period, Chanute had graduated fewer than nine hundred men, but now with a new urgency to their mission Chanute would go on to certify seven hundred thousand men in all aspects of aircraft maintenance by the end of the war.[2] After months in specialized training for the nearly indestructible B-17 bombers, known as Flying Fortresses, George did an additional four weeks of training to become an instructor at Chanute.

For this responsibility, in June 1942, four hundred men, including George, transferred to the military's new Air Mechanics Technical School in Lincoln, Nebraska. Later, George was sent to Boeing Field in Seattle, Washington, then to Salt Lake City again for additional training, and next to Rapid City, South Dakota. By 1943, however, with the Allied air offensive mounting, more mechanics were needed overseas.

George was reassigned to the 731st Squadron in the 452nd Bombardment Group. After short stays in Spokane, Washington, and at Pyote Army Air Field in West Texas, in 1943, the 731st was ordered to report to Camp Shanks, New York, for deployment overseas. George sailed out of New York's harbor one day after New Year's Day 1944 aboard the RMS *Queen Elizabeth*.

Although commissioned as an ocean liner, the *Queen Elizabeth* made its maiden voyage and every subsequent ocean crossing until 1946 carrying troops or shuttling supplies between the United States and Britain.[3] The spartan quarters bore little resemblance to the accommodations the future luxury liner would offer. To be sure, with the eighteen thousand men on board far outnumbering the bunks, many of the troops slept not in cabins but wherever they could find a flat surface—on deck, in the hallways, and beside the stairwells.

Where they lay their heads was the least of their worries. There was the ever-present threat of a German U-boat attack. But, George said, the young troops feigned indifference. The *Queen Elizabeth* was "too fast" and could easily outrun the Germans, or so they thought. They were lucky, despite one encounter with heavy seas and spray breaking over the bow of the ship. George recalled, "It was a comfortable voyage and a beautiful trip."

Once in Europe, he made his way to the airfield at Deopham Green in southeastern England. George was nearly five thousand miles from Cosmopolis, Washington, where he was born. It was as far away as he could ever imagine living and working. Yet, Deopham Green was exactly where he wanted to be. Far better to be there than fighting in the hedgerows of France, where he imagined the infantry would have taken him.

George and his team—less a designated unit than one or two men from the pool of mechanics—were assigned to one of the 731st's Flying Fortresses. The men rarely knew what to expect. They might wake in the morning or be called to the airfield at a moment's notice to find anywhere from one hour to twenty-four hours of work waiting, depending on the status of their aircraft. They worked quickly, sometimes needing to have their plane ready for its next mission in hours, and they worked nonstop until they completed the needed repairs and the aircraft could return to the skies. Then they slept. "We would just find a place to curl up and go to sleep," George said, as if sleep were optional.

George's crew conducted routine maintenance and repaired damage to every part of the B-17 except structural damage to the airframe, which a separate crew handled. Although their instruction manual contained over five hundred pages of charts, illustrations, tables, and detailed instructions, he said, "It was pretty straightforward." The ground crews repaired most issues on the spot. They had no choice. They could not contact the factories in United States, so if they needed help, it had to come from someone at the field.

Over the course of the war, the 452nd Bombardment Group flew 250 missions and lost 110 of its bombers.[4] George's planes flew on almost half the missions, but he lost only two aircraft. The first was a Flying Fortress: *Tangerine.* "Named after the song," he said—a 1940s jazz favorite performed by Jimmy Dorsey and his orchestra, Frank Sinatra, and a host of other Hollywood luminaries. In 1944, carrying a full load of bombs, the *Tangerine* crashed on takeoff. All aboard survived, with little more than a few scratches.[5] "We had some pretty inexperienced pilots," George said. "The flight crew claimed the *Tangerine* wouldn't fly, but the flight engineer told me, 'Keating, it wasn't your fault.' A later investigation proved there was nothing wrong with the controls and listed the cause as pilot error."

George's second plane, *Johnny Reb,* met a similar fate, although with less fortunate results. After crash-landing in Holland on September 9, 1944, the copilot, navigator, bombardier, tail gunner, right waist gunner, and radio operator fell into German hands and were imprisoned. Horace Bradshaw, the pilot, and Frank Doucette, the ball turret gunner, escaped capture and were rescued by members of the Dutch resistance. A later skirmish with German soldiers left

Frank dead. Horace, however, survived. On his way back to the United States, Horace stopped in England and made a trip to Deopham Green to thank George and to assure him nothing had been wrong with the *Johnny Reb*.

For the ground crews, each day passed in much the same manner as the previous day, epitomized in scenes familiar to fans of classic war movies. When the Deopham Green–based bombers were due to return from their missions, the crews scrambled to the airfield to wait and watch. The men scanned the skies, squinting to read the tail numbers as the planes approached, hoping to spot their aircraft in the group. As each B-17 rolled to a stop and its engines quieted, the flight crew disembarked and turned the aircraft over to the ground crew. Other than to report any mechanical issues, the two exchanged few words. "They had seen the face of death," George said, recalling their drawn and pale faces.

While far from the front lines, Deopham Green was bombed once and hit on another occasion by a German V-1 flying bomb, dubbed a *doodlebug* or *buzz bomb* for the pulsating sound of the unmanned craft's engine. "It was as close to combat as I came," George said.

> The night we were bombed was the one time we had fueled the aircraft and loaded their bombs the night before their scheduled mission. For security, one man from each crew stood guard on the airfield. As crew chief, I volunteered for the duty and was standing guard in the middle of a group of five planes when I heard the *putt putt* of a single-engine plane approaching at a low altitude. Then, just like you hear in the movies, came the whistle of a bomb falling. The enemy aircraft was flying a diagonal path across the runway from the gas dump on one side to the bomb dump on the other, but the plane dropped its bombs early and made only a few holes in the runway.

With characteristic humor, George added, "I hit the concrete—beating the bomb to the ground." The next day, a fellow crewman showed George a large piece of shrapnel he had retrieved near where George had stood guard.

During some rare free time, George visited London and once traveled to Ireland. Of London, he remembered the threat of air raids but never felt in danger of losing his life. He visited pubs where whiskey flowed around the clock and indulged in "cress sandwiches," which, he said, due to shortages, featured more "cress" than egg salad.

Most of his time, however, passed caring for his aircraft. Ensuring the aircraft was free of mechanical problems took on more than just a sense of duty. It was an obsession, urged on, his son, Patrick, believes, because he harbored a bit of guilt for not serving in harm's way himself. It was also a source of tremendous pride. In their 120 missions, George's planes never encountered a mechanical failure. For this achievement, the military awarded him a Bronze Star Medal, although he did not learn of the award until he returned home and was discharged. "I guess I did a satisfactory job," he said as another smile spread across his face.

The citation accompanying the medal reads, "For his outstanding performance of his duties in aircraft maintenance in seventy-six bombardment operations against the enemy which resulted in no plane being forced to return because of mechanical failures."[6]

With much humility, George said Milton Applebaum, his immediate supervisor and the best friend he ever had in the service, deserved much of the credit and should have received a medal. "It was his training that allowed me to get the award."

George also was the beneficiary of several other awards, including the American and European-African-Middle Eastern Campaign Medals, a Good Conduct Medal, a National Defense Service Medal, a World War II Victory Medal, and the French Legion of Honor Medal (Chevalier). He downplayed the latter, one of France's highest honors, saying anyone who served to defend France in any capacity received the Legion of Honor Medal.

To George, the Bronze Star stood apart from the rest. "My service was routine. It was nothing exceptional," he said, lowering his eyes. But, he added, "I did my job and did it well," which the Bronze Star attests. He couldn't protect his aircraft from attack or artillery fire. He couldn't prevent pilot error. But he could do everything in his power to give his flight crew a reliable aircraft. And he did, with a perfect record.

As the war in Europe wound down, George worried the military might send him to the Pacific rather than home. He feared his B-17 bomber maintenance skills would not transfer to the B-29s flown in the Pacific and that he'd be transferred to the infantry and never return. Thankfully, however, in September 1945, George went home. He returned aboard the third of his three planes and brought along his sleeping bag. After eighteen months with only short bursts of sleep, he said, "I found a spot in the forward section of the aircraft, unrolled the bag, and slept the whole way home."

George was discharged at Fort Lewis, Washington, on September 13, 1945. In 1946 he married Lois Russell, a former welder in a Portland, Oregon, shipyard. Lois had helped build Liberty ships as one of the six million women known as

"Rosie the Riveters." The women did their part during the war by taking jobs in aircraft and tank manufacturing plants, ammunition factories, and shipyards.[7] The couple made a fitting match—they were both proud of doing their duty.

For a decade after the war, George continued to work around aircraft. He earned his pilot's license and became a certified airframe and engine mechanic, working at Boeing and later at Northwest Airlines and United Airlines in Seattle. With the advent of lower-maintenance jet engines in the late 1950s, however, the demand for his skills declined. George put the military behind and tried his hand at several entrepreneurial endeavors.

In 2004, at his son Patrick's urging, the two attended a 452nd Bombardment Group reunion in Savannah, Georgia. At first, Patrick said his father feared he would have little in common with the men, most of whom George imagined served in combat. The general camaraderie and joy of reminiscing with other participants, however, triumphed. For years afterward, father and son attended every group reunion and several Eighth Air Force events. George enjoyed the experience and being recognized for his service alongside his fellow veterans, regardless of their roles.

George Keating died on May 26, 2019, three weeks after celebrating his ninety-ninth birthday. While George had been unable to travel to attend recent Eighth Air Force and group reunions, his son, Patrick, remains active in celebrating the contribution of his father and George's fellow bombardment group veterans.

CHAPTER NINE

With a Welder's Torch for a Weapon

James K. Neyland

* * *

The skies over London were so full of planes, they blacked out the stars. The invasion had started.

JAMES K. NEYLAND,
Private, US Army Air Forces

From the day he graduated from high school in 1940, James Neyland knew exactly what he wanted to do: join the military and fly. But he was only seventeen, and his mother refused to give her consent. From the seventeen years he spent under Mary Neyland's roof, James had learned not to ask twice and not to argue with her. She'd seen the results of war. Her brother Walter had fought in World War I and been gassed. During that most cruel war, Germany had used tear gas, chlorine, and mustard gas against its enemies. Fortunately, while a million soldiers and civilians suffered from exposure to chemical weapons during World War I, less than a hundred thousand died from gassing. Still, many suffered respiratory ailments and related illnesses for the rest of their lives.[1]

Mary had watched Walter suffer and did not want to see the same happen to James. Her son would not join at seventeen or eighteen or nineteen—not as long as Mary had a say. James would have to find something to do for a few years. "I just knocked around a bit," he said.

With a population of less than two thousand, Gloster, Mississippi, his hometown, offered few job opportunities, so James moved to Lake Charles, Louisiana, to live with his sister, Inez. Her husband offered James work painting houses. He took the job and painted until he stumbled on an opportunity to become a welder with Reed Roller Bit Company. Reed manufactured bits for oil drillers, an industry entering its heyday. Welding was steady work and paid forty cents an hour, even for an apprentice welder. Shortly after James started work, a union organized workers at Reed. His wages rose to seventy-five cents an hour. "I thought I was rich," James said. Rich and another year closer to twenty-one.

November 13, 1942, proved to be James's lucky day. On that day, Congress passed legislation to lower the draft age to eighteen and raise the upper limit to thirty-seven. By then, with the country fully engaged in the war, the military had a better appreciation for how many men they needed. That number was far more than they had expected in 1940 at the start of the peacetime draft.

Nineteen-year-old James no longer needed his mother's approval. He extinguished his welder's torch and hurried to Lake Charles Army Air Field just a few miles away. After taking and passing a three-hour test for training as a pilot, James was sworn in, becoming a proud member of the US Army Air Forces. With the training school at capacity, James returned to work to wait for an opening. In March 1943 a slot opened for preflight training in San Antonio. "Preflight was all book work, no flight time," James said. Book work and physical training.

On completing preflight training, James moved to Coleman, in central Texas, for primary training at the Coleman Flying School. James remembered walking up to a PT-19 on the tarmac at Coleman. The low-wing, open-cockpit aircraft "looked marvelous just sitting there," he said. In no time, James and an instructor were airborne, flying over the horizonless brown landscape of Texas, the plane's blue and yellow colors sparkling in the afternoon sun. During his first weeks in training, James flew with an instructor in the backseat. Sometimes they swooped low over farm fields, and once they startled a farmer who shook his fist in the air and yelled from his tractor.

"One day the instructor landed, jumped out of the plane, and said, 'Take her up!' One of the greatest sensations of my life was when I reached three hundred feet and looked back. The backseat was empty. A cold chill went up my back. It was up to me now. I landed and took off three times without a problem." James had soloed after eight and a half hours of instruction, sooner than most of his fellow recruits.

Although excited to fly, James experienced excruciating headaches every afternoon. When he couldn't stand the pain any longer, he sought help. The army air forces sent James to nearby Camp Hood for tests. There, doctors found his sinuses did not respond to changes in pressure or at least did not respond as fast as a fighter plane changed altitude. James refused to allow a sinus defect to derail his plans and returned to Coleman to give flying another chance. The headaches returned.

With so many hours invested in the young recruit, the army air forces offered James the chance to go to gunnery school in Colorado and train as a gunner aboard a bomber. While James's body might not tolerate a fighter plane's quick altitude changes, the doctors thought he could withstand a bomber's more gradual changes. James was eager to make the switch but had reservations about going to Colorado. It took a bit of convincing, but after his older brother, Gerald, described Colorado's beautiful mountain scenery, James packed his bags.

In a twelve-week program at the Lowry Field Army Gunnery School near Denver, James learned to operate .50-caliber machine guns. As the military reserved live ammunition for men in combat, again, book work filled much of the training time. "It wasn't until about the sixth week," James said, "that we got to fire live rounds—to see and hear the real thing." Real bullets or not, James took to the gunnery role, drawing on the untold hours he had spent hunting in the backwoods of Mississippi as a young boy.

By this time, James thought things were looking up, but shortly the army air forces pulled aside James and two other men who the army said were the "best gunners in the school." They asked the three to transfer to MacDill Field in Florida to become .50-caliber gun instructors. "I'd been called one of the three best in gunnery school. I was excited." His excitement lasted for a week. Then the army air forces canceled all training at Lowry Field and sent the school's students, including the three best gunners, back to Denver for transfer to Europe.

"We didn't like that one bit," James said. "We didn't know anything except that we were going overseas as part of the Ninth Air Force." In Denver, along with hundreds of other anxious young men, James boarded a train bound for the East Coast. The men remained on the train for the three-day trip, passing the time sitting, staring out the window, and playing endless card games. Finally, they disembarked at what James called a bleak, uninviting spot, a New Jersey marshaling station with tents pitched across a low field. "The land wasn't good for anything else. We called it the swamps of New Jersey." Each miserably cold February morning during his stay, James awoke to see ice on the blades of coarse saw grass encircling his tent and then passed the rest of the day staring at the landscape and playing more card games. New York City lay a short distance away, and some of the men headed for the city lights. James resisted the temptation, however, and chose to stay at the camp.

After three uneventful days, the military ordered the men to the New Jersey docks where they discovered their troopship was none other than the cruise liner *Queen Elizabeth*. Operating as a troopship, the immense ship had surrendered her Cunard Line colors for a coat of wartime battleship gray. It was impossibly large, measuring a staggering three football fields long. A photographer of the day claimed the *Queen Elizabeth* strained the limits of his box camera, forcing him to take multiple shots of the ship and paste them together to capture the behemoth.[2] James, like others who spotted the ship for the first time, was stupefied. He could do nothing but stand stock still and stare upward and then take a long gaze from one end to the other.

When he recovered from the initial shock, James spotted what he said was a "huge black hole in her side." The open cargo hold was the tallest, blackest object he had ever seen. On regaining his composure, James started thinking about the German U-boats searching the seas for Allied vessels. He turned to the soldier beside him and asked, "Where's our convoy?"

"Convoy?" the man replied. "We're by ourselves."

James frowned. "But what about all the subs I've been reading about?"

The man told him not to worry. With a top speed of twenty-eight knots, the *Queen Elizabeth* could outrun anything else in the ocean, including German submarines.[3] Still, to outwit any potential attacker bearing down on her, like other ships, the *Queen Elizabeth* made turns every eight minutes when at sea. Submarines, as the Allies knew, needed at least that long to change course, get a bearing, and set their torpedoes. Reassured, the men shrugged off concerns for U-boats, worrying more about holding their poker chips and cards in place as the ship veered sharply right, then left, then right again.

The ship packed the men into very close quarters. "We didn't have it too bad, though," James said. The *Queen Elizabeth,* designed to carry two thousand passengers as a cruise liner, could accommodate fifteen thousand troops when outfitted for war. "We had only fourteen thousand aboard," said James.[4] In each stateroom, canvas bunks, stacked three or four high, stood in the place of beds meant for two. "But we had a pillow and a blanket," James added, making light of the conditions.

"The British cooking was the worst part. Bully beef and hash. We had that for breakfast every morning." Half the men couldn't stomach the food. Although James managed to down the meal once or twice, he soon found his way to the canteen at the front of the ship where he could choose from a limited menu of snacks and drinks. Orange Crush and cookies sustained him for breakfast, lunch, and dinner for the rest of the voyage.

On the third day at sea, somewhere in the North Atlantic, the *Queen Elizabeth* encountered a ferocious storm. The ship rolled so violently that dining hall tables broke from their floor moorings and crashed across the hall. Many passengers became seasick. One unfortunate soldier, James remembered, ran to the rails and heaved his bully beef and hash over the side, only for the mess to land on a dice game under way on the deck below. But James soon found his sea legs, developed, he thinks, from his days learning to fly. He enjoyed being on deck even during the storm and went forward to stand at the rails and watch the sea for hours. "The ship would go up, up, up, up, hang at the top of a wave, then drop down, down, down, down. My knees buckled when we reached the bottom." Then the next wave would come.

In March 1944 the *Queen Elizabeth* dropped anchor in the bay outside Glasgow, Scotland. The troops disembarked and then boarded a train bound for Bournemouth, England, to rendezvous with the Ninth Air Force. The Ninth had completed its duties in the invasion of Sicily and Italy and was now assigned to support the assault on Normandy.

Within days of arriving in Bournemouth, James's sergeant called the men together to make assignments. James drew the role of welder and could not have been more delighted or more relieved. With the welding experience he had gained at Reed Roller Bit in Louisiana, he would have an advantage over those new to the task. And welding would keep from the front lines. He wouldn't be facing fire.

Soon, however, James and some of the other crewmen confessed they had second thoughts—concerned they were not doing all they could. "When the first casualties came back from the front lines, some soldiers without an arm or a leg or with other serious injuries," James said, "those thoughts disappeared. We were more than relieved. We were thankful."

Despite his prewar welding experience, the military sent James to a welding school in London. At Reed Roller Bit, he had welded cast iron, but to work on aircraft, he needed to know how to weld aluminum. "Working with aluminum is much different, much harder. You have to do it just right or it drops away," James said. He explained, "If the metal gets too hot, a hole opens up. You learn how to tell when to stop by the color of the metal, the temperature of your torch, and the thickness of the piece you are working."

During his six weeks in London, James lived with a local family, sharing a bedroom on the second floor with another soldier also learning to weld. Although the worst of the German bombing had ended by this time, London remained on constant alert. Air raid sirens sounded daily, warning of potential Luftwaffe attacks. "The sirens would start and then we'd hear the pom-pom guns firing." Pom-pom guns were the British autocannons used as antiaircraft guns, so named for the sound they made on firing. "One night we heard a loud *ka-thunk*. We didn't think much about it, but the next day on our way back from class, we watched a bomb squad remove an unexploded bomb from the garden behind our quarters. We could only imagine what would have happened had that bomb exploded. Whew!"

Mr. Kerr, James's host, worked as a conductor for one of London's famous double-decker buses. Often when the two young Americans returned from a day at school, Mr. Kerr took them to see the sights. Once they stopped at 10 Downing Street, Prime Minister Winston Churchill's official residence and the seat of England's power. It was more than an address to James. It was more than where Churchill lived. It was where men decided his fate.

School or no school, James was still on active duty. "Everyone below the rank of sergeant did guard duty. We stood four-hour shifts in a rotation." On June 6, 1944, he was standing guard at a petroleum storage facility. "It was close to two o'clock in the morning when I heard the engines," he said. "It wasn't like the sound a single plane makes as it comes toward you then dies off as the plane passes. The sound filled the air and went on and on. The sky was so full of planes [that] they blacked out the stars. All I could see were the dark outlines of the aircraft. Bombers, fighters, tow planes pulling gliders. The noise continued until dawn." The invasion had started.

When he got off duty, James hurried to a nearby airfield to watch for planes returning after their first sorties and others taking off for their next. "One of the planes landed with twigs and leaves caught in its cowling. A ground crewman advised the pilot not to fly so low the next time," James said.

By mid-July, six weeks after the invasion, the Allies succeeded in clearing the Normandy beaches and pushing the Germans back from the coast. Support troops from southern England, including James's group, transferred to the continent to set up repair depots closer to the front lines. With the facilities operating in France rather than in England, the military could put planes back into the skies more quickly.

When James landed on Omaha Beach on July 20, most of the signs of combat—the aircraft, tanks, trucks, jeeps, and fortifications—were gone. As he walked the beach with his fellow soldiers, all that was visible were the jagged edges of the remains of one or two ships sunk offshore to act as breakwaters. But, James said, "We knew we were walking on hallowed ground where three thousand of our boys lost their lives."

On his first night in France, James came as close as he would to earning a Purple Heart. His squadron had set up their pup tents and dug foxholes next to a farm field where, earlier, James watched a bull graze. He recalled the situation:

> That bull weighed 1,100 to 1,200 pounds, I'd say, and was wearing a blindfold to keep him from tearing down the wire enclosure. At about eleven o'clock that night, 'Bed Check Charlie' roused us from our tents. Bed Check Charlie was what we called the German fighter planes that strafed and bombed our camps at night, hoping to find us asleep in our tents. Well, our *ack ack* guns started firing. We had jumped up at the sound of the strafing and thrown ourselves into our trenches. The trenches were supposed to be three or four feet deep, but we'd run into hard chalky soil, so most were only two feet deep.

That bull panicked too. Still blindfolded, he tore down the wire fence and came charging toward us. I could hear him stomping through our tents. When I looked up, there he was standing right over me with his hooves on the edge of my foxhole. The side gave way, and those big hooves started down toward my chest. As much as it scared me, it startled him too. He jumped back and retreated.

James emerged from his foxhole, his carbine in hand, and said, "If you come over here again, we'll be having beef for dinner."

With their camp established, the men turned to setting up the airfields and their maintenance depot. They unloaded and laid perforated steel planking into place, connecting the pieces to form emergency landing strips. Shortly afterward, the maintenance technicians began their duties, with James and a fellow mechanic repairing cracked aluminum air scoops for the P-38 Lightning aircraft. As a sign of how hard the war was raging, the two spent every waking hour of every day repairing P-38 scoops. Other mechanics repaired other damaged aircraft parts.

"Our next move was to central France, following the troops inland," James said. "We set up operations there only to receive orders to move out the next day." James moved several times during his stint in France, billeting in northern and central France. During one transfer, he remembered passing through Saint-Lô, a town devastated by German and American artillery after a battle in July 1944. The battle had been a turning point, marking the breakthrough of Allied forces from the Normandy beaches to the interior of France.[5] "When we wheeled through," James said, "I could see only one chimney standing."

His only break from welding occurred in the winter of 1944. Snow blanketed the airstrips, preventing the military from flying. "When the order came to clear the airstrips, we had to improvise. The sheet metal group manufactured shovel blades, and I welded the part that holds the stick to the blade."

The work never ended, but when the situation allowed, the military gave the men a furlough. James had a fleeting thought that he might get to go home to see his family, but instead the army air forces returned him to London and back to welding school. "The army wasn't going to send me home, so when they said I could go to London, I said yes without a second thought." In London, James learned of the German offensive later known as the Battle of the Bulge. "It was the last big push for the Germans. I hated not being there, not being a part of it."

Germany surrendered a few months later, and the army air forces sent James and his group to a marshaling area in Marseille, France, to wait. Once again, they weren't going home, as they had hoped. Instead, the rumors had them going from Marseille to the Philippines without a side trip or single day off to see their families. "Nobody was happy about it. I wrote a letter to my brother and complained," James said. And during a routine inspection of troop mail, one of the officers read James's complaints and called him in to explain. Sympathetic to James's plight, the officer reprimanded him nonetheless but agreed to throw the letter out if James promised not to write another similar letter. James gave his word.

Not expecting their outbound transport to arrive for a few days, James and several fellow soldiers went to Paris for the weekend. To no one's surprise, they drank more than they should have. James stumbled back to his hotel and heard nothing until the next morning when he walked into the hotel lobby. "Everyone was running around. It was buzzing. I asked what was going on. Someone said, 'Haven't you heard? We dropped a twenty-thousand-ton bomb on Japan.' 'So what?' I said. 'We've been bombing Japan for two years.'" James got drunk again. "They poured me onto a truck and poured me off at the camp. Whew!" he said, recalling the celebration.

Fifteen days later, on September 4, 1944, James arrived at Camp Miles Standish in Massachusetts. The war was over. The military, however, did not release James for another two months. During that time, while on furlough, he did visit his family. Then, on November 8, 1945, he was discharged at Camp Shelby, Mississippi, and went home to Lake Charles.

Reed Roller Bit offered James his job back on the condition he move to Houston. James declined, choosing instead to stay near family and in the familiar surroundings of Lake Charles, where he started his own floor-sanding business. He planned to settle down and have a family, which is exactly what happened. In 1947 his sister, Inez, introduced him to Ruby Pierson, whom he married in February 1948. When he wasn't working or tending to his family, James became active in his church. His Christian faith grew ever more important in his life until, in September 1953, with his pastor's help, he decided to pursue religious education. He enrolled at the Southwestern Baptist Theological Seminary in Fort Worth, Texas, the best school in his chosen field. After graduating, James worked full time for eight Southern Baptist churches across the South. He moved to Georgia and retired there in 1990 at the age of sixty-eight. Unfortunately in 2000, after fifty-two years of marriage, James lost his wife, Ruby. But two years later, he met and married Judy Abouchar. The two have enjoyed sixteen years together.

At ninety-six years old, James has a knack for remembering the tiny details of his time in the war. Without a moment's hesitation, he can recall minor details of his service, the Kerrs' street and house number in London, for example, and where he went, what he saw, and just how close the bull's hooves had come to his heart. He said he has few regrets and displays a wonderful sense of humor. James doesn't play cards anymore, but he reads the newspapers and keeps up with current events, good news and bad. Mostly, he has a positive outlook driven by his faith. And he boasts that his second daughter, Debra, followed in her father's footsteps. She joined the seminary, served as the children's director for the Southern Baptist churches for thirty years, and lives just a few miles away.

James Neyland lives in Marietta, Georgia, with his wife, Judy. He takes comfort in his faith, which has sustained him through the loss of his first wife, Ruby, in 2000 and the loss of two daughters—Cheryl in 2010 and Debra on Christmas Day 2018. Debra's obituary notes she was proud to be known as James Neyland's daughter, a fitting tribute to someone who proudly served his country and his church.

CHAPTER TEN

One of Five

Orin F. Buffington

It was your Dad's mechanical expertise and skill which made those missions possible—and kept me getting back safely.

Howard Gurley
about Orin F. Buffington,
Staff Sergeant, US Army Air Forces

Five stars hung behind the rippled-glass window, clearly visible to anyone who wandered up the hill to Emma Buffington's front porch. Emma displayed the stars proudly, each a reminder of one of her five sons serving in the military. James Victor had been the first to join, enlisting with the air corps in 1940. He planned to make a career of military service. Emma hadn't worried too much about him then, but by late summer in 1943, with the war very much a reality, Emma had more reason to be concerned. Four other Buffington siblings had followed James's lead. Kenneth and Wayne were army privates first class but still in training. Tom, a paratrooper, was jumping from planes over Fort Benning, Georgia. Although Tom was also still in training, Emma feared he would soon be jumping out over Berlin. The one she worried most about, however, was her fourth-born son, Orin Fred. Orin, whom everyone called Randy, had enlisted in the army air forces and was willing to do just about anything the military wanted. The military promptly sent him for training to Chanute Field in Illinois, as far as he had ever ventured from the family home in north Georgia. Emma took small comfort that, as an aircraft mechanic, even in Europe, he would not be on the front lines.

A year later, much to Emma's delight, Randy came home to visit. It was a short visit, with just enough time to see a few old friends and to meet a young lady named Bennie Lee Coffey. The two bumped into each other at a café in Ellijay, and despite the ten-year gap in their ages, they fell in love. When his leave was up, Randy returned to his station in Illinois to finish his training. In the fall, expecting he might soon deploy to Europe, he returned home again. He lost no time in asking Bennie Lee out and took her to a basketball game at Ellijay High School. Randy loved sports and enjoyed seeing his hometown team play, but he had trouble following the action on the court, as he had other things on his mind. Minutes into the game, Randy and Bennie Lee left the gymnasium and headed to the local minister's home. Later that evening, Randy led his new wife through his mother's front door, and, in keeping with his reputation as a practical joker, said, "Mother, I've brought you one hundred ten pounds of coffee." Emma would have been happy with a pound of the rationed goods, but a new daughter-in-law left her speechless.

Randy had to return to his base, but Bennie Lee soon followed, catching up with him in Baltimore, where the army air force trained mechanics for the P-47 Thunderbolt. The newest of the military's fighters, the Thunderbolt would become the workhorse of the army air forces. Although it lacked the sleek lines, nimble handling, and speed of other American fighters, the Thunderbolt boasted a wider, longer, heavier, and more rugged body—a true juggernaut, giving the aircraft the moniker "Jug." The P-47 boasted a 2,000-horsepower engine, a top speed of 460 miles per hour, a fast climb rate, and good high-altitude performance. With eight .50-caliber machine guns mounted on its wings and the capacity to carry 2,000 pounds of bombs, the Jug was viable as both a fighter and a bomber. Heavily armored, it also proved difficult to down.[1]

With Randy buried in his books and tools, Bennie Lee spent her days sightseeing in the nation's capital. Once she took a day trip to climb the Washington Monument only to find her way blocked. A sign at the entrance noted the stairs were closed. As part of the country's conservation effort, the government decided the climb inflicted unnecessary wear and tear on shoe leather, an extravagance the public could do without.

Bennie Lee brushed her disappointment away. She imagined she would have other opportunities ahead. (She did, although perhaps not as scenic.) The military sent the young couple through a series of bases. From Maryland, they went to Millville Army Air Base in New Jersey; then to a base in Buffalo, New York; Richmond, Virginia; and, finally, to Camp Kilmer, a staging area in New Jersey. Randy, now with the 365th Fighter Squadron of the 358th Fighter Group, waited at the camp for his orders. Then, on October 8, 1943, after saying a tearful goodbye to Bennie Lee, Randy boarded a troopship and sailed for Liverpool, England.

The men survived an uneventful crossing, disembarked, and made their way east to USAAF Station F-345, a Royal Air Force (RAF) base at Goxhill in Lincolnshire, England, and one of the 140 airfields the US military constructed or improved in the United Kingdom during the war.[2] Within a month, the unit moved to Station F-373 at Leiston on the southeastern coast of England. As their quarters were not ready, the men pitched in to set up operations in a group of Niessen huts. The half-cylinder structures of corrugated steel, first introduced during World War I, served as their barracks, showers, and mess. As time passed, the men added greater creature comforts to their primitive home away from home, including a dayroom where they could read and write letters home. Over the following weeks, they built card tables and a ping-pong table to create what the squadron's diary described as an "enjoyable recreational room." Even more enjoyable, the diary added, were the weekly dances at Leiston. "The girls seem to be on the spot, coming from neighboring villages and towns."[3]

Despite the distractions, in the first weeks in England, the pilots and ground crews were learning to work together as a team and to build their trust in each other and their planes. With a bit of luck, the pilots might return from a bomber escort mission in France needing only to refuel, add oil or water to the plane's reservoirs, and reload their ammunition. More often, they arrived with broken windshields, fuselage damage from flak or bullets, or engine damage. Either way, the crews had to work swiftly, sometimes with less than an hour to put a Thunderbolt back in the air.[4]

Randy became crew chief for P-47s flown by Howard Gurley and Leslie Boze. On his first B-17 bomber escort mission, in December 1943, Gurley ran into trouble. "We rendezvoused with the bombers," Gurley wrote after the war, "and I had never seen such a sight, hundreds of B-17s in formation, each leaving a contrail." Gurley's engine quit, however, and he dropped back. In minutes, he remembered he could switch to a second, auxiliary fuel tank. Too late to catch up with the bombers, Gurley restarted the engine and flew back to his base. "My crew chief asked if there was a problem. I said, 'Yes, the problem was the pilot in the cockpit.' I was really embarrassed."[5]

Gurley would go on to fly 141 missions, more than any of the other pilots in the squadron. But the aborted mission was the one that helped cement the lifelong relationship between Gurley and his crew chief, Randy. Many years later, Gurley wrote Randy's daughters, to explain his admiration for their father. He said, "It was your Dad's mechanical expertise and skill which made those missions possible—and kept me getting back safely."[6]

Leslie Boze also befriended Randy. After the war, he wrote:

Orin Buffington, my crew chief, was a prince and a genius of a mechanic. His one concern was for that airplane to be ready to go and to perform like a Swiss watch, which it just about always did. Pete Bianchi, my assistant crew chief was equally dedicated. Many times, the three of us would just talk in long bull sessions about all kinds of things, like when would the war be over . . . guessing about how the families were making out at home and wondering what we would be doing after the war.[7]

Boze also mentioned Randy's thoughtfulness: "He made an aluminum case that would hold two packs of cigarettes and a lighter. . . . When I mounted the airplane to fly the mission there were always two fresh packs of Philip Morris in that case. What a guy!"[8]

The 365th moved two more times, each move taking them closer to the channel separating England from the continent. The first move was to Raydon and from there they transferred to High Halden, both RAF air bases. In High Halden, the men bivouacked in tents set beside slit trenches. They slept on metal cots, and each morning they filled their steel helmets with cold water to wash and shave. It wasn't for lack of better facilities. "Roughing it on a grand scale" was designed to introduce the men to conditions they might experience after going ashore in France.

At the beginning of April 1944, although there still was no word on when the invasion would occur, the men expected the orders to come at any moment. Finally, on June 5, 1944, one day before the Normandy invasion, the 365th Squadron pilots sat through a first briefing on the plans and their duties. The P-47s were to provide high cover over the beaches. Randy and the rest of the ground crews sprang into action, working around the clock to ensure their aircraft were ready. To save time and effort, the ground crews did not return to their tents. Instead, they slept beside their aircraft in shacks constructed from discarded fuel tank boxes to which they had added lights and radios.[9]

In the first hours after the pilots took off, the ground crews had little to do except wait and watch for their aircraft to return, hope, and pray. That and dodge V-1 doodlebug bombs. Germany began launching the unmanned explosives-loaded aircraft into southern England about the same time as the Allied invasion. The 365th's diary reports the doodlebugs caused a bit of excitement. As the flying bombs approached, the base's antiaircraft guns fired deafening, nonstop salvos of artillery. If a V-1 penetrated the defenses and crashed to the ground, it could explode and spew shrapnel in all directions. The men made good use of the slit trenches beside their tents—their purpose now clear.[10]

During the first week in July, the ground and other rear-echelon crews began their move across the English Channel into France, settling at the town of Cretteville. While the officers quartered in a nearby chateau, the enlisted men stayed in tents in an orchard next to the airfield. The weeks of roughing it at High Halden had prepared the men well. But in no time, they again made their tent city comfortable with showers and small firepits in the ground to heat water and warm their meals. The clean and comfortable conditions did not last for long. Following close behind the advancing army, the men moved to Vitry, east of Paris, and to an airfield subject to flooding in heavy rain. For decades after the war, Randy remembered how the mud had caked his boots, his equipment, and his living quarters, both at Vitry and later in Toul, near Germany.[11]

In his favorite memory, a story Randy told often after the war, he and a fellow soldier borrowed a motorcycle for a ride through the French countryside. As they cleared the top of a hill, they forced an oncoming jeep to veer from the narrow road to avoid a collision. Randy glanced at the jeep's occupants. The man in the passenger seat was Gen. Dwight Eisenhower. "I was just sure we were busted," Randy said. Gathering his courage, he looked back in time to see the jeep pull back on the road and Eisenhower smile and give the men a salute.

The 365th's last move took Randy to a former Luftwaffe base at Sandhofen, Germany, about one hundred miles inside the German-French border. He was there when Germany surrendered. With the hostilities ended, the squadron's group command took the opportunity to praise the ground crews, saying:

> The conditions that our ground crews worked under were difficult to say the least, and at times horrendous. At each of our airfields they always lacked protection from dust, rain, snow, mud, heat, and cold. The winter at Toul went on record as one of the coldest in one hundred years and those guys worked on aircraft in the open. It was a team effort with the pilots being an extension of all the efforts and work of the ground personnel and crews. There was never any doubt in the pilots' minds that the aircraft they are taking into battle were as worthy as human hands could make them.[12]

With Germany's surrender, the men could relax, although the question on their minds remained the same—whether they would go home, stay behind for occupation duty, or transfer to the Pacific where the war continued unabated.

In August 1945, Randy got his answer. He headed home, this time aboard the *Queen Mary* and with a duffle bag full of awards. The 358th received a Presidential Unit Citation, three Distinguished Unit Citations, and the French Croix de Guerre with Palm for assisting in liberating France. Brig. Gen. O. P. Weyland, commanding general of the XIX Tactical Air Command of the Ninth Air Force, presented Randy with a Bronze Star with an oak leaf cluster for meritorious achievement in direct support of combat operations. Besides this award, Randy earned the European Theater Medal, a Good Conduct Medal, and a Silver Service Star with two oak leaf clusters—for his perfect record of one hundred missions without his aircraft suffering a mechanical problem. In fact, with 168 missions successfully completed, Randy had come close to making his second series of one hundred flawless missions when the war ended.

All five of the Buffington brothers survived the war and returned to their homes. Randy came home to Ellijay and slipped back into the community as if he had never been away. He went to work, as might have been expected, at J&C Spread Company, later Universal Carpets, with north Georgia and the Ellijay area being major producers of carpeting and other woven fabrics. Randy worked his way up the organization and retired as a vice president after forty-five years in the industry.

But Randy didn't settle for merely working and supporting his family—which by 1954 included two daughters. He was committed to his community. He knew everyone in town, and everyone in town knew him. Young children knew Randy carried spare change in his pockets, and if the youngsters hung around he'd often part with a few quarters. Teenagers knew Randy loved the game of football and rooted for the local high school team. They knew, too, if they played football and needed a job, Randy would find them something to do to earn a few dollars. Parents of sons drafted for the Vietnam War came to see Randy, who served for twenty-five years on the local selective service board. Although he did what he could to help, his hands were most often tied. And during hard times, when the local mill-based economy slipped, Randy found jobs for men and women out of work.

Hardly a day passed without someone encouraging Randy to run for public office, but Randy declined. He much preferred helping others achieve their public service dreams, contributing time and effort to the campaigns and political lives of Senators Sam Nunn and Zell Miller from Georgia and President Jimmy Carter. Each of these statesmen had occasion to thank Randy for his help in carrying a community or a county in an election.

Bennie Lee passed away in 1984 and Randy a year later. His daughters remember the outpouring of kindness from the community. In the days before he died, while Randy lay in intensive care, the small Ellijay hospital's phone did not stop ringing. One after the other of the people Randy had helped called to express their support.

"He always gave me a job and spending money," one former high school football player said.

"He bought shirts for me when I was in school and had nothing to wear," said another.

"When we were facing a layoff," one man said, "your father would see that either my wife or I kept our jobs."

Later, after connecting with a few of the veterans of the 365th at a squadron reunion, Patricia Buffington began a correspondence with her father's pilots, Howard Gurley and Leslie Boze. In one letter to Patricia, Howard Gurley wrote, "Those planes and engine sounds bring tears to our eyes."[13] And, at the next reunion in 2003, he stood beside Patricia on the runway in Knoxville, Tennessee, as two beautifully restored P-47s took off. The 2,000-horsepower engines roared to life. Howard set his tears aside and said, "Isn't that the nuts! Isn't that the nuts!"

Randy died at the age of seventy-two in 1985. He would no doubt have shared Howard's enthusiasm for the old Jug and would be pleased to know his two daughters have preserved his memory for his grandchildren and ever-growing number of great-grandchildren. Randy is a legend in the Ellijay community—more than thirty years after his death, people there still think of him as a friend.

CHAPTER ELEVEN

Bearing Witness

William A. Scott III

✮ ✮ ✮

*Some moments cannot be forgotten or
dimmed by the passage of time.*

WILLIAM A. SCOTT III,
Reconnaissance Sergeant, US Army

When asked, many people would claim the day they married or welcomed their first child into the world as the most memorable of their lives. But William "Bill" Alexander Scott III had known his wife, Marian, since second grade. They had their first official date in the tenth grade, had fallen in love, and then married in 1944. The following nearly forty-eight-year period was one long string of memorable days. And he cherished the days his two children were born. But there were two days that stand out from the many others in Bill's life. The first was the day his father, whom he adored and for whom he was named, was killed. The second was the day he entered Buchenwald with a handful of other men from the US Army's all-black 183rd Engineer Combat Battalion.

Bill was born to William Alexander Scott II and Lucile McAlister in 1923 in Johnson City, Tennessee. Five years later, his parents divorced and Bill moved with his father to Atlanta, a city he would come to call home.

An ambitious businessman, Bill's father tried his hand at several publishing ventures before he borrowed five hundred dollars to launch a newspaper, the *Atlanta World*. The paper found a following in the city's black community and in 1932 expanded from a weekly to a daily paper, the *Atlanta Daily World*. As such, it became the first successful black-owned daily newspaper in the country.

A family photo from the early days of the paper shows Bill sitting on his father's lap in the newspaper's Auburn Avenue, Atlanta, office. Bill grew up in the newspaper business but started at the bottom—sweeping floors and delivering papers. He and his younger brother, Robert, learned many of life's lessons from their father through his business. When the boys wanted a few pennies to spend, Bill's father sent them out the door with stacks of newspapers under their arms. As children of a prosperous business owner, they might have certain privileges, but they would have to earn their way.

The idyllic life did not last. In 1934 tragedy struck. As Bill's father arrived home from a long day at the office, he was shot. Rushed to the hospital, he lived just long enough to create a hastily written will, later contested by Bill's uncle and executor of the estate, Cornelius Scott. Cornelius won control of his brother's assets and took the helm of the newspaper. In doing so, he also gained control of the family's financial well-being and their daily lives, wielding power over Bill, Robert, and their mother, Lucile, who had come to Atlanta to look after her sons.

Looking back, Bill's daughter, M. Alexis Scott, believes those tension-filled years contributed to Bill's premature death at sixty-nine in 1992. But Bill persevered through the turmoil, finished high school, and then enrolled at Morehouse College. Like his father, Bill had an ambitious streak. He took courses in business administration, which would help with the future he imagined for himself at the *Atlanta Daily World,* and mathematics, his passion. He also became the photographer for the *Maroon Tiger,* Morehouse's campus newspaper, maintaining ties with the newspaper world. His path forward seemed clear, until the middle of his second year at Morehouse, when he received his draft notice.

It wasn't a lack of patriotism or that he didn't feel a sense of duty to his country, but Bill was not eager to join the army. He knew plenty of young men his age who had enlisted when the war started and others who wanted to join now, even with hostilities in full swing. Perhaps those other men did not have as strong a yearning for a college degree or as bright a future in business as he did—or a childhood sweetheart they planned to marry.

With few viable options available, in January 1943 Bill reported for duty at Fort Benning, Georgia, and was inducted without delay. His experience was far different from blacks who sought to enlist at the start of the war. While the 1940 Selective Training and Service Act prohibited discrimination (though not segregation) in terms of race or color, loopholes allowed the practice to continue. To serve, black recruits had to be deemed "acceptable to the land or naval forces" and could not be inducted until separate shelter, medical and sanitary facilities, and water supplies were available.[1] Rather than confront those obstacles, draft boards often took the easier route, passing over blacks and filling their quotas with white soldiers.

By 1943 the army had worked through these constraints and was on target for black soldiers to constitute 10 percent of all US Army troops, a racial mix mirroring the population at large. Nevertheless, discrimination persisted. Blacks were assigned almost exclusively to existing or newly created all-black units overseen by white officers. And also with rare exception, their units were designated noncombat units.[2] On the brighter side, at least with a noncombat unit Bill had a better chance of coming home safely, back to Atlanta, back to Morehouse, and back to Marian.

Initially, Bill joined the 318th Air Base Squadron at Tuskegee Army Air Field in Alabama—home to the group of aviators and support personnel who would find fame as the Tuskegee Airmen. After scoring well on a battery of tests, however, the army sent Bill to the Army Specialized Training Program at Howard University in Washington, DC. There, he completed a nine-month basic engineering program in six months and was assigned to the 183rd Engineer Combat Battalion at Camp McCain in northern Mississippi.

From Mississippi, his new unit traveled to Texas, then to Louisiana, and finally to Arkansas for further training.[3] The interminable transfers and the weeks and months of delays the 183rd endured before being deployed to Europe was common for all-black units. Despite manpower shortages in Europe, some commanding officers and some foreign governments refused to accept black units when they became available. Even during the spring of 1943, only seventy-nine thousand of America's five hundred thousand black troops had deployed overseas. But public pressure was mounting to balance the number of whites and blacks sent abroad and to include blacks as full-fledged participants in the war.[4]

When his orders to deploy arrived, Bill decided it was time to marry his sweetheart. In August 1944 Bill and Marian married in New York City. Shortly afterward, Bill boarded a troopship and crossed the Atlantic with the 183rd to Liverpool, England, where they transferred to the continent and to the VIII Corps under Gen. George Patton's Third Army. The 183rd, as a headquarters, or non-divisional unit, did not operate on the front lines. Instead, they followed closely behind the infantry divisions to maintain roads, landing areas, and bridges and to manage communications and water supplies. As a reconnaissance sergeant for the group's intelligence section, Bill was charged with surveillance of roads and waterways, camouflage, and photography. Little did he know at the time, his duties as photographer and archivist for the 183rd would soon place him at the center of history.

In the hectic final campaigns of the war, the 183rd rotated from one command to another, first transferring to the Ninth Army and then to the First Army.[5] By December 1944, the group again fell under the command of the Third Army. With them, the 183rd advanced across France toward Belgium and the heavily forested Ardennes region where the Battle of the Bulge took place. Although he did not participate directly in the battle, for the fortieth anniversary of the engagement, Bill wrote a column for the *Atlanta Daily World* about what he witnessed. "It is with great sadness," he said, "that I remember the devastation and death that raged across the snow-covered hills of Belgium and Luxembourg."[6]

Despite the 41,000 American casualties, including 4,000 killed and 16,000 missing, by the end of the battle, the Wehrmacht was all but destroyed.[7] The Allies took advantage of the situation and pushed deep into German territory—the

Americans and British from the west, the Russians from the east. To prepare troops for what they might encounter as they entered enemy territory, the army played films with footage of conditions in Germany's political, forced-labor, and extermination camps and the atrocities performed there. The films came courtesy of the US Office of War Information, which had worked hard since 1942, commissioning, acquiring, censoring, and distributing newsreels for information and propaganda purposes and to counter enemy propaganda.[8]

Like most of the men who sat through the films, Bill said he could not believe what he saw. As the army advanced, however, they entered and liberated camps dotting the landscape and learned of the Holocaust. Bill witnessed firsthand the extent of the savagery that had taken place, erasing his earlier doubts. In April 1945 he and a few other men from the 183rd received orders to go to Buchenwald, a camp in the heart of Germany, near Weimar. The name *Buchenwald* meant nothing to him. He asked what he was supposed to do at Buchenwald, but the commanding officer offered no explanation, saying only, "Just go there and see."[9]

On that clear, sunny day, Bill later wrote, after losing their way, his small convoy came within sight of Buchenwald. Bill recalled thinking, "There is no place as horrible as we have been told—no atrocities—we should turn around, stop wasting time, go back to Eisenach and establish our battalion headquarters." Then, he and the others spotted a throng of survivors walking aimlessly around the enclosure.[10]

"We got out of our vehicles and some began to beckon to us to follow and see what had been done in that place—they were walking skeletons. The sights were beyond description. What little we had been told . . . was nothing in comparison and I had thought no place could be this bad."[11]

Bill picked up his camera to capture what he could not find words to describe. As his photographs reveal, the survivors, still in dirty and tattered striped uniforms, were little more than flesh and bones with prominent cheekbones, shoulders, elbows, and knees and sparse hair on their heads. Overcome with emotion, Bill said, "As the scenes became more gruesome, I put my camera in its case and walked in a daze with the survivors."[12]

The few photos Bill took and the copies he retained testify to what later became familiar to the world: the ovens, strewn with bones in an unfinished incineration attempt, elsewhere the remains of tortured limbs, and outside, a tangle of bodies—more like fallen branches with their twig-like arms and legs than human beings. "My mind closed the door on this horror," he said. Bill tried to put aside what he had seen at Buchenwald. He focused instead on finishing his tour of duty. It was his way of coping.[13]

In May, after Germany surrendered, the army disbanded Bill's unit, and to his disappointment, ordered them to the Pacific. Bill boarded a ship in Marseille, France, for the six-week voyage traveling halfway across the world. To pass the time, he learned to play chess and found he had an aptitude for the game. He played his way across the Atlantic, through the Panama Canal, and on to Okinawa, when he heard Japan had surrendered.

Now, just one of the one million blacks who served in the war, Bill made his way home aboard another troopship.[14] During the voyage, one of his shipmates asked what rights he thought he would have when he got home, referring to the many black soldiers who returned earlier only to be denied the jobs they wanted and the housing they sought. Bill hadn't given much thought to the question. In some respects, he was fortunate—he had a job waiting for him at the family business. After receiving his discharge in 1946, Bill returned to Atlanta, to his studies at Morehouse, and to Marian.

The fighting had ended. The camps had been liberated. To Bill, it seemed everyone had moved on. The memories of Buchenwald, however, remained and forced him to question almost everything he believed. He had always thought the key to success and self-improvement lay in education. Yet the highly educated German people committed genocide and treated human beings with depravity. He tried to explain away the Holocaust by comparing it to slavery, but, he said, "It all seemed to pale in comparison to the glaring impact of what I had witnessed at Buchenwald. My slave ancestors, despite the horrors they were subjected to, had value and were listed among the assets of a slaveholder."[15]

He had no answers to his questions, and doubted anyone else did either. Bill finished his studies at Morehouse and went to work for the *Atlanta Daily World* as the paper's circulation manager. In his spare time throughout the 1950s and 1960s, he played competitive chess. He won numerous tournaments, became a chess master, and achieved the United Chess Federation's "expert" rating. The awards are all that much more remarkable for their being earned during a period of intense racial strife in America. Bill's daughter, Alexis, remembered more than one occasion when her father traveled to play in chess tournaments and was denied admission to a segregated hotel or relegated to staying in a back room, separate from other players. Nevertheless, at one event she recalled the players threatened to walk out if Bill was not admitted. "If *he* can't play," they said, "then *we* won't stay."

Like many other black veterans, Bill was dismayed to find he'd fought a war for a country that continued to deny him the basic privileges white citizens enjoyed. His predicament was exactly what the *Pittsburgh Courier,* another

American black newspaper, understood in 1942 when it launched the Double V Campaign. The two *V*s stood as symbols of the two wars blacks faced and fought: one for America's victory over the Germans and Japanese and one for their own victory for civil rights at home.[16]

Bill's approach to this second war was not to be angry, not to be bitter, not to give up, but to help lead the fight for civil rights as a social activist through his words and deeds. His efforts were recognized in his later years when he served on several boards and commissions, many of which supported the civil rights movement, including the National Association for the Advancement of Colored People, the Educational Foundation of Metro Atlanta, and the Greater Atlanta Council of Human Relations.

Ultimately, Bill turned to writing accounts of his experience as a witness to the Holocaust, sharing his photos of the war, and lecturing extensively, all of which brought him some measure of satisfaction. As the years passed, more and more veterans came forward with stories of what they witnessed during the war, many claiming they liberated one of the German camps. The claims were often unsubstantiated. A controversy developed, eventually forcing the military to define the requirements for being considered a liberator. In terms adopted in 1985 by the US Holocaust Memorial Museum and the Center for Military History, only division-level units, not individuals, and only those who arrived at one of the camps within forty-eight hours of the initial division's encounter, were recognized as liberators.[17]

Thanks to Bill's photos and despite his having served in a non-divisional unit and having no official time-stamped records, there was no question the 183rd entered Buchenwald in the first days after liberation. One of Bill's cousins, Asa Gordon, could not leave it there. He was determined to see Bill credited with his role as a liberator. Asa conducted years of research to document the movements and timing of the 183rd's activities in Germany and at Buchenwald.[18]

Setting all arguments aside, there might have been a strategic reason for black units to play the role of liberators. Although he admits he cannot substantiate the claim, Dr. Paul Parks, a black soldier and liberator of Dachau, claims Gen. Dwight Eisenhower purposefully arranged for black soldiers to lead the camp liberations. Eisenhower, Parks reasoned, believed that on seeing black soldiers, the survivors would understand instantly the men were Americans and not Germans disguised as Americans, dispelling the notion that the liberation was nothing more than another cruel German hoax.[19]

There was also the symbolism to consider. Stories and scenes of America's black soldiers being among the first to venture into the camps and of Jewish survivors seeing their first black soldiers and calling their liberators "black angels" made for good newspaper and magazine copy.[20]

Regardless, what Bill witnessed in his twenties at Buchenwald (and likely what he encountered in episodes of racial strife before, during, and after the war) stayed with him and left its mark. "My life," he said, "as I have contemplated the impact of past events on it, has evolved into a character that exhibits an attitude to fellow humans that they have nothing to fear from me or my family." He did not want to be seen as an aggressor against his fellow man.[21]

For his service, and specifically his role in liberating Buchenwald, Bill received numerous honors. The US Holocaust Memorial Museum in Washington, DC, captured his story on tape and placed his photographs on display. Later, following his death, the Georgia Commission on the Holocaust created a traveling exhibit of his memories as a witness to the Holocaust. The exhibit was still touring in 2019.[22]

A year before Bill died, Governor Joe Frank Harris awarded him a charter membership in the Georgia Commission on the Holocaust. In that same year, President George H. W. Bush appointed Bill to the US Holocaust Memorial Council.

For his part, Bill had made peace with his experience in the war. He might not have wanted to join the army or fight in the war, but he could look back proudly on his service, his career, and his life. His attitude is manifest in his demeanor in the videotaped interview of him at the Holocaust Memorial Museum: his clear and calm voice and his measured words, even as he speaks of Buchenwald and the deplorable state of the survivors.[23]

Until his death in March 1992, Bill was active on the lecture circuit and working with the Atlanta Daily World *as the paper's public relations and advertising manager. His obituary mentions his "refusal to be downcast or embittered" and his "buoyancy." He left behind his wife, son, daughter, and five grandchildren. His descendants would later include seven great-grandchildren.*

CHAPTER TWELVE

On Foot, on Horseback, or in a Sampan

Jack T. Coyle

✸ ✸ ✸

I was a sailor in the US Navy. I walked, rode horses, drove jeeps, rode sampans, flew in planes, but never served on a ship.

JACK T. COYLE,
Radioman First Class, SACO Navy

A woman's voice rose from the vinyl disc on the turntable in the Coyle living room. Ida leaned close to capture each word. "It's 1944 in California, and courtesy of the US Navy, here's your husband, Jack." A scratchy second later, Jack spoke. "Hello sweetheart. . . . I thought I'd take this opportunity to make a record as it's much cheaper than making phone calls every five minutes. The weather out here is not so good; about all I've seen is rain, and it's pretty chilly. . . . We rented a station wagon to run around and see Los Angeles and the vicinity. So far all we've seen is Hollywood. However, it's all very beautiful. Every time you feel lonely, play this record and think of me. Don't you know, I wish I could take one with me where I'm going. . . . Well, honey, I'll sign off for now. Don't forget how much I love and miss you. Bye."[1]

Similar short messages were the last contact many wives had with their husbands for weeks after the men departed California for the Pacific. If you had asked anyone in his outfit, including Jack, where they thought they were headed, not one of them would have guessed China. Not one would have imagined serving in the Sino-American Cooperative Organization (SACO), a wartime collaboration between the US Navy and the Chinese Army. SACO's existence, its mission, and the men who staffed the organization were carefully guarded military secrets. Even decades after the war, few people had heard of the 2,800 Americans (including 2,000 navy personnel and 300 marines) who served their tours of duty with SACO in India, Burma, Indochina, along the coast of China, and deep in China's interior.

Jack T. Coyle was born on March 18, 1920, in Bloomington, Illinois, in the heart of America's vast grain belt—a town where Abraham Lincoln once practiced law. Bloomington was a small city in the 1920s. One hundred years later, with fewer than a hundred thousand residents, it was still small. Although his family resettled to Florida, Jack always called Bloomington home. He met his future wife, Ida Jayne Griffin, in Bloomington and returned there after the war to work for State Farm Insurance Company, one of Bloomington's largest employers.

In 1937 Jack graduated from Dade County High School in Florida. Four years later, he graduated from the University of Miami and started law school. Before he could finish, however, war appeared on the horizon and his draft notice arrived in the mail. Jack was eager to serve and started making plans to put his studies aside, but he failed the army physical and received a medical deferment. The deferment was a stroke of luck—it gave him time not only to have the medical condition corrected but also to finish law school. After graduating, Jack decided instead of waiting to be drafted, he would enlist in the branch of his choice—one that he imagined offered better opportunities: the navy. Jack T. Coyle, juris doctor, joined in March 1943 with the distinction of being one of the most highly educated enlisted men in his class. His JD notwithstanding, Jack started like everyone else—in basic training. In a letter home, he complained of the constant marching. But he also reported good news: an early promotion. "I am company clerk for 130 men. It is an honor of some sort involving a lot of extra work but is given only to older more educated men . . . and I will be called 'Sir.' My rate will be apprentice petty officer." Another promotion followed. With it came more work and more privileges. "All I do now is work . . . but, I get to eat and smoke whenever I want," Jack wrote, "and they have to salute me when I'm at my desk."[2]

The official US Navy enlisted ratings for World War II include apprentice seaman, seaman second class, and seaman first class, but there is no rating of apprentice petty officer. Nor does the protocol call for seamen or petty officers to be saluted. Perhaps there were exceptions made in the field—or perhaps Jack embellished his story to impress his wife. Regardless, the taste of privilege and respect shown to higher ranks might have triggered Jack's decision to apply to the navy's Officer Candidate School (OCS). Despite forwarding copies of glowing letters of recommendation from several of his former law professors, he was not accepted. Instead, in August 1943, the navy sent Jack to radio school at the US Naval Training School at Miami University in Ohio. Jack described the work as tiresome—all he did, he said, was sit for hours copying code sent from Washington, but he found it interesting. "We hear all sorts of things," he wrote, without elaborating.[3]

Two months later, bored and perhaps disappointed with not having been accepted to OCS, Jack ignored the age-old military advice never to volunteer. When the call came for a top-secret assignment, Jack raised his hand. He soon found himself among a group of daring young men on their way to Maine without an inkling of the nature of their mission or where it would take them. Jack's letters to his wife, Ida, and to his mother grew vague. "I can't tell you anything about my work," he wrote in November, "except that I enjoy it very much. It is more interesting than anything I've done yet. . . . It's the first time since I've been in the navy that I felt like I was doing something worthwhile."[4]

Whatever the work was, on completing an initial phase of training, Jack and the other volunteers went to Washington, DC, for screening by the Federal Bureau of Investigation. Those who passed faced more intense and specific training at a school operated by the Office of Strategic Services (OSS), forerunner of the Central Intelligence Agency.

As expected, the OSS operated under tight security. The men had code names and traveled in covered trucks to training exercises at unnamed tracts of land isolated from roads and the public. It was not until 2009 that the Central Intelligence Agency acknowledged the OSS had used Maryland's Catoctin Mountain Park and Virginia's Prince William Forest Park for training during World War II.[5]

Years after the war, Jack spoke of his OSS training in a speech he made to the Winter Haven, Florida, Rotary Club. "[We were trained in] espionage, sabotage, guerrilla warfare, demolition, and hand-to-hand combat, the object of which was to kill armed enemies silently with our bare hands." He went on to say he learned how to assemble and operate almost every type of small arm the Allies possessed and how to establish and hold beachheads. Jack learned other specialized skills, too, including radio operations, code breaking, weather forecasting and reporting, radio direction finding, boat operations, and some foreign language. To Ida, back in 1943, he simply said, "I'm knee deep in all sorts of scientific shenanigans and experiments."[6]

Of his location, on December 9, he said only that "It is a military secret." Then, realizing what he wrote might itself violate military rules, he followed with a letter asking her to destroy the earlier letter. Jack made it home to see his family for Christmas but left for the West Coast immediately after the holiday. In California, he learned his destination was China, although he could tell no one, not even Ida.

In the two hundred letters Jack wrote from his first weeks in basic training until the end of the war, he spoke repeatedly of his concern for Ida, how much he missed her and his then one-year-old son. All the letters began with the salutation "My Dearest Darling Sweetheart" or "My Dearest Darling Wife" and close with "With all the love in the world to my honey." A poignant farewell note of March 9, 1944, read, "Now that I am actually faced with the possibility of a several-month absence from you, sweetheart, I can hardly bear the thought. . . . I find that I almost lack the courage to go on."[7]

Jack's trip across the Pacific took six weeks. While a direct route would have been faster and more efficient, Japanese warships and submarines ploughed the waters around China from the East and South China Seas north to the Yellow Sea, and Japan controlled most of China's ports. Forced to take longer and more circuitous routes to their destinations, many Allied ships stopped for supplies and fuel, as Jack's ship did, in Australia.[8]

Well aware of the military prohibition on disclosing his location, Jack sent word to Ida using a prearranged code—one they might have devised while he had been home on leave at Christmas. As soon as the mail arrived, Ida grabbed a red pencil and circled the first letter of each sentence in selected passages. I-N P-E-R-T-H A-U-S-T-R-A-L-I-A one letter revealed and C-A-L-C-U-T-T-A another, referring to the US Navy base Camp Knox in Calcutta, India.

In Camp Knox or other bases in India, the men waited sometimes days and often weeks for transport onward. The next leg of their journey was aboard aircraft operated by the US Army Air Forces India-China Division of the Air Transport Command or the China National Aviation Corporation (CNAC). Pilots for CNAC included many former Flying Tiger pilots, men who flew for Col. Claire Chennault's American Volunteer Group in China until 1942.[9]

Eventually, a Douglas C-47 Skytrain, a Douglas DC-3, or a C-46 Curtiss Commando transport would find space for a few men along with much-needed supplies for the military, the supplies having the highest priority. Their route took them over the Hump, although aircraft of the day could not actually carry a heavy a load over the thirty-thousand-foot-high Himalayan peaks. Instead, the planes wove their way through the valleys and between the mountain peaks to their destinations.[10]

The route was treacherous, due not only to the high altitudes but also to the extreme weather, primitive navigation equipment, and threat from enemy aircraft. Over the course of the war, the Allies lost seven hundred airplanes in the route. Twice that number of crewmen perished. Barely recognizable pieces and parts of aircraft fuselages, wings, and tails lay strewn across the mountainsides. On sunny days, pilots flying the treacherous route could catch glints of silver reflecting from the debris far below. They dubbed the route the "Aluminum Trail."[11]

Guy Tressler, a SACO veteran who in 2013 recorded his memories with the Veterans History Project, recalled the flight vividly. The men, none of whom had trained to parachute, found themselves strapped into and sitting on their parachutes for the five-hour flight. Many of them wondered what they would do if they had to abandon their transport. Guy thought he might actually have to jump. "I looked out the window, and I seen this oil coming out of this motor. . . .

I said to Whitlock, the man sitting next to me, 'Come look out this window.' He said, 'That's no good.' I said, 'I didn't think it is either.'" After throwing out all but their essential gear to lighten their load, Guy's flight limped safely into the SACO airfield at Nanning, China.[12]

Of his flight, Jack wrote, "We flew over the Hump and it was about the nicest trip I ever had." Later, after months in the country, he discovered how lucky he had been. Jack witnessed several planes landing with bullet holes in the fuselage from small-arms fire. One arrived with burns to the underbelly from flying too close to a mountainside forest fire.

On reaching his camp in China, which Jack described as "way out in the sticks about ninety miles from nowhere and where there is absolutely nothing to do," he was officially a member of the "Rice Paddy Navy"—the name the men gave to SACO.

Two men spearheaded the organization: Capt. Milton Miles (later a rear admiral) representing the United States, and Gen. Tai Li the Chinese. Tai Li, a much-feared and revered strongman and head of Chinese intelligence, reported directly to Chiang Kai-shek, the leader of the Republic of China. The Chinese people considered Tai Li omnipotent, wielding "terrifying and dreadful power." As such, the Allies saw him as useful to the United States and SACO.[13]

The SACO Navy's stated objectives were to gather weather information and intelligence to support the military in defeating Japan, but they had broad latitude in defining and executing the mission. Miles expanded the effort to include laying mines and harassing Japanese shipping along the Chinese coast, gathering weather information for the US Navy's Pacific Fleet, and identifying potential sites for invading Japan.[14] Miles needed a secret army to set up and maintain the weather reporting network, guerrillas to protect the men operating the stations, and Americans to train the Chinese. SACO would be that army.[15]

Once in China, the men learned their assignments and flew, drove, took sampans, rode horses or cattle, or walked to one of SACO's fourteen camps, some in territories the Japanese controlled.[16] In notes he made, Jack claims to have run, walked, or crawled for five thousand miles during his tour in China. His missions took him to Chungking (Camp Nine), Kunming (Camp Fourteen), and Nanning (Camp Five) in China near the Indochina border, and to Burma.

The nature of the camps varied, with some situated in or near cities and others spread across the countryside. The complement of Americans ranged from one or two men at the smallest sites to hundreds in the larger camps. Conditions in the "Happy Valley" headquarters near Chungking were extensive. There, the men enjoyed running water, sanitary and permanent dwellings, regular meals, movies once a week, religious services, and, perhaps the most treasured amenity of all, a post office for mail call.[17]

Other camps were plagued with poor sanitary facilities and tainted food. Dysentery was common, due in part to the Chinese practice of using human excrement for fertilizer. Jack wrote, "We tried to cook out the bacteria but were not always successful." He added, "My main trouble is eating with those damned chopsticks." Besides large quantities of rice, the menu included dog, octopus, and water buffalo. Jack developed beriberi—a disease associated with a limited diet and thiamine deficiency. He said it "rotted the skin off my upper torso and arms."[18]

SACO radiomen manned their radio stations around the clock, listening to and intercepting Japanese transmissions. At the Kunming and Chungking camps, Jack maintained and operated the radio receiving and transmitting station and learned to operate direction finders, rotating antennas from which he could triangulate signals and locate Japanese radio station sites.[19]

With the intercepted messages in Japanese or in code (where dots and dashes represented Japanese characters or syllables), the radiomen had little idea of what the messages contained. Their job was not to decipher the messages but to intercept, transcribe, and forward the messages to SACO's Chungking headquarters. In Chungking, cryptologists decoded the messages, analyzed the contents for pertinent information, coded them again, and forwarded the messages to the Pacific Fleet, to the Fourteenth Air Force headquarters in Kunming, and to Washington. The messages provided valuable intelligence, including Japanese weather broadcasts or the enemy's reports of US military plane and ship locations.[20]

Although officially a radioman, Jack also took part in Chinese guerilla instruction. The training included how to set up radio stations, maintain and operate radio equipment, gather intelligence, and carry out sabotage, such as demolition of Japanese camps. The SACO men in camps close to the coast or along rivers occasionally took part in covert missions to observe Japanese troop and shipping movements.[21]

Despite the secrecy surrounding SACO, Japan and its allies knew the Americans were in China. Spies lurked everywhere, whether Japanese, Communist Chinese, or puppet Chinese (Chinese cooperating with the Japanese in areas of China under Japanese control), and would shoot any American on sight.[22] The enemy placed a bounty of $300 (equivalent to $4,000 today) on each SACO man's head and over $1 million ($13 million today) for capturing or killing Miles or Tai Li. To help protect the SACO men, Tai Li assigned a guard to each American. Despite the attractive monetary incentives, only four attempts were made on

Miles's life and one on Tai Li's and only three of the 2,800 SACO operatives were captured. After the war, the grateful Americans credited Tai Li with keeping the SACO men safe.[23]

For added protection, the men did what they could to blend in with the Chinese villagers in their camps. They did not wear their uniforms or any insignia designating rank or branch of service. Instead, in camps and on missions around their camps, they wore Chinese clothing. Jack's slight build (he stood just over five feet and a few inches and weighed 130 pounds) and his black hair, when cropped short to eliminate the prominent wave at the center of his forehead, helped, as did his jaundiced skin—the result of taking atabrine tablets to combat malaria.

When in transit between camps, the men also tried to mimic their native companions. As they crossed open terrain and rice paddies, they balanced yo-yo poles (long poles with baskets suspended at each end) on their shoulders. The baskets held their guns and ammunition buried beneath their food and clothing. During these treks, the SACO men gained an appreciation for their hosts who could walk thirty miles a day carrying heavy packs with little more than a handful of rice to eat.[24]

In his later Rotary Club speech, Jack said the men blended into their surroundings in more ways than they wanted to: "We smelled from the garlic in the food and the lack of bathing." But their clothing, lack of insignia, sallow-colored skin, and garlic odor were more than a means of disguise. They were a source of pride. As Miles summarized the SACO code: "We hoisted no flag. We sounded no calls. We practiced no salutes and wore what was handy. We walked, hiked, and scrambled, but we never marched. It was a place to forget spit and polish but never cleanliness—to forget rank but not discipline."[25]

Miles left an indelible stamp on the organization. He made a point of greeting men on their arrival in China, shaking their hands, and wishing them well. Further, Miles's pennant, flying at any camp where he billeted, served as a rallying point across the SACO organization. The pennant bore three question marks, three exclamation marks, and three stars on a white field as symbols for (at the time) unprintable words meaning "What the hell?" Later, SACO adopted the pennant as its emblem. It expressed the attitude of the men operating behind the lines, reflecting not only their loneliness and deprivation but also their spirit of nonchalance and indifference to the dangers they faced.[26]

Jack spent from July to November 1944 in Chungking and from November 1944 to October 1945 in Kunming, the capital of the southwestern China province of Yunnan. Those who saw Kunming on first landing at the eastern terminus of the Burma Road described the town as a "brown jewel displayed on a jade-green velvet cloth." Kunming housed the busiest airfield in the world during the war along with restaurants, bars, and its share of less reputable places, or as one SACO man said, "sights in the winding alleys only to be talked about in hushed whispers . . . with the boys."[27]

Jack took part in activities outside the camps as well, including training Chinese and making reconnaissance sorties. Accounts from other men illustrate the variety of assignments and their risks. While Shanghai was under Japanese occupation, Radioman First Class Bill Bartee hid in the attic of the chief of police's home where he relayed coded messages from the fleet to Chungking. He broadcast the messages twelve hours a day from August 4, 1945, until the end of hostilities on August 14.[28]

Kenneth Brown operated a communication station near Shenpa in Camp Four and helped establish communications capabilities for coast watchers. In a trip aboard a paddle wheeler, he fought off pirates to complete his journey. Later the infamous Tokyo Rose exposed Brown by name and location in a broadcast, but he escaped capture.[29]

Ignored by the US military, even after the war, the SACO men did not gain the recognition their brothers in other branches did. Their lone medal, the Sino-American Cooperative Organization Medal, was awarded by the Nationalist Chinese Ministry of National Defense. US Navy regulations, however, prohibited the men from displaying the unofficial medal on their uniforms. Regardless, the SACO Navy made a considerable contribution to the success of the war. SACO Navy–led Chinese guerrillas killed 23,000 Japanese, wounded 9,000, captured 300, and destroyed 200 bridges, 84 locomotives, and 140 ships and rivercraft, as well as many depots and warehouses.[30]

Over a hundred thousand Chinese contributed to SACO's mission, serving as guerillas, weathermen, radiomen, and coast watchers and conducting sabotage against the Japanese. Ten thousand Chinese were killed and another ten thousand wounded.[31] The group helped rescue downed American pilots as well, saving seventy-six lives.[32] Further, SACO played an uncredited role in General MacArthur's invasion of Leyte, supplying word to the general of an approaching Japanese carrier task force in October 1944.[33]

Miles commented, "The war, of course, would have been won even without our efforts, but I am confident that no other military unit as small and inadequately supplied as ours contributed so greatly to the outcome."[34]

Although the war ended in August 1945, Jack had to wait his turn to go home. In October 1945 he made the return flight over the Hump and then sailed back to California. From there, he came full circle, returning to Bloomington, Illinois, to work for State Farm. Later the company transferred him to Florida, where he served as deputy vice president of operations. Not one to retire fully, he dusted off his law license and in 1984 practiced law part time, writing wills and handling other minor legal matters.

In 1959, realizing the potential strategic value of the SACO experience, the US chief of naval operations asked to interview a group of SACO Navy veterans including Jack. The military wanted to hear firsthand of the challenges SACO, men faced working day after day and face-to-face with the Chinese people.[35]

Jack passed away in 1996 but left photo albums chock-full of tiny black-and-white snapshots of his time in China. His son, Jackson, has taken on the task of making sense of the photos, most of which bear no inscription. With a fervent desire to have his father's story told—and the stories of all the men in the SACO Navy—and to obtain recognition for them, even posthumously, Jackson works in his spare time as historian for the SACO Navy.

Jackson notes a handful of books exist on the SACO Navy, but Hollywood made only one film on the unit, *Destination Gobi*. In the 1953 film, actor Richard Widmark plays US Navy chief petty officer Sam McHale, who leads the men in the camp. Widmark adds a bit of glamour to the story, but the film bears little resemblance to what the men on the ground experienced, whether at the Gobi Desert station or the other camps.

Jack died in 1996 at the age of seventy-six, leaving behind his wife, three children, and five grandchildren. With his military experience in communications and weather reporting, he would be interested and perhaps proud to know that one of the country's National Oceanic and Atmospheric Administration radio towers stands in the center of his hometown of Bloomington, Illinois. The 420-foot, Eiffel Tower–like structure reminds all of the importance of communications and the expertise of US weather reporting—and maybe of men like Jack Coyle.

CHAPTER THIRTEEN

Defying the Odds

Howard O. King

✳ ✳ ✳

*We had absolutely no basic training. We took off
civilian work clothes and put on uniforms.*

HOWARD O. KING,
Steward First Class, US Navy

With only grade school educations to guide them, Willie and Lula King relied on instinct and hard work to raise their three children, Willie Seymour (Junior), Bessie Marie, and Howard Oley, the youngest. "I gained a strong sense of values from them," Howard said later. "Honesty and dedication to family were among the most important." Unfortunately in 1936, when Howard was only ten, his father died. With his death, Howard lost his role model, the man he adored and respected. In his 2017 memoir, *In Spite of the Odds,* Howard was blunt about his prospects. "As a ten-year-old fatherless black boy, my life had all the appearances and circumstances for failure."[1]

Fortunately, Howard's mother helped fill the void in his life. And, at thirteen he quit school to help his mother support the family. He worked a series of jobs—first as a delivery boy for a local grocer and then as an iceman's helper, adding an evening job at the Pensacola, Florida, YMCA, where he stoked coal for the building's hot water boilers. Later, he shined shoes for YMCA residents and washed clothes for businessmen who exercised at the YMCA. By working diligently at these and other similar jobs, Howard established a reputation for being thorough and dependable. And by keeping his eye out for opportunities and adding jobs when he could, Howard parlayed his initial five dollars a week into thirty-five. Most of his earnings went to his mother. The rest he put into savings.

Two timely blessings changed the family's circumstances. One was a government bonus Congress agreed to pay World War I veterans to compensate for the difference between the veterans' military and civilian pay—one dollar and twenty-five cents per day for men who had served overseas and one dollar per day for those who had served at home. Although enacted into law in 1922, Congress had no obligation to make the payments until 1945, except in the case of deceased veterans. Their next of kin were eligible to receive the "tombstone bonuses" immediately. The bonus due Howard's father became payable in 1936 to his widow, Lula. Others, including twenty thousand unemployed veterans who marched on Washington during the Great Depression, went through a lengthy battle to claim their bonuses. The government eventually yielded to the veterans' demands and made the long-overdue payments in 1937.[2]

The second blessing came in the form of Howard's aunt Bessie King Wheeler, his father's sister. Bessie lived in Detroit but owned a house in Pensacola on E Street and needed a caretaker for the property. She looked no further than to her sister-in-law Lula. With their improved financial situation, Lula quit her job as a domestic and focused on raising her children.

Although Howard doesn't list other blessings, his good fortune to be born in Pensacola and the dominant US Navy presence in the port city might qualify as such. Throughout the city's history, people of diverse backgrounds flocked to Pensacola to find work at the city's thriving port. Blacks and whites lived in close proximity, as Howard recalled, and in a harmony not found in nearby communities. The gainfully employed population had little time to mire in social discord. Further, the navy, with a personnel demographic mirroring the city's mixed-race population and a generally more progressive attitude, helped blunt the edge of racial prejudice.

In September 1941, at the age of sixteen, Howard took a new job, signing on as a waiter at the Naval Air Station (NAS) Pensacola cadet mess hall. Chief boatswain's mate Winfred Beaudette, who supervised the civilian workers at NAS Pensacola, took an interest in Howard. He liked the young man's diligence and his even disposition. Under the seasoned veteran's guidance, Howard learned more than just how to wait tables. He learned to do his job and by extension any other job to the best of his ability. He said, "I was motivated to dispel the myths that blacks were not able or willing to show up and be responsible. I wanted to prove that I can."

Beaudette soon offered Howard a higher-paying job as a driver for the mess. "There's no doubt in my mind," Howard said, "that it was not my doing but an act of God that put me in touch with Beaudette and empowered him to be a surrogate father."

As the Second World War continued, the military's need for troops rose. Recruiters scoured the country for eligible men and turned to the military's civilian workers. "They promised us we could stay at NAS Pensacola for two years and keep our jobs in the mess hall," Howard said. One of the most compelling enticements to Howard, however, was the possibility of retiring at the age of thirty-seven—far earlier than he imagined if he pursued any other endeavor. In September 1942, weeks after his seventeenth birthday, Howard enlisted as a messman first class.

Initially, the navy had offered Howard a steward second class rating. During his swearing-in ceremony, however, the presiding navy official noted Howard's age on the roster and told Howard he was too young to hold the steward second class rating. Chief Beaudette pulled aside a disappointed Howard and counseled him to accept the lower rating of mess attendant first class. Beaudette promised to "take care of matters" as soon as he could. With Beaudette's word on the matter, Howard agreed. With that, he became a member of the navy's food services group, a group almost exclusively of blacks and Filipinos.[3]

Although perhaps more tolerant than society as a whole, the military was not immune to racism. Blacks and whites were assigned largely to separate units—blacks often to those handling menial tasks. Further, blacks and whites lived in separate barracks. Segregation at that time was not considered discrimination.[4]

Indeed, Howard witnessed racism firsthand during his time in the navy. He said he rarely saw whites praise minorities when in the presence of other whites and seldom heard of white officers recommending minorities for advancement or bothering to complete the necessary paperwork. "Still," he said, "it is fair to say some white officers were decent and respectable."

The numbers speak for themselves. In 1940 no blacks served in the marines or army air corps, only a handful in the coast guard, four thousand in the army, and four thousand in the navy. All those in the navy were enlisted men, and all but six of those were steward's mates.[5] Blacks serving outside the military food services were "scarce as hen's teeth," Howard said. The numbers caught the attention of the National Association for the Advancement of Colored People (NAACP). With the rising demand for military enlistment, the NAACP found the perfect opportunity to raise the issue of black recruitment and increase opportunities for blacks in both the army and the navy.

The organization approached the Roosevelt administration but was rebuffed. President Roosevelt found himself in a nearly impossible situation; while sympathetic to the civil rights leaders, he was in the middle of an election and could not afford to take on the controversial social issue. Both Roosevelt's secretary of war, Henry Stimson, and secretary of the navy, Frank Knox, argued the difficulties of integrating the military, particularly in Knox's case with the close quarters aboard navy ships. The issue took years to resolve, and even behind-the-scene influence from Eleanor Roosevelt, the president's wife, but finally, in June 1942, blacks were allowed to enlist in all general service units.[6]

Howard describes his entry into the navy as unorthodox by today's standards. "We had absolutely no basic training. We took off civilian work clothes and put on uniforms." His duties did not change—he continued driving mess hall vehicles to deliver food, supplies, and men to their destinations. Soon, although content with his current position, Howard started thinking about his future, wondering whether doing sea duty might enhance his career prospects. Standing a relatively small five feet seven inches, Howard imagined he'd be perfect for a job in the cramped quarters of a submarine mess. In the mess, even on a submarine, Howard would still be in a noncombat role, but to his mind that wasn't the issue. No one then or later ever encouraged him to seek a combat role or disparaged his position as a messman or his serving in a noncombat role. Quite the contrary, he said, "I was surrounded by officers who made me feel comfortable in my role."

Still, he believed sea duty might be the best career choice, and in the spring of 1943 he requested a transfer to the navy's submarine school in Connecticut. Lt. William Bogar, the officer in charge of cadet messes, took Howard aside and told him his role at NAS Pensacola was more important than anything he would do on a submarine. "Can you think of anything more important than food?" Bogar asked, echoing the statement paraphrased and variously attributed to Frederick the Great and Napoleon: "An army marches on its belly." Howard could offer no argument, not with Lieutenant Bogar, not with the navy. He stayed on at NAS Pensacola. Reflecting later on his decision, Howard said, "We did what we were told." In doing his job to the best of his ability and setting an example for others, Howard was convinced he contributed to the war effort as honorably as anyone.

By August 1943, Howard had received two promotions and carried the rank of steward second class. His pay increased from sixty-seven to seventy-eight dollars a month, allowing him to increase his aid to his mother and put more into savings. Despite the promotions and pay increases, Howard felt he was unprepared should the escalating war need his services abroad. "I was concerned about getting shipped out without knowing anything about cooking and the other duties of a steward first class," he said. With his characteristic determination, Howard applied himself to the task. He rose long before necessary and went to the NAS galley. There, on his own initiative, he followed behind the cooks on duty, peering over their shoulders, learning everything he needed to know by observing and asking questions but staying out of the way.

Lieutenant Bogar rewarded Howard's drive and determination with privileges not extended to others. When the long hours of driving and the strain of lifting heavy supplies caused Howard back pain, Bogar found him an alternative position. He designated Howard as assistant master at arms, shifting his responsibilities from driving to making personnel assignments, inspecting work and living areas, and planning leaves. Soon afterward, Howard received yet another promotion. A grin spread across Howard's face when he remembered becoming a petty officer first class. "Quite an accomplishment for a school dropout," he said.

Then, toward the end of the navy's promised two-year assignment to NAS Pensacola, Lillie Marie Pollard walked into Howard's life. Howard knew a few members of the Pollard family and remembered Lillie as a cute young girl. She was now an attractive high school senior. In a few short weeks, Howard decided to propose. First, though, he needed to buy an engagement ring. He was in a quandary about what ring to buy and how much to spend until a fellow sailor solved his problem. The sailor had been jilted and had a ring he was eager to part with—the sailors made a deal. Lillie and Howard married weeks later on January 15, 1945. Neither Lillie nor Howard considered the ring with its history of a broken relationship a bad omen. They looked forward, not backward, and trusted in each other.

In March, Howard's name appeared on the transfer manifest from the Naval Bureau of Personnel. Although the Allies were gaining the upper hand in Europe, the war continued at a fever pitch in the Pacific. As he had done a few times earlier, Lieutenant Bogar offered to intercede on Howard's behalf and request the supply officer remove Howard's name. This time Howard declined. Expecting he would be transferring sooner or later, Howard wanted to transfer with men he knew and among whom he was comfortable.

In April 1945 families from across Pensacola gathered on the railroad station platform to see their loved ones off. Lumps welled in their throats, and despite the overcast skies, most, including Howard, wore dark sunglasses to hide their tear-filled eyes. When the signal to board came, Howard said his good-byes, kissed Lillie on the cheek, and hopped on board the military troop train bound for California. Exactly where in California and where he would go from there remained a mystery.

The train made several changes in direction and stops on its way, picking up other troops and adding railcars to the ever-lengthening chain. Their first stop was Memphis; the second and longer stop was Saint Louis, where some of the men took advantage of the layover and ventured into town. The nineteen from Howard's car split up, the eleven blacks going one way, the eight whites another.

At midnight everyone returned. Shouts, laughter, and the sickly sweet odor of alcohol filled the train car. The men who had been drinking were confrontational and ready for a fight. "Those were the times when deep-seated feelings about race surfaced," Howard said. One of the white men used a racial slur, and a drunken scuffle ensued. Although far from home and its tolerant environment, Howard—in typical Howard King fashion—carried on, as he had learned to do. He chose not to worry about what he couldn't control and focused on doing the right thing.

"There were three teetotalers in the group," Howard said—two whites and Howard. Together the three men restored the peace. The next morning everyone was sober, and feelings on race stayed under wraps. But, Howard said, "The cordial relationship had fractured."

The train pulled out of Saint Louis, continued on to Kansas City, and then paralleled Route 66 into Las Vegas and on to Albuquerque. On April 24, six days after leaving Pensacola and without further incident, the train came to a stop in Vallejo, California, where the men disembarked and settled into an embarkation camp.

Rumors about their final destination circulated, but no one knew anything for certain. While they waited for their orders, the men attended a survival training program at the navy's amphibious training center. The rugged program, intended to build the men's endurance for surviving in extreme conditions, was perhaps a hint of what waited for them.

Two weeks later, Germany surrendered. Although the war had ended in Europe, it was far from over in the Pacific. A month later, in the sixth week of his nine-week training program, Howard's orders came. "Pack your gear. You will be shipping out tomorrow." Amid a sudden crush of knees, elbows, and shoulders, Howard rushed to the nearest telephone bank to call home and tell Lillie and his mother he was off to somewhere in the Pacific.

With hundreds of other transient troops, Howard shipped out aboard the USS *Menard* attack transport and stood on deck to watch as they passed beneath the Golden Gate Bridge. Later the men sat down to a meal of red beans and rice. The dish—a staple of the South and a favorite of Howard's—did not mix well with the pitch and yaw of the *Menard* in the Pacific's rough seas. "In just a few minutes, red beans and rice covered the deck of our living quarters," he said. By the next morning, the seas had calmed, and the men found their sea legs, if not their appetite for red beans and rice. Howard swore off the dish for years.

During the first general quarters, the officer in charge of the troop transport asked for chief petty officers to step forward. When no one moved, he called for petty officers first class to come forward. Howard stepped up, one of four but the smallest and youngest. "You're the mustering petty officer for your detachment," the officer in charge said. Along with accounting daily for the members of his group, making work assignments, and inspecting living quarters, being the mustering officer gave Howard privileges. "I was permitted to take fresh-water showers and to eat with the ship's company, the officers' stewards and cooks. It was like being able to eat in the officers' mess."

When the *Menard* reached the Marshall Islands in the central Pacific, the ship joined a convoy and zigzagged its way to the Philippines to avoid any Japanese submarines operating in the area. On June 23, 1945, the *Menard* paused at Samar Island, south of Manila, to drop off Howard and his group. Nine months earlier, the island had been at the center of the Battle of Leyte Gulf, the largest and fiercest navy battle of the war.[7] But by late 1944, like the other islands surrounding the Gulf, Samar had been secured and construction of naval facilities was under way. Nevertheless, the station was far from ready to accept troops. "The entire area was overgrown with knee-high weeds and unfamiliar jungle vegetation," Howard said. And, with a shiver, he added, "large lizardlike reptiles wandered through the camp." Despite the high humidity, temperatures of over one hundred degrees, and the threat of remaining Japanese troops, work parties set out to remedy the conditions.

The Allies had cleared the vast majority of Japanese troops from the islands, but a few enemy soldiers remained, lurking outside the camp. "They would sit in the trees and watch the movies we played on an improvised screen," Howard said. Although the snipers seemed harmless, the men did not let their guard down. At night, after making a foray to the latrine, they identified themselves or sounded an agreed-upon signal before entering their tents. No one wanted to be mistaken for a sniper.

Living off the land and their meager food stores, the Japanese soldiers were always hungry. They tried to infiltrate the mess hall, stepping in the lines, hoping to blend in with the Filipinos or other islanders working in the camps. The white guards couldn't tell the Japanese from the islanders—neither could the black guards. "Finally, we switched to using Philippine soldiers as guards," Howard said. The infiltration ended.

Next, Howard moved to Tubabao and then to Calicoan, two small islands just off the southeastern point of Samar Island. On Tubabao, the navy assigned Howard to the 143rd Naval Construction Battalion (Seabees). Most of his days were spent making the daily menus and procuring food supplies and ingredients, sometimes crossing from one island to another on pontoon bridges the Seabees had constructed. Seabees were famous for *cumshaw*—a navy term for making do with what they had and procuring goods by swapping, bartering, mutual back-scratching, and "midnight requisitions."[8] Howard fit right in. The ever-enterprising young man traded supplies he had in abundance, including beer, for Coca-Colas, fresh meat, and eggs. And, with an eye for a chance to make an extra dollar or two, Howard, the teetotaler and nonsmoker, also sold his beer and cigarette allotment to his fellow sailors. "It was my little hustle," he said, "and the demand was high." Then in August, when he thought his next move was to Indochina, the war ended.

Howard sailed home aboard the carrier USS *Bunker Hill* with close to nine hundred men wedged together on the hangar deck, their bunks stacked four high. As it had on his outgoing voyage, the sea churned. This time, however, it was far worse. The ship sailed through a typhoon, and one man was swept overboard.

After making it to the West Coast safely, Howard faced a long and arduous cross-country journey. The trains were full and there were long delays due to traffic jams. By some estimates, 94 percent of travelers in December 1945 were soldiers trying to make it home. With a bit of luck, Howard found a seat on a train headed east.

Americans across the country were ready to welcome the men home. Some opened their homes to the soldiers and, when trains stopped over for long periods, they threw parties. Truckers and taxi drivers drove soldiers to their destinations—some going thousands of miles out of their way and accepting nothing more than the cost of the gas.[9]

After Howard arrived in Jacksonville, Florida, he was discharged. It was December 22, 1945. He left immediately for Pensacola and his nine-months-pregnant wife, Lillie. "I kept telling Lillie, 'Wait till I get there.'" She did. Lillie gave birth to their son, Howard Oley King Jr., three days later, the day after Christmas.

Although he could have rejoined the navy, Howard decided he would be a better husband and father at home than somewhere faraway on a ship. He tried his hand at several jobs, including driving a taxi. None suited him, and eventually he returned to work as a civilian at NAS Pensacola.

As he had throughout the war, Howard continued to think about his education. Now, twelve years after dropping out of the ninth grade, he took advantage of funding from the GI Bill and went back to school. He earned his high school equivalency diploma and then, while working full time at the naval station, attended Washington Junior College. Four years later, in 1956, he became the first male in his family to earn a college degree, graduating with distinction from Florida A&M. "It was the great equalizer," Howard said of having an education. Now, with a college diploma in hand, Howard had no intention of working as a carpenter or mason or auto mechanic. He aspired to a future in business where he could create a better life for his family and set an example for his children.

He submitted his name for every civil service opportunity he was qualified to fill and was interviewed but never selected. Then, deemed ineligible for a position he knew he was qualified for, Howard had had enough. He appealed his case. After months of legal wrangling, the Washington, DC, Civil Service Commission upheld his appeal, awarding him eligibility as a supervisor in the supply department at NAS Pensacola with pay retroactive to the day of his appeal. The department tried to ignore the ruling and denied Howard a hearing on the matter. Undeterred, he appealed his case to the commanding officer in Pensacola.

The officer ruled in Howard's favor and offered him his choice of positions. Howard chose one in the civilian personnel office, from where he thought he would have more opportunity to help others. He became the first nonwhite to occupy a staff position in the office. "My faith in human beings received a tremendous boost. I acted because I thought I was right and that right would triumph ultimately over wrong."

Howard earned several promotions in his personnel role and was once appointed to the Pensacola City Council's Biracial Committee to address integration issues in the community. Later he took a job in contract compliance with the army matériel command in Atlanta. Howard's congenial manner, common sense, and polite and respectful approach helped him win victories over clear issues of bias for companies under government contracts, ending segregation at company drinking fountains, restrooms, and lodging and dining facilities.

Still later Howard worked as a regional intergroup relations specialist for the US Forest Service. He successfully initiated the course for a degree-granting program in forestry at the Tuskegee Institute (now Tuskegee University), ensuring more opportunities for black students in forestry. He also helped upgrade Moton Field in Tuskegee, Alabama, where the Tuskegee Airmen trained, bringing additional business and educational programs to Tuskegee University. Both efforts, in his opinion, stand at the top of the long list of his achievements.

Finally, in 1972 Howard transferred to the Federal Aviation Association (FAA) in Washington, DC, where he helped carry out the mandates of Titles VI and VII of the Civil Rights Act and became the deputy director of the Department of Transportation for the FAA's Office of Civil Rights. After retirement, Howard served his community in business ventures and volunteer capacities, and as a deacon at his church. As he looked back over his career, Howard said he was most proud of helping others find opportunities and improve their lives.

In January 2019 Lillie and Howard celebrated their seventy-fourth wedding anniversary, Lillie wearing a diamond on her finger—not the jilted sailor's ring but a new ring she chose on the couple's fiftieth anniversary. Howard laughed, remembering when as a teenager in 1945 he wondered if the relationship would endure. "It might last a weekend or two," he said, "if we're lucky." But it was the example he followed and set, not luck, that saw all three of Howard and Lillie's children retire after successful careers and all six of his grandchildren attend college.

PART IV

Going Home

When a thing is done, it's done. Don't look back.
Look forward to your next objective.

GEORGE C. MARSHALL,
General, US Army

As early as January 1942, the United States began planning for demobilization and redeployment. Planning continued throughout 1942 and into 1943 and culminated with a report to the president in June 1943 in which the government assumed Germany would surrender by September 1944 and Japan would continue to fight for another twelve months.[1]

Of course, Germany didn't surrender until May 1945. But with victory in Europe, the Allies had the liberty to concentrate their efforts on a single battlefront, ultimately resorting to using the atomic bomb to end the war. And although America's decision to use the bomb was questioned, supported, and railed against in later years, few doubted the fighting would have continued and more lives would have been lost without it.

Besides, there was a particular urgency in releasing the atomic bomb when the United States did. The country knew Germany had been working to develop more powerful weapons, including an atomic bomb, and feared the Germans would succeed and gain the upper hand. In response, in one of the most closely guarded secrets of the war, America launched its own atomic bomb plans. Joyce Maddox, like her fellow workers at the Manhattan Project's Oak Ridge Tennessee facility, knew little more than rumors about how their jobs supported the war. Her job paid well, better than the other jobs she had had, and the recruiter had promised her she would be helping the country win the war. At eighteen, that was all she needed to know.

In September 1945, after Japan surrendered, troops in the Pacific joined the already long line of soldiers from other theaters of war waiting to go home. The enormous task of transporting millions of men involved nearly as much planning as the war itself had. A points system (the Advanced Service Rating Score) was devised to determine the order in which men and women went home. Under the system, members of each branch of the military accrued points for the length of their service, overseas service, combat service, awards, and the number of children they had at home. In keeping with the mores of the time, women received some deference, requiring forty-four points to be eligible to ship out, while men needed eighty-five—and if a married man went home, his wife serving abroad moved to the top of the list.

On paper the plan sounded perfect. Execution, however, was anything but perfect. Individual personnel records were often inaccurate or outdated and although the plan was revised multiple times, officials failed to communicate changes to the field on a prompt and even basis.[2]

Despite the plan's problems, the military had good intentions. They hoped to bring anyone who could be spared back to the United States, back to their homes and families, back to the lives they led before the war as soon as possible. Operation Magic Carpet (sometimes referred to as Operation Santa Claus) involved an eighteen-month transportation effort to maximize the number of men arriving home by Christmas 1945. As they had during the deployment phase of the war, most troops returned by ship with 370 carriers, battleships, and conscripted ocean liners participating. The USS Saratoga alone carried 29,200 troops home in multiple voyages during the operation.[3]

For some, of course, the war ended with their untimely death before Germany or Japan surrendered. Such was the fate of Frank Cone, a battalion surgeon with the cavalry who served in hospital wards in the Philippines during the Japanese invasion and in the field as US forces "withdrew" from their stand on the Bataan Peninsula and Corregidor. After being taken prisoner, and until the day he died, Frank considered it his duty to tend to the Americans and Filipinos around him in Camp Cabanatuan, a Japanese prison camp. His fellow surgeons, people who lived and worked beside him in the deplorable conditions, tell much of his story.

In this final group of stories, army nurses Josephine Sanner Davis and Marie Touart Stepp share their perspectives on ministering to the wounded. Josephine had jumped at the chance to join the Army Nurse Corps. She and the three women who would become her lifelong friends, Orpha Mae Riggle, Margaret "Janie" Moore, and Helen Budzak, enlisted in the army, in part, to see the world. The group of four young ladies defied the odds and stayed together for the duration of the war aboard one of America's hospital ships, crossing the Atlantic six times, bringing the wounded home, and caring for them during their crossing. When the war in Europe ended, the four returned home, waited for their ship to be overhauled for service in the Pacific, boarded again, and sailed for the Pacific, where they served until the end of the hostilities.

Marie, however, simply wanted to do her part. She was well trained and an expert at bandaging wounds, having worked in a Mobile, Alabama, shipyard's infirmary. When President Roosevelt threatened to conscript the country's nurses if they didn't volunteer, Marie's mother signed her up at the nearest recruiting office. Although the epitome of a young lady from the South, Marie discovered she had a backbone of steel and a spirit to match. She spent part of her service in Washington, DC, at Walter Reed General Hospital, tending to the wounds, both physical and mental, of the young men who had fought in Belgium at the Battle of the Bulge.

Randy Bostwick, like Frank Cone, had trained as a battalion surgeon, but when he arrived in Italy, the Seventh Army needed a medical supply clerk more than it needed a battalion surgeon. Unfazed, Randy and his unit went to work gathering medical supplies the army had off-loaded on the beaches of Italy and later France and sped them to hospital wards and aid camps scattered behind the advancing army. Randy's service did not stop in the summer of 1945. Lacking sufficient points to join the line of men and women going home, he stayed behind to organize the mountains of medical supplies left in the army's wake and to help the millions of displaced persons who were homeless and hungry, wandering the countryside.

The veterans' stories end with Pete Peterson. His was the first story captured and is one of the most poignant of the group. Pete served in the Quartermaster Corps, Graves Registration Unit. Few can imagine volunteering to do Pete's job, yet he picked up the mantle and began caring for the fallen American soldiers, regardless of branch of service or role in the theater. He helped collect, identify, and prepare soldiers' remains for burial, and he designed the cemeteries where he laid them to rest. He and his men did their duty to the utmost of their ability, intent on providing the fallen the dignity and respect they deserved.

CHAPTER FOURTEEN

Inside the Secret City

Joyce Maddox Lunsford Kellam

*This is to certify that Joyce Maddox has participated in work
essential to the production of the Atomic Bomb, thereby
contributing to the successful conclusion of World War II.*

Henry L. Stimson,
Secretary of War, to Joyce Maddox,
Corps of Engineers, Manhattan Project, US Army

In modern neonatal wards, heat plays a critical role in caring for premature babies. Their thin skin allows water to evaporate faster than in full-term babies, subjecting the babies to life-threatening heat loss. In poor and less-developed countries, mothers of preemies compensate by wrapping their babies in blankets and placing them on their chests in the first hours after birth.[1] In rural Georgia in the winter of 1926, Mittie Belle Maddox devised her own solution. She warmed two bricks in the fireplace, the sole source of heat in her home. Then she buried the bricks among the blankets in the chest of drawers where Joyce, her newborn daughter, slept.

Joyce told the tale on a videotape her son Ray Lunsford made a decade ago, before her memory clouded. Tales of the good and bad times in Joyce Maddox Lunsford Kellam's life fill the tape. But, for some reason, Joyce remembered the story of sleeping among the warm bricks more clearly than most of the other stories of her life, including those about her life before and after World War II and her contribution to the war effort.

In the video, Joyce laughs and claims she's the runt of the family, blaming her short stature and plain looks on her premature birth and difficult upbringing. It's a self-deprecating statement because 1940s photos of Joyce reveal her to be an attractive young woman with fair skin and a high, bright forehead with a crown of brunette curls. Perhaps her manner and dress in the photos define Joyce better than her physical characteristics. In one black-and-white snapshot, she stands, hand on hip, in a "just dare me" pose. In another, her confidence evident, she strides along a sidewalk in fashionable bow-topped, open-toed high heels. "I never wore sneakers," she said. Ray confirmed Joyce's "girly girl" persona, saying, "She even gardened in heels."

The stories of Joyce's early childhood read like those of many other children who grew up in the rural South of the 1920s and 1930s. They are bleak but filled with good times and peopled by a loving family. Her parents, Mittie Belle and Philip Russell Maddox, raised cotton, corn, peppers, and okra. Joyce remembered helping harvest the crops, pulling a cotton bag twice her size across the field. She picked muscadine grapes and beans and won prizes for her jars of sliced peaches, the sections of fruit arranged in precise, even layers. She attended a one-room schoolhouse, carried around a doll that'd lost its head, and in the summer made trails through honeysuckle vines and built playhouses from fallen pine needles.

In her teens, Joyce attended "nickel nights" at the theater in Griffin, Georgia. Once a week, she and her friends took their places in the center of the dark theater and watched newsreels. She remembered one featuring Adolf Hitler. "We knew about him years before the war," she said. And then, as all America watched Europe descend into war, things changed at home. For the first time, Joyce's classes included a physical education program. "The principal wanted to make us more able bodied," she said and laughed, the unfeminine shorts and sneakers no doubt crossing her mind.

One day in December 1941, the principal called the students into the auditorium. He announced the United States had entered the war. "There was a long period of silence," Joyce said. "No one knew what to say."

Philip Jr., Alton, and Chester, three of Joyce's four brothers, were eligible to enlist. One signed with the navy, another entered the maritime services, and the third enlisted in the army. A year and a half later, after graduating from high school, two friends talked Joyce into joining the US Army Nurse Corps. They wanted to serve their country too. The women drove to Atlanta but discovered a flood of applicants waiting at the recruiting office doors. Joyce returned home a civilian. As she pondered her next move, she attended the Ruth E. Mitcham Shorthand and Business College, learning dictation and typing—skills she thought would bolster her chances of finding a job. Shortly afterward, she landed a position at Warner Robins, a new military facility seventy miles from home.

"It was an elite place to work," she said with a hint of pride in her voice. The Warner Robins Air Service Command, a repair depot for US Army Air Forces aircraft, maintained the army's parachutes and radio systems and trained military maintenance and supply personnel.[2] With the war effort gearing up, Warner Robins became a hive of activity, much of it involving sensitive military information. Joyce worked in the inspector general's secretarial pool, handling the office's correspondence on war preparedness and documenting the military complex's efficiency reports. To this day, Joyce, who claimed to have held top-secret clearance at the installation, keeps tight-lipped about what she did at the depot. She may not recall the details, but she remembered being ordered not to talk about them then, and she doesn't talk about them now.

While Joyce took dictation, typed, and filed reports at Warner Robins, three hundred miles north Brig. Gen. Leslie Groves and the US Army Corps of Engineers were busy as well. In a remote eastern Tennessee valley, the army was engaged in its own top-secret effort, ambiguously named the Clinton Engineering Works (CEW).

The facility, located at Oak Ridge, Tennessee, became the headquarters for the Manhattan Project—the army's code name for the effort to develop a weapon capable of mass destruction, the world's first atomic bomb. Besides Oak Ridge, the Manhattan Project included two other planned sites, one at Hanford, Washington, and another at Los Alamos, New Mexico.

The Oak Ridge site proved ideal, offering everything the army needed: relative isolation, vast amounts of electricity via the Tennessee Valley Authority, clean water, and good rail lines and roads for transportation. The seventeen-mile valley winding through Roane and Anderson Counties had another feature in its favor. The designers believed the high parallel ridges running through the area might buffer the surrounding communities in the event of a catastrophic explosion at the facility. Further, the sheer length of the property meant the town could sit at one end and the uranium processing plants could be widely dispersed at the other.[3]

Nuclear science was in its infancy in the 1940s, and despite having tapped some of the brightest scientists in the field, disagreements persisted on all fronts, including the best means to develop enriched uranium. As a result, the project called for not one but three processing plants at Oak Ridge, each with a code name—X-10, Y-12, and K-25—and each using different processing methods. The planners grossly underestimated the number of workers needed as well, sending recruiters scrambling across the country to meet the demand.[4]

Army recruiters targeted high school–educated girls from rural backgrounds, presuming the young women would do what they were told and not ask too many questions.[5] To a large extent, they were correct. After hearing the Oak Ridge jobs would help win the war and offering attractive salaries, few needed to know anything more. Not about what the job entailed or the purpose of the work or the potential risks—of which little was known for certain.

Joyce was the perfect candidate. She knew how to follow orders and had experience handling confidential government matters. After finding and interviewing Joyce at Warner Robins, the recruiters offered her twice the $1,400 a year she earned at the Georgia facility. Whether the high pay, the intrigue of taking part in a top-secret war effort, or the chance to see another part of the country was the deciding factor, the strong-willed, ambitious Joyce Maddox signed on.

In early 1945 Joyce joined Roane-Anderson Company, whose offices were in the town of Oak Ridge, away from the uranium processing plants. The company operated the town, or the "secret city" as some called Oak Ridge, with responsibility for living conditions, including cafeterias; schools; transportation; the water, electrical, and steam systems; sewage and waste disposal; the town's hospital; and its public safety and security system.[6]

The police and the fire departments—where Joyce worked—were major elements of the Oak Ridge security system. As secretary for the fire commissioner, Joyce attended many of the commissioner's meetings and there, among the Manhattan Project's scientists, military advisers, and public safety authorities, Joyce caught an earful. Fire control was understandably a very serious matter. Roane-Anderson had no interest in seeing a fire break out in one location, spread to another, and cause an explosion. Joyce dutifully sat through the meetings, took notes, filed reports, and said nothing.

She also made frequent trips deep into and across the project's operations, keeping records on the location and condition of each of Oak Ridge's 350 fire alarm boxes and handling classified files for alarms reported. Thanks to the fire commissioner's watchful eye and thoroughness—as well as luck and maybe Joyce's diligence—Oak Ridge boasted a record of fire damage well below that for cities its size. In fact, the community had no incidents of radiation exposure, while Los Alamos had two such events in the late 1940s.[7]

Oak Ridge had grown to a peak workforce of close to 80,000 by the time Joyce arrived in 1945. Roane-Anderson managed the town's 35,000 homes set aside for families and dormitories that could house 15,000 single men and women. Eight company-supervised cafeterias served 40,000 meals a day, and a fleet of 800 buses carried over 100,000 passengers a day during peak periods—equivalent to the sixth-largest bus system in the United States at the time.[8]

The men and women working at CEW had to accede to high levels of secrecy, constant supervision, and austere living conditions. Single men and women lived in dormitories with men segregated from women and, in keeping with the times, blacks from whites. Despite the conditions, many of the former employees have fond memories of Oak Ridge. Although some women say they had little time to themselves, most, like Joyce, were young and "freewheeling" and spent night after night socializing and dancing until the early morning hours.

Joyce even met her future husband at Oak Ridge. One of her friends had been dating Bill Lunsford, a young man working at the K-25 processing plant, but was now dating his boss, leaving Bill available. The friend offered to introduce Bill to Joyce. Suspicious, Joyce questioned her friend at length about the young man she had described as funny, smart, and nice looking. Her concerns satisfied, they set a date. On Ray's videotape Joyce recalled the first date as if it were yesterday. She had chosen to wear a sunny yellow cotton dress, her ever-present white platform heels, and matching white purse. Bill arrived dressed in a red plaid shirt, khaki slacks, and field boots, anything but smart and nice looking.

Despite his dress, Bill, a former marine staff sergeant who had seen combat in World War II, had a way about him, a certain charisma. Joyce later described him as a charmer. Bill and Joyce danced the evening away, and the evening after that, and the next. She was smitten.

In the summer of 1945, when word of the explosion over Hiroshima spread across Oak Ridge, employees spilled out of their homes, dormitories, offices, and plants to celebrate. Finally, Joyce and Bill and the thousands of their coworkers discovered what they had been working on at CEW and the reason for the years of secrecy.[9]

Work did not stop with the bombing, but the number of employees plummeted. Joyce stayed on, as did Bill. The two were a couple. Bill wanted to take the next step, but when Joyce learned there was already a Mrs. Bill Lunsford, she kept Bill at arm's length until his divorce came through. As luck would have it, in 1951 the military intervened, reactivating Bill for the Korean War. He left Oak Ridge and a tearful Joyce for duty at Cherry Point, North Carolina.

Thinking she might never see Bill again, Joyce threw caution to the wind and followed him to North Carolina. But the marines did not send Bill to Korea. Whether the threat of his being sent to war had been real or a ploy to win Joyce's sympathy, she would never know. Regardless, the two young lovers returned to Oak Ridge to be married at the Chapel on the Hill on March 13, 1951.

Sadly, Joyce and Bill's story did not include a happily ever after. When the Korean War ended, Bill separated from the marines and took on a series of jobs. The combat-hardened former marine was used to having his way. When things didn't go as he liked, he walked off the job—never mind that he had a wife and, by 1963, five children to support. The meager times led to alcohol, arguments, and abuse. Joyce and Bill separated, got back together, separated again, and then divorced in 1967.

Undaunted, she held her broken family together, doing whatever she could to feed, clothe, and shelter her children. Joyce took in laundry and ironing to make ends meet. Although she came close to losing her children and her home several times, somehow she prevailed. Eventually, she met, fell in love with, and married another strong-willed World War II veteran, Seth Kellam. In time, he, too, turned to alcohol and the marriage spiraled into trouble.

Joyce, however, refused to surrender. She had an equally strong will from years of growing up with little means and making her own way through life. Joyce had survived one marriage to a demanding bigger-than-life marine. She could do it again. Joyce redoubled her efforts to take care of her children. She brought them up and saw them through school, marriage, and having children of their own.

At ninety-two, Joyce lives just doors away from her son, surrounded by her children and grandchildren. She showers all with love, holds their hands tightly, and hugs them often. She wants nothing more for her children and grandchildren than to have the happily-ever-after she sought. Still, she won't say a bad word about Bill or Seth and remains tight-lipped about Oak Ridge.

CHAPTER FIFTEEN

Helping, Helping, Helping

Frank Cone

☆ ☆ ☆

Everything has been fine and this has been a lovely war.

Frank Cone,
Captain, US Army Medical Corps

J amie's memories of the five short years he shared with his father flicker in his head like clips from vintage home movies. In one, the two build a snowman after a rare snowfall covers Texas. In another, they stand side by side and watch floodwaters course through the streets of Houston. A third recalls his father parading on horseback during maneuvers at Fort Bliss, near El Paso. To the side, a group of Native Americans huddles under blankets.

He has a binder full of newspaper articles, military records, and letters from his father to his mother and to Jamie on his birthday. He has Frank Cone's dog tags and one black-and-white photo of Frank from the Philippines in 1941. In a wicker chair, the dark-haired army officer sports a perfectly starched uniform while perusing a copy of the state of Texas medical journal.

Frank Cone was born on June 24, 1910, in Pikesville, Maryland, northwest of Baltimore, at the family home known as Pomona. At Park School in Baltimore, Frank showed all the signs of a future leader; he became an Eagle Scout, class treasurer, and assistant business manager of the yearbook. He followed his interests and natural athletic ability, playing on the football, basketball, and lacrosse teams. Frank graduated from Park School in 1927 and from Johns Hopkins University in 1931, with a bachelor of science degree and as a member of the Omicron Delta Kappa Fraternity, a national leadership honor society. Not satisfied and perhaps influenced by his father, also a graduate of and professor at Johns Hopkins, Frank continued his studies. He earned a bachelor of arts from Johns Hopkins in 1933 and then a medical degree from Johns Hopkins Medical School in 1938. While at the university, Frank met and married Marian Jones. Actually, they married twice—once in Annapolis by a Baptist minister and then at her family home in Joplin, Missouri, by a Methodist minister.

By the time Frank finished his internship, the couple had two sons, Jamie and Alan. Then, in September 1939, just as he was establishing a medical practice in Houston, the US government called, "requesting" he serve in the army medical corps. Frank "volunteered" and reported for duty. Perhaps his athletic build or the note on his records indicating he played polo in college led the army to place Frank with the Twelfth Cavalry Regiment, First Cavalry Division. He would be one of the last men to serve with horse-mounted troops. The cavalry had served in America's wars through World War I, but by 1940 its days were numbered.

Frank spent 1940 and the spring of 1941 with his family, first at Brownsville, Texas, and then at El Paso. For Valentine's Day 1941, while in El Paso, Frank gave Marian a handwritten card with the message, "Houses are rare, rents are high, but remember, dear, you still have I." In truth, she had him for another three months. In May 1941, along with twenty-seven other medical officers, Frank shipped out from San Francisco, California, to Fort Stotsenburg in the Philippine islands. A few active horse-mounted units still operated in the Philippines, but the men of the Twelfth Regiment left their horses behind. They sailed aboard the SS *Washington,* a former Austrian luxury liner, fully furnished, complete with stewards. "It was some trip," Wade Robinson, a fellow medical officer and passenger, reported in a letter to Frank's brother Maxwell after the war.[1]

In the early days of his appointment to the Philippines, Frank penned a poem, sent it to Marian, and encouraged her to send the work on to Ogden Nash, the famous and widely imitated American poet. Apparently, Frank thought he might have similar skills. An excerpt from "Lament of a Medical Officer Isolated by a Typhoon" reads:

> In a lonely little field camp
> On a well secluded ridge
> The hero of this story
> Was cut off by a bridge
> He was restive, he was angry
> He was lonely, he was wet
> Do you think he thought of home?
> It's an even money bet.
> He thought of little Marian
> Of Jamie and of Bink,
> And the more he thought of these folks
> The lower he did sink.
> It was raining, it was misting
> And the mildew, it did stink.
> And all that he could really do
> Was think, and think, and think.[2]

Things were about to become far more serious. In 1941 the Philippines was transitioning from status as a US possession to independence, planned for 1946. In the process, America began drawing down its military presence and transferring responsibility for defense of the islands to the Philippine government. By midyear 1941, when Frank arrived, limited US armed forces remained—their primary purpose was to protect Manila Bay, a strategic port. Should the islands come under attack, the plan called for American forces to withdraw to the Bataan Peninsula, a spit of land forming the western boundary of Manila Bay, and to Corregidor Island in the bay. Should the US forces fail to maintain control of the bay, the ultimate plan was to sacrifice the Philippines. At the time, the United States had no desire to fight on multiple fronts—in Europe and in the Pacific.[3]

The United States had reason to believe an attack on the Philippines was coming. In July 1941 the Japanese assumed a protectorate over French Indochina. In retaliation for the blatant aggression and to hamper Japanese military plans, President Roosevelt froze Japanese assets in the United States and incorporated the Philippine Commonwealth Army into the US Army. Gen. Douglas MacArthur, whom the president called out of retirement to organize the Philippine Army, became commander of the US forces in the Far East. The forces under his command included the Philippine Scouts, units of Filipino soldiers led by American officers.[4]

Frank was assigned to the medical ward with the Twenty-Sixth Cavalry, Philippine Scouts at Fort Stotsenburg, a former artillery and cavalry installation. The post sat a half mile from Clark Field and housed the Clark Field hospital. Despite the beauty of the setting with giant acacias surrounding a large parade field, there were ominous signs. As the new arrivals disembarked from the *Washington,* Wade wrote, officers' families from Manilla and Stotsenburg were boarding to return to the United States.

Still, the men made the most of their time. Frank, Wade, and another medical officer, LeMoyne Bleich, billeted together at the post. And in a setting reminiscent of a more genteel era, the three engaged in an active social life. Wade wrote, "We wore our formal white dinner jackets with gold epaulets . . . for parties and receptions and we wore our 'whites' for dinner in the evening." The men made trips into Manila and saw more remote parts of the Philippines, thanks to the Chevy coupe Wade brought with him from the United States. They furnished their living quarters in Philippine style, purchasing native rattan furniture and decorating the walls with handmade knives, bolos, bows, and arrows. In the nearby town of Angeles, Frank ordered a handmade credenza from a local furniture maker and had planned to bring it back home with him. Wade added, "I don't think it was ever finished."

A few of Frank's letters home survive and provide a sense of his understanding of the events leading up to the hostilities in the islands. As late as November 1941, Frank wrote, "We aren't the least worried about the Japs now because we have plenty of what it takes to put them where they belong and they know it as well as we do. Six months ago, they could have walked in and taken these Islands without a 'by your leave.' Today there isn't a single one of the several thousand islands of this group which they can take and hold—so let them come and they'll learn plenty fast that they missed the boat."[5]

Then, nine hours after the attack on Pearl Harbor, on December 7, 1941, the Japanese attacked Clark Field, destroying or damaging seventeen of the Far East Air Force's thirty-five B-17 bombers, fifty-three P-40 fighters, and three P-35 fighter aircraft.[6] Two weeks later the Japanese landed at Lingayen Gulf and Lamon Bay, dashing hopes for an Allied victory. The United States activated its plan to withdraw to Bataan.[7]

A letter from Frank to his wife on December 30 showed no sign of concern. Quite the opposite. Frank wrote of his Christmas dinner with twenty men at a small hotel overlooking a lake backed by mountains and a distant coastline. For dinner, the men gorged on fried chicken, baked ham, yams, and fruit salad; drank coffee and champagne; and topped everything off with Sauterne and cigars. Mostly, however, Frank longed for the time when he would be back home for Christmas with his family, playing with his sons' toys.[8]

Not all meals were as sumptuous. "One breakfast," Frank wrote, "consisted of a great big swallow of whiskey & a black cigar. This was followed that night by a can of grapefruit juice & 3 bananas, but my waist line seems to 'hold its own.'" The letter ends with a wish for the new year, and Frank's words, "I am well and busy."

March 2, 1942, found Frank somewhere on the Bataan Peninsula. He kept his letter to his mother, Bess, lighthearted, describing his Filipino orderly, driver, and launderer and his living conditions. He described his bunk as being "under a thatch of banana, nipa, and bamboo, matted against a sharply rising hill in a grove not far from our bathtub." Frank went on to explain that by "bathtub" he meant a nearby stream of clear, cold water. He told Bess about his meals: for breakfast he had stewed raisins, corned-beef hash, French toast, and coffee; for dinner, rice, stewed jackfruit, sardines, cocoa, biscuits, and cake, as well as ketchup, mustard, and other condiments. "In short we live quite well," he wrote.[9]

Frank had been in the field, presumably near the fighting, returned to Fort Stotsenburg, and then rejoined a field group. In the field, besides his primary duty as battalion surgeon, Frank acted as a forward observer, tractor driver, telephone lineman, messenger, mechanic, and airplane lookout. At various times, he had been strafed but missed by a Japanese plane, shelled by the enemy while checking on his men in the field, and thrown against a tree after a bomb exploded nearby. He survived another Japanese bombing and a sniper who had shot the windows out of his car.

Frank had a chance to laugh at himself too. Earlier, he wrote home of an escapade near Luzon, the largest of the Philippine islands, where he took shelter in a Catholic church. Despite Frank's disheveled appearance—he describes himself as "filthy, smelly, sleepy, wearing a steel hat, cover-alls, GI shoes, a gas mask on his back, and a pistol on his hip"—the priest invited him inside. Weary, he told the priest, "I have driven two nights and a day without rest and without food." The priest welcomed Frank, offering him a Coca-Cola and a glass of one-hundred-year-old brandy and then a bath, towels, soap, and a bathrobe. Later they sat down to eat, and typical of someone for whom good food is a luxury, Frank took pains to document the meal: "soup, boiled eggs in Spanish sauce, sliced ham, smoked sausage, fried meat of some sort, papayas, bananas, Spanish wine and then coffee and brandy." The evening ended on less than a happy note. Minutes after he laid down to sleep in a two-hundred-year-old Spanish bed, he awoke, "burning all over as though his robe was on fire." What looked like an entire colony of stinging ants covered Frank's body.[10]

Another time, when he was playing cards with a colonel, enemy artillery shells screamed overhead. While Frank hit the dirt, the colonel never left his seat or dropped his cards. He looked at Frank and laughed. The shells exploded miles away. "Aside from the above . . . everything has been fine and this has been a lovely war," Frank wrote. "We have had less than 1.3% of our command killed, less than 2.3% of the command killed and wounded, no epidemics, very few days lost from illness. . . . A good number of cases in my hospital should be diagnosed 'constipation, acute.'"[11]

The scant records don't say if Frank had been in the field with the Twenty-Sixth Cavalry Regiment, his original group, or another unit. If he was with the Twenty-Sixth, he may have taken part in the horse-mounted cavalry action. After the Japanese rout of soldiers defending the Philippine beaches, Lt. Gen. Jonathan Wainwright turned to the Twenty-Sixth Cavalry, Philippine Scouts. Their primary mission was to delay the inevitable, giving the United States time to withdraw.

When the Japanese attacked next, the horse-mounted soldiers dismounted and took cover, set up position, and returned fire, proving the accuracy of their rifles and machine guns and giving the Japanese their first real fight. The cavalry successfully delayed the enemy, but the relentless Japanese soon took control of the peninsula. Historians report the Twenty-Sixth's performance at Lingayen Gulf, at Binalonan, and on Bataan "wrote a glorious final chapter to the proud history of both the Philippine Scouts and the American horse cavalry."[12] The Twenty-Sixth was the last traditional horse cavalry regiment to go into a battle in a US war.[13]

Despite Frank's optimism, the United States surrendered at Bataan on April 9, 1942. After gathering the captured Americans and Filipinos, the Japanese forced the prisoners to walk a seven-day, sixty-five-mile trek across the Bataan Peninsula to Camp O'Donnell, a former Philippine Army installation. On the Bataan Death March, as the maneuver became known, an estimate of 600 of the 10,000 American troops and between 5,000 and 10,000 of the 70,000 Filipino troops died.[14]

N. H. Blanton, a survivor of the march, wrote decades after the war, "Sick, beaten, wounded, and starved, they staggered on under the prodding of the Japanese bayonets, filling their canteens with green stagnant water from the drainage ditches. I saw the compassionate Filipino endeavor to help with food . . . only to be beaten back by the captors. On the march many fell, never to rise again."[15]

Wade Robinson saw Frank near San Fernando, Pampanga, where the Japanese loaded the prisoners onto railroad boxcars for the final twenty miles to Camp O'Donnell. Wade wrote, "He had obtained permission to set up a little aid station by the roadside and was busy helping, helping, helping, as usual. He looked well at that time."[16]

Somehow Wade, LeMoyne, and Frank survived the march and found each other at Camp O'Donnell. The doctors lived in a "barracks-like section of the camp," with the men sleeping on the wooden floor cushioned with a pad of grass they had picked. "This was a hell-hole and I can only tell you that we were starved, sick, and half dead." Everyone was hungry and could think only of food. Wade wrote, "Everyone from buck private to general carried a recipe note-book with him and talked food-food-food all day long—also listed names of good restaurants all over the US."[17]

In June 1942 the Japanese moved the Camp O'Donnell prisoners to a larger facility at Camp Cabanatuan. From the day he arrived, Wade remembered Frank felt tired and ran a fever. Tapping the Filipino black market, the men smuggled food for Frank. An egg, rice cake, or banana. Despite their efforts, Frank grew more ill and developed a tender mass in his lower right abdomen. Frank went into the camp hospital and later transferred to the Provincial Hospital of Cabanatuan where, on August 13, 1942, Col. Jack Schwartz performed surgery and found an inoperable form of intestinal cancer. Although put in a "miserable corner of the hospital to die," Frank hung on. Five days later, the Japanese returned Frank to the camp. During a rough ride on a bumpy road, his surgical wound split open and did not heal. The cancer took its toll, too, but Wade noted Frank remained free of pain and was lucid.[18]

A month later, Wade saw Frank for the last time. Frank knew he was dying. "This is it," Frank said. "You won't see me again." Frank gave his personal effects (a watch, a fountain pen and pencil, and a "few treasures") to Wade and asked to have Rev. Samuel Donald, a chaplain in the camp, read the Twenty-Third Psalm over his body. Frank died the next day, on September 13. His friends LeMoyne and Wade shaved and bathed Frank and wrapped his body in a sheet. He was buried in a common grave at the prison.[19]

Wade concealed Frank's effects and kept them safe, despite repeated, surprise inspections by the Japanese prison guards. After the war, he sent them to Marian. As Wade described to Marian in a letter dated November 10, 1945, his possessions included a watch, fountain pen, and pencil; a notebook containing a sketch of a brooch (in the shape of Luzon with a pearl inset where Bataan lay) that Frank planned to have made for Marian; a note of debts owed; lists of recipes, places to eat, and household furnishings; a coin purse with three checks for debts owed by fellow soldiers in the camp; a medical brassard, US and medical corps insignia; and a leather thong holding a pearl. "Frank carried that pearl in the little leather case," Wade wrote, "attached to his dog tags around his neck and the Japs never spied it."

In May 1942 the army notified Marian and Bess that Frank was missing in action. Weeks later, they learned he was alive but a prisoner of war. What little hope the women clung to was dashed months later when they heard of Frank's death in the camp.

Years later, on January 30, 1945, in arguably one of the most daring and successful missions of the war, the US Army's Sixth Ranger Battalion, a "new, relatively untested unit of elite infantry," led the rescue of the remaining prisoners in Cabanatuan. Alamo Scouts, a reconnaissance unit of the Sixth Army, preceded the Rangers and Filipino guerillas who approached on foot after a twelve-hour march to the camp. As the men prepared to assault the prison in the early morning hours, one of the newest US fighter aircraft, the Northrup

P-61 Black Widow, flew over the camp, distracting, confusing, and terrifying the guards. The pilot in the unusually shaped, black-painted aircraft flew back and forth over the camp, cutting and restarting the engines to give the impression he was about to crash. The ruse helped, and five hundred prisoners escaped.[20]

Finally, months after the war ended, Gen. Douglas MacArthur sent Marian a letter of condolence. The letter, dated November 1, 1945, reads:

> My deepest sympathy goes to you in the death of your husband, Captain Frank Cone, while a prisoner of war of the enemy. You may have some consolation in the memory that he, along with his comrades-in-arms who died on Bataan and Corregidor and in the prison camps, gave his life for his country. It was largely their magnificent courage and sacrifices which stopped the enemy in the Philippines and gave us the time to arm ourselves for our return to the Philippines and the final defeat of Japan. Their names will be enshrined in our country's glory forever.
>
> In your husband's death I have lost a gallant comrade and mourn with you.

Four days later, another letter arrived at the Cone home, this time from Le-Moyne Bleich. LeMoyne provided the details of Frank's death, explaining he died of cancer of the large bowel. He described Frank as someone liked by all who knew him and said Frank had done his job well and did not "suffer excessively." In a statement often echoed by many survivors of the Japanese prison camps about fellow prisoners, LeMoyne wrote that Frank, though in pain, "insisted upon working to take care of those whom he considered were less fortunate than he was."[21]

The men took care of each other. Edward Konik, another survivor, explains, "You got to know each other very well and you kind of helped one another. If you got sick, your buddy usually kicked you in the butt to get you on your feet, to keep you going. If he got sick, you reversed it. That's the reason you survived because one took care of the other."[22]

The army made a retroactive award of a Bronze Star to Frank Cone for his involvement in the defense of the Philippines. Frank's son Jamie (now Knox Glass, having taken the name of his stepfather, whom Marian married in 1956) received the award at the 1984 convention of the American Defenders of Bataan and Corregidor. He accepted the award on behalf of the family: Knox and his brother, Alan, and Candace Glass Cox who devoted much time and effort to finding acquaintances and records of their father.

Frank Cone is buried in the Manila American Cemetery and Memorial at Fort Andres Bonifacio in the Philippines. The cemetery holds seventeen thousand fallen American men and women and the names of thirty-six thousand missing, the largest number of graves and names of the missing of any cemetery built and administered by the American Battle Monuments Commission. In some respects, Frank is home. The grass covering the cemetery was propagated from two square yards of sod from Beltsville, Maryland, Frank's home state.[23]

CHAPTER SIXTEEN

To See the World

Josephine Sanner Davis

★ ★ ★

*We had a sincere desire to serve our country and a romantic
dream that we would see the world while doing so.*

JOSEPHINE SANNER,
First Lieutenant, US Army Nurse Corps

Josephine Sanner Davis's exquisite watercolors grace the walls of her sunny apartment. Most are landscapes—including one of a stand of dark conifers that may have reminded her of her native Pennsylvania. Of late, as she said in her studio in 2012, she had been captivated by mandalas, Hindu or Buddhist graphic symbols of the universe. She had painted a series of mandalas in a rainbow of colors. "I studied painting in New York after the war," she said, "and I've been painting ever since."

Her head and eyes shifted as she returned to the subject at hand, her "war story," a story of great luck and lifelong friendship. In 1941, when the war started, twenty-two-year-old Josephine Sanner and her best friends, Orpha Mae Riggle and Margaret "Janie" Moore, had enrolled at the Western Pennsylvania Hospital School of Nursing in Pittsburgh. Citing a "sincere desire to serve our country and a romantic dream that we would see the world while doing so," Jo and her friends enlisted in the US Army Nurse Corps.[1]

The trio joined the ranks of nearly two thousand US military nurses, a small group at the time when compared with the sixty thousand nurses who would serve by the end of the war.[2] Their first assignment fell far short of Jo's expectations—Fort Indiantown Gap, near Harrisburg, Pennsylvania, sat a mere two hundred miles from home. Not what anyone would consider romantic or "seeing the world."

Fort Indiantown Gap was a staging area for troops on their way to Europe and where the nurses trained for war duties, practicing on troops too ill to deploy. There, too, Josephine's group of friends expanded to include a fourth, Helen Budzak, a young woman with a similar background and outlook on life. Within weeks, the four women became fast friends, hoping against hope they could stay together in the coming months.

With each nurse responsible for a nearly overwhelming thirty-three patients, the daily routine became a juggling act of working, eating, sleeping, and enduring the army's traditional white-glove inspections, as Orpha Mae remembered in her book, *Kindred Spirits in the Service of Uncle Sam.* When the opportunity for foreign service surfaced, Orpha Mae wrote, "We jumped at the chance!"[3]

In typical army fashion, however, more transfers, additional training, and months of delays followed. Finally, in November 1942, the group settled at Camp Kilmer, New Jersey. With their training completed, the women's lives returned to some degree of normalcy. They enjoyed an active social life, attending parties at the officers' club and taking short trips to marvel at the sights of New York City. There was ample opportunity to meet young men, and while at Camp Kilmer, Josephine met Dent Davis, a determined young army air forces officer who kept in contact with her through the months and years of separation to come.

Six months later, in May 1943, the nurses deployed to North Africa, traveling aboard the USS *West Point*, the former luxury liner *America* converted for military use. With eight thousand troops on board, the nurses had little time to think about the windswept deserts, spice-laced breezes, and exotic animals that awaited them at the first stop on their journey to see the world.[4]

Besides the good fortune of being able to remain together to this point, by the time the *West Point* docked at Casablanca, the fighting in North Africa had ended. The four women transferred by train four hundred miles east to Oran, Algeria. On the journey across northwest Africa, Josephine marveled at the sight of camels and people in Middle Eastern dress. It was a far cry from Fort Indiantown Gap. As full of wonder as it might have been, Josephine was also struck by the rampant abject poverty and, on a personal note, appalled at the limited and primitive toilet facilities for women.

Months of tending to wounded troops followed. The cases of flu and digestive maladies they'd treated at home were a thing of the past; in North Africa, the nurses treated stomach and chest wounds, broken bones, and amputations.

Despite being far from home and in the middle of a war, the women's social lives continued. Josephine even found a chance to reunite with Dent Davis. While in Oran, Jo learned Dent was stationed at a nearby base. The determined young lady went AWOL, hopping aboard a military transport for the short flight to his Atlas Mountain station. Jo garnered much attention from the servicemen on the base. She was, after all, the only Western woman for miles. As her short visit neared its end, Jo realized she hadn't thought about how to return to Oran. Dent came to the rescue, borrowing his commanding officer's jeep to drive Jo back across the mountains to Oran. Many years later, no matter how many times she told and retold the story, the desert adventure would be the favorite of her son Kent Davis.

In late 1943 Josephine and her fellow nurses were assigned to the USS *Santa Rosa* to escort casualties back to the United States. Then, in May 1944, the four-some transferred to the USAHS (United States Army Hospital Ship) *Charles A. Stafford*, on which they made seven more crossings of the Atlantic, traveling most often between Charleston and Liverpool or Bristol, England.[5]

The *Stafford* was one of forty-four American hospital ships, twenty-nine operated by the army and fifteen by the navy during the war. Most of the ships were converted cargo ships, troop carriers, or passenger liners. The *Stafford* was converted from an East Coast passenger ship, the *Siboney,* and had seen duty in both World War I and earlier in World War II. It could carry 700 patients in addition to 150 ship's crew and 200 medical staff. Painted white with large red crosses on the sides of the hull and the stack to distinguish them from destroy-ers, battleships, and troop carriers, the hospital ships were protected from attack by provisions of the Hague Convention of 1907. But in fact, before the end of the war, ten army hospital ships would be torpedoed and seven destroyed after hitting mines.[6]

Life aboard ship—whether going to or from Europe—was anything but glamor-ous. In the nurses' living quarters, four bunks and small sets of drawers occupied most of the space, and only one nurse at a time could stand comfortably. Had they not been the best of friends, the situation would have been untenable. On duty, the *E* ward became their least favorite work rotation, being below the waterline, with low clearance and no portholes; the ambulatory ward on the *B* deck, closest to the main deck, was the best.

Shuffleboard, movies, card games, and letter writing or worrying about their sweethearts on some distant battlefield filled the nurses' idle time on trips to Europe. Josephine and Dent maintained an almost daily campaign of letter writing, and what she saved fills boxes in Kent's attic today.

On occasion, the women took advantage of being in foreign ports. Orpha Mae wrote of sojourns in Liverpool and Bristol, although Josephine said she saw little of the ports when their ship docked. Instead, from the ship's deck, she would watch one set of passengers disembark while hundreds of new patients onshore waited their turn to board for their voyage home. At those times, the *Charles A. Stafford* became a hive of activity—with quarters cleaned; bunks, free of their prior inhabitant, readied for the next; food and supplies loaded; and papers checked for those coming aboard.

As each new patient boarded, the medical staff assessed the level of treatment they required. Some needed only a few good meals to regain their strength and the weight they had lost. Others were seriously malnourished or needed dental treatment or wound care. The trip home, whether to England or the United States, took from a few days to two weeks. The long process of healing and regaining their former lives could only begin aboard ship.

Many of the men lacked physical wounds but suffered, instead, from trauma. In all, Josephine remembered a third of the patients aboard a typical voyage on the *Stafford* being psychiatric patients and housed in a separate locked ward.

With a full load of wounded soldiers, for the nurses, the return trips were far different from the earlier leisurely outbound voyages. On these trips, the nurses had little to no idle time, a day and a half off each week, and when working night duty, they served without a day off for thirty days straight.[7]

Most often, the ships carried American or British troops from Europe. But on one voyage to Europe, Josephine's ship carried German soldiers. These soldiers had been among the 425,000 prisoners of war, mostly Germans, Italians, and Japanese, captured in battle and held in one of the 500 prisoner of war camps dispersed across the United States.[8]

Josephine remembered the German prisoners' mixed emotions about returning to their homeland. Many had come to enjoy life in America and dreaded returning to Germany. Despite being deemed the lucky ones because they had survived and were heading home, the men did not feel lucky. As the *Charles A. Stafford* approached Gibraltar and the straits leading into the Mediterranean and to their port at Marseille, one German soldier disappeared. The crew presumed he jumped overboard under the cover of night. Regardless, by morning the roster held one less name, saddening all aboard. Someone would have to prepare an explanation for the Swiss guards responsible for the prisoner exchange.

But Josephine had good memories too. One soldier she attended and befriended had been evacuated from a German prisoner of war camp. He brought with him a set of tiny figurines and told Josephine how he made them. During captivity, he explained, he and the other soldiers in his camp scavenged bits of solder from ration cans, squirreling away one small particle at a time, and later assembled the pieces into various shapes. This soldier's figures included females and males, the males easily distinguished from the females by the tiny rifles they carried.

The nurses made their last trip to Europe in May 1945. Three days out of New York City, word of Germany's surrender reached the ship. Orpha Mae remembered the "explosion of excitement" as a celebration began.[9]

The *Stafford* sailed on, picking up waiting patients in Liverpool, returning to New York, unloading the troops, and going immediately to the shipyard for overhaul before continuing to the Pacific. The layover afforded the nurses time to visit with family and friends and for Josephine to reunite with Dent, who was waiting on the pier in New York when the *Stafford* docked.[10]

The two spent six weeks together and, near the end of the period, married. Josephine, her three best friends, and the groom all wore their uniforms for the simple ceremony at the Church of the Transfiguration, better known as the Little Church Around the Corner. Formed prior to the Civil War, the church later became popular with the theater crowd in New York. Theodora Roosevelt held her wedding at the Little Church, as did other famous couples. In 1942 and 1943, with throngs of young men and women passing through New York, the church hosted many wartime weddings, sometimes conducting as many as six a day.[11]

Luck stayed with the women on their next duty. After tending to patients across the Pacific from Leyte to Mindoro and a side trip to Corregidor, the nurses headed home. As the *Stafford* crossed the Pacific, news arrived of the bombing of Nagasaki and, a few days later, of Japan's surrender. The war had ended, and the four women were discharged from service in January 1946.[12]

Despite the travails, not one of the four nurses would have traded her experience for a safer, more comfortable role back in the United States. All four returned home and carried on with their lives. Helen married Joe Neidinger, whom she had met during the war under circumstances similar to Josephine and Dent's. Joe became a florist after the war, and the couple settled in New Jersey. Orpha Mae married Roy Blood and moved with him to Texas, where she continued her nursing career. Janie wed Reinhart "Yup" Krebs. She had passed many of the days crossing the Atlantic and Pacific by knitting and developed a passion for spinning and weaving, which she practiced in her later years. And Josephine went to art school in New York.

The adventure, as the young women thought of their experience, went far beyond what any of them had imagined at the outset. They had fulfilled their dreams of serving their country, finding romance, and seeing the world. For decades after the war, the four maintained their friendship through correspondence and annual reunions with their spouses, last meeting together in 1988.

Josephine passed away in Atlanta, Georgia, in 2014 at the age of ninety-five. She was the third of the four lifelong friends to pass, but not before Orpha Mae Riggle Blood preserved their story in her book and Helen Budzak Neidinger recorded her experiences with the Veterans History Project. Josephine left two sons, Kent and Dent, six grandchildren, and four great-grandchildren as well as scores of lovely watercolors that grace their homes.

CHAPTER SEVENTEEN

A Southern Lady in the Ranks

Marie Touart Stepp

We broke rules we didn't know existed.

MARIE TOUART,
Second Lieutenant, US Army Nurse Corps

I n 1945, as a first aid station nurse in the shipyards of Mobile, Alabama, Marie Touart earned seventy dollars a week, whereas buck privates in the army earned the not-so-princely sum of thirty dollars a week. "Roosevelt said that if we didn't enlist [as officers in the Army Nurse Corps], he would drag us into the army as buck privates." At least that's what Marie remembered of the scuttlebutt spreading through the shipyards. She felt she had little choice and would have to enlist.

Casualties in late 1944 and early 1945 had mounted. Some of the fiercest battles of World War II occurred during that period, including the Battle of the Bulge in the Ardennes in Belgium, the Colmar and Ruhr Pockets in central France and Germany, Luzon in the Philippines, and Iwo Jima in Japan, straining the Allies' medical resources.

"The care and treatment given to our wounded and sick soldiers have been the best known to medical science. Those standards must be maintained at all costs," President Roosevelt said in his January 1945 State of the Union Address. But to illustrate the inadequacy of nursing care, he noted more than a thousand nurses were hospitalized, many from overwork, leaving army hospitals under-staffed. One nurse tended to twenty-six beds in army hospitals, far more than the recommended fifteen beds. Shortages of trained personnel placed the care and lives of the wounded in jeopardy.[1]

The statement that made Marie and her fellow private nurses stand up and take notice, however, was the president's appeal to the people's sympathy. His words were a thinly disguised admonishment and a threat to the country's nurses. "It is tragic that the gallant women who have volunteered for service as nurses should be so overworked," Roosevelt said. "It is tragic that our wounded men should ever want for the best possible nursing care. The inability to get the needed nurses for the army is not due to any shortage of nurses; 280,000 registered nurses are now practicing in this country."[2]

Those nurses worked in civilian hospitals and, as Marie did, for public and private entities. They just weren't volunteering for military service. As a result, the president took an unprecedented step and asked for an amendment to the Selective Training and Service Act to induct nurses into the armed forces. He hoped to add twenty thousand nurses to the army, bringing the total to sixty thousand. Twenty thousand, he claimed, would hardly be missed from civilian duty.[3]

As a young girl, Marie had learned etiquette and proper elocution from her grandmother Mary Naomi Touart, one of Mobile's well-mannered ladies. From her grandfather Louis Touart, who lost everything in the 1903 cotton market crash, she learned to make do with what she had and to never stop trying. After the crash, Louis had started over, taking a job as a night watchman. Marie's father, Eugene Touart, was also a hardworking man determined to make a good life for his family. He worked as a fireman and later a streetcar motorman, until he lost his sight. Then in 1935, just as the country was recovering from the Great Depression and Eugene thought a better future lay ahead, he died from a heart condition. Marie and her mother, Winifred, were on their own, but Winifred was an enterprising woman. To make ends meet, she began renting spare rooms in the family home, charging her boarders five dollars a week.

The mere threat of war had brought prosperity to Mobile. Men and women from across the South flooded the city seeking steady shipyard jobs and wages four times what they earned elsewhere.[4] Demand for lodging outstripped the supply, with the less fortunate forced to sleep in parks, alleys, and even chicken coops. It was not uncommon for men to rent a bed by the hour, sleeping in shifts—as soon as one man vacated his bed for work, another took his place. Winifred could have made more money renting by the hour, but she had her limits and the principles her mother-in-law, Mary Touart, had set for refined southern women—even those who needed to work to support themselves. Marie, still a teenager, helped out as well, wrapping packages at the Kress Department Store and selling beauty products behind the store's cosmetics counter. She also worked at the local theater where, for a bit of extra money during the 1939 opening of *Gone with the Wind,* she dressed in a replica of the white and green hoop-skirted dress Scarlett O'Hara wore for the movie's barbecue scene.

Then in 1941, on graduating from Bishop Toolen High School. Marie did what many young women of the day did. She enrolled in Mobile's Providence Hospital School of Nursing. Even Mary Touart might have approved. Marie received her license in the summer of 1944 and began working as a registered nurse at the shipyard's first aid station. That's when the rumors started, culminating in Roosevelt's pronouncement about dragging nurses into the army.

A flood of nursing applicants followed, overwhelming the recruiting offices. "You'll hear from us," the army told Winifred when she registered her daughter on Valentine's Day 1945. Six weeks later, on Easter Sunday, which Marie remembered ironically fell on April Fool's Day, she was in the army—or at least in basic training at Camp Rucker in southeastern Alabama.

Until mid-1944, nurses held only quasi-military status and had the barest of military training. An army bulletin explained: "The duties of a nurse in a military hospital do not differ in any important particular from the duties . . . in civil hospitals. Preliminary military training is not essential therefore."[5]

Already a practicing nurse, Marie's four weeks of training focused on book-keeping, saluting, and marching. "They just pulled out some books and said, 'Here's our books' and 'Here's how to keep them,'" Marie remembered. As the numbers in the Army Nurse Corps grew, more formal, if not more rigorous, training evolved, mostly through trial and error. Nurses following Marie and her cohort trained in far more diverse topics, including "military courtesy and customs, uniform regulations, dismounted drill, physical training defense against chemical, mechanized, and air attacks, army and medical department organization, military administration, first aid, field sanitation and communicable disease control, ward management and routine hospital procedures." In 1945 the army added instruction in malaria control and tropical diseases for nurses like Marie who expected to see duty in the Pacific theater.[6]

At a slender and petite five feet five inches tall, Marie tended to let the other nurses take the lead. "I always got in the back and kept my eyes open for trouble," she said. "I wanted to be ready to go if we had to get away." Her philosophy served her well.

During one outdoor training exercise, a march on a packed-sand road through the area's savannah of longleaf pine, turkey oaks, and wiregrass, Marie occupied her usual place at the rear. Without warning, the women at the front of the line came to a complete halt. The puzzled drill sergeant asked why they had stopped. A woman responded, "There's a snake in the road."

The sergeant stepped to the middle of the road and glanced at his feet. "Ladies," he said, "the snake is dead."

"Then take it away," the woman said, the entire column refusing to proceed until the perplexed sergeant obliged.

Later, for a mustard gas demonstration, Marie stood again at the back of the group, staying away from potential harm. "We were supposed to get just a whiff of the gas so that we would recognize the odor if we smelled it later. But the wind whipped around, and the gas came at us. Luckily, I was so far back, it didn't get to me."

Camp Rucker graduated two thousand nurses between October 1943 and August 1945, including Marie in April 1945, all receiving full commissions after completing basic training.[7] Now a second lieutenant, Marie took what seemed a never-ending trip by train across the South to Camp Butner near Raleigh, North Carolina. There, she and the other fresh army lieutenants disembarked and formed a long line beside an equally long line of footlockers. A truck for their footlockers and a bus to take the ladies to their quarters idled some yards away. The women looked at each other, at the vehicles, then back at the footlockers. "I guess this is the army," Marie said. She reached down, grabbed the handle of her footlocker, and dragged it to the truck, then hopped aboard the bus for the short ride to her quarters.

One of the larger army installations in the country, Camp Butner sprawled across forty thousand acres of farmland acquired from local communities in 1942. Besides the hospital where the nurses worked, the camp housed facilities for troop training and served as a staging area for troops bound for the western front and as a marshaling point for troops waiting discharge. Like Camp Rucker, Butner also contained a prisoner of war camp for captured Germans and Italians.[8]

"The prisoners served our meals in the mess hall. They were very polite but didn't talk. They didn't speak very much English," Marie remembered. The women communicated with the prisoners largely by sign language. Once, when they thought they'd reached an impasse in asking for milk, one nurse resorted to mooing and pumping her hands up and down as if milking a cow. The prisoner smiled and returned in minutes with a tall glass of fresh milk.

In return for the kindness shown them, the nurses gave the prisoners tobacco. Camp protocol did not allow the nurses to give the prisoners their cigarette rations. Instead, the nurses purchased cigarette packages, removed and discarded one cigarette, and then left the "used" packages beside their plates at the end of their meals.

While at Camp Butner, Marie treated her first wounded soldiers, monitoring and recording the men's vital signs and changing their dressings. She was an expert at bandaging, having had much practice during her days in Mobile. There, injured men did not have the luxury of time to recuperate in a hospital bed. After seeing the first aid nurse, they had to report immediately back to work, so their bandages had to last. Marie's skills did not go unnoticed. Soon, the other Camp Butner nurses were coming to her for help—something she regarded with pride even decades later.

Most of the women at the camp lost weight from the long workdays and with only minutes to eat between shifts. Marie was no exception, losing precious pounds from her already small frame. "We did have one day off each month and a half day off each week," she said.

On one of those half days in August 1945, Marie and a friend went to Durham to shop and to see a movie. A few minutes after the film started, they heard shouts. The movie stopped, and the lights went on. "People were running around, screaming, 'The war is over, the war is over!'" With, as she described, "lots of wild celebrations erupting," the two well-mannered young ladies hurried back to camp.

The war might have been over, but the nurses were needed as much as ever. Marie transferred to Lawson General Hospital in Chamblee, Georgia, north of Atlanta, where wounded American soldiers arrived by military transport. One of the most tragic cases she remembered was a soldier whose feet had been badly injured from frostbite. The man, the lone survivor of a battle in Germany, said little and spent most of his days thumbing through a book of photos of friends who had died in the battle. When one of the German prisoners of war entered the ward to repair a ceiling fan, the wounded soldier eyed the prisoner, watching his every move. As the prisoner set up and then climbed a ladder in the middle of the room, the soldier dangled one foot over the side of his bed and pawed and pulled at the ground, inching his bed toward the ladder. His plan to topple the ladder and injure or kill the German failed, and he was taken away. Marie never saw the soldier again but heard later he had been transferred to a mental ward.

In July 1946 Ann Turbeville, a friend at Lawson, transferred to Walter Reed Hospital in Washington, DC. Marie applied for and received permission to transfer along with Ann so they could stay together. In Washington, the pair found themselves in a very different environment. Their superior officer, a female captain, had been at Walter Reed since the hospital opened at the end of the First World War. "She had her own ways of doing things," Marie said. Her ways were very much at odds with those of Ann and Marie, who shared a fun-loving streak and frequently ran into mischief. "We broke rules we didn't know existed," Marie said, laughing.

The women purchased bicycles and rode across the grounds and into town whenever they had the opportunity. At the end of one sojourn, fearing they would be late for duty if they didn't hurry, they pedaled frantically back to their dormitory and sped straight into the basement storage area, nearly colliding with the captain. Ann and Marie caught the stern look on their superior's face but hurried past without a word, stowed their bikes, changed clothes, and ran to their wards. Laughing all the way, the women arrived just under the wire.

Life at Walter Reed, however, was for the most part hard work. One of Marie's wards housed dozens of men who had fought in the Battle of the Bulge. Most had suffered severe frostbite, leaving their feet with few or no toes and grotesque scars. Some had received initial care in German prisoner of war camps. "Those soldiers fared better than the soldiers treated first by American doctors," Marie said. "The German doctors had preserved the ball of their foot and their big toe. When it came time to try to walk, they just hopped up and walked." However, American doctors amputated all the toes of frostbite victims, and those men needed much more care and the nurses' help as they relearned to walk.

By late 1946 the demand for nurses declined. Bloated from years at war, the army carried out a reduction in force, offering not a carrot and a stick but a stick and a stick. If they volunteered for five more years—which seemed like a very long time for most of the young women—they could receive a promotion to first lieutenant. If not, they would be subject to the reduction in force and separated without a promotion. Plus, they would run the risk of being called up later at a lesser rank. Marie said, "I thought, hmm, Mother's getting old." She decided to take her chances, separate, and go home.

"I didn't get a promotion, but I did get a ruptured duck," Marie said as she delicately plucked the tiny gold-colored medal from her box of keepsakes. The Honorable Discharge Medal given to World War II soldiers on separation with good conduct was known colloquially as the "ruptured duck" for the shape of the medal: an eagle with wings spread and positioned partially outside a circle, the breast of the bird protruding from the plane of the medal. "And," she continued, "the army even shipped my bicycle back."

Marie's good conduct notwithstanding, she said she did something not quite honorable. On discharge, the army handed her a train ticket home. At the station, Marie traded the Pullman class ticket for a less expensive coach ticket and pocketed the difference. That and the money the army paid for her mileage onward would prove a tidy sum to help her mother. It was a small transgression.

Emaciated and exhausted, Marie arrived home in November 1946. After months of care and her mother's home cooking, she regained her health and returned to work as a private duty nurse. Twenty-six, single, and attractive, Marie had had little time for a social life—until her cousin insisted she get out and meet people. She started by attending a dance school, which led to an evening at the Rose Room.

"Everyone's been to the Rose Room but you," her cousin said.

"So we went," Marie added.

Music filled the local hotel's ballroom, and soon a brash young man asked Marie to dance. After a single spin around the dance floor, Ralph Stepp grabbed a chair, made space at Marie's table, and spent the rest of the evening by her side.

Ralph, a navy veteran, worked for a passenger cruise line and was absent from Mobile for weeks at a time, returning for a few days at the end of each cruise. The two continued their relationship on those handful of days each month. "Once I took him to see some land I was buying. I wanted to get his opinion. And that night, he asked me to marry him. I always teased him that he wanted my land more than me," Marie said, laughing in her easy, genteel way.

After a courtship of a few months, Ralph and Marie married in 1950. In their first years together, the couple moved often, living in North Carolina, Tennessee, and Mississippi before returning home to Alabama. They built a house by the river in Mobile on the same plot of land Marie had first shown Ralph. They also cared for Marie's mother in her final years and raised two daughters, both of whom, Marie notes proudly, became nurses. In failing health and a widow, Marie lived in the north Georgia mountains with her eldest daughter, Rita. The two passed the time talking of Marie's service and their shared passion in caring for others, mother and daughter equally proud of each other.

Over the last few years of her life Marie suffered several strokes, leaving her fragile. Her memory never faltered, however, and the events of her life, the broad sweep of the war, and the tiny details—Roosevelt's threats, bandaging the wounded, and her ruptured duck—shone clear and bright until her death on April 30, 2019. She left behind two daughters, two grandchildren, and boxes of memorabilia.

CHAPTER EIGHTEEN

Innovating and Improvising

Randell A. Bostwick

The Quartermaster said, "If someone came in here with a bottle of bourbon, they could have just about anything they wanted." I returned with one, for medicinal purposes of course.

RANDELL A BOSTWICK,
Captain, US Army

Niles, Ohio, sits halfway between Cleveland and Pittsburgh in the US industrial belt. Like the region, the town's fortunes depended on iron ore processing and thus suffered the ebbs and flows of the economy, including an economic collapse in the late 1890s. Then, in the early 1900s, an epic flood ravaged the area, and in the 1920s ethnic and racial conflicts erupted across the small town. But Niles also held with traditional American values like self-reliance and hard work. It had produced William McKinley, the twenty-fifth president of the United States, and Harry Mosely Stevens, the inventor of the all-American hotdog. It was a resilient town that could easily weather the economic and social storms.

For Clifton and Ann Bostwick, Niles was a good place to live and raise their children: Donald, Virginia, and Randell "Randy" Bostwick, the youngest, born in 1922. Clifton worked as an insurance salesman. He knew almost everyone in town, and everyone knew him, Randy said. "He was one of the nicest guys you'd ever want to know." The family was a loving one, their happiness marred only by the tragic loss of Virginia at the age of ten.

In 1939 Randy started high school. With his slight build, he eschewed the football and basketball teams to join the drama club. He also took up the clarinet and played for the Mineral Ridge High School marching band. Randy claimed he marched better than he played the clarinet. Perhaps he said this tongue in cheek, perhaps not, as he later joined a hundred-piece boys' marching band that performed at the 1939 World's Fair in New York City.

On graduating, Randy enrolled at the University of Michigan. With a chuckle, he described himself as someone never quite sure what he wanted to do. He added that, today at ninety-five years old, he still didn't know. "Pretty much everyone knew we were going into the military anyway," he said.

One fall afternoon during his sophomore year, despite the threat of rain, Randy headed to the Michigan Wolverines stadium. As he cheered from the stands, rain began to fall and soon soaked his wool coat. The temperature dropped and a crust of ice formed over his shoulders. Randy came away with a cold he couldn't shake and developed pneumonia. Seriously ill, he withdrew from Michigan for the rest of the school year. When he recovered, both his doctor and his mother encouraged him to transfer to Westminster College in western Pennsylvania. Westminster, they argued, was closer to home and would be quieter and easier for him to handle. Randy agreed, although he thought he would miss the Big Ten campus and all the advantages Michigan offered. To his surprise, Westminster's down-to-earth style suited him well.

In December 1941, the midpoint of his junior year, the attack on Pearl Harbor changed everything. Together with thirty of his college friends, Randy headed for the local recruiting office and enlisted in the US Army. They were soon called to active duty. The only clues Randy had about where he was going or what he would be doing came from the typewritten words on the last line of his enlistment papers: Medical Administration Corps.

A whirlwind of activity ensued. Randy traveled to New Cumberland, Pennsylvania, for induction into the army and then to Camp Pickett, sixty miles southwest of Richmond, Virginia, for basic training. At Camp Pickett, Randy and his fellow recruits honed their marching skills. The recruits marched before breakfast, lunch, and dinner. And then they marched some more. Randy said, "I thought about it a long time and came to understand the purpose of so much marching. You developed an automatic, involuntary response to commands." Presumably, when they completed their training and reached the battlefield, the men would be conditioned to follow a superior's order without question or hesitation, regardless of the circumstances.

In the following few months, Randy rose from private to corporal and had the opportunity to attend Officer Candidate School at Camp Barkeley outside Abilene, Texas. He graduated in 1943, one of the more than twelve thousand officers Camp Barkeley produced over the course of the war.[1]

With his newly minted commission, Second Lieutenant Bostwick deployed for several short-term assignments. The last, in early 1944, was northeast of Sacramento, California, where he helped open Dewitt General Hospital, an army facility built specifically to treat war casualties.[2] Randy barely had time to settle in before the army ordered him back to Camp Barkeley—this time to attend Assistant Battalion Surgeon Training School. The school's curriculum focused on emergency medical treatment for men injured on the battlefields. He learned everything from bandaging blisters to treating major wounds—enough for Randy to decide his future was not in medicine.

As soon as he completed his prescribed courses, he shipped out to Europe aboard a converted cruise ship. The crossing was uneventful but unforgettable too. "A dozen of us shared state rooms designed for two people. But we had it good," he said. "We were officers."

Randy disembarked the ship's cramped quarters in Naples, Italy, to join Gen. Alexander Patch's Seventh Army as the Allies prepared for the invasion of France. "In the first few days after landing, I still had no idea what I was supposed to be doing," Randy said. "I felt like the least informed man there." Not only was he one of the "least informed," but he was also one of the youngest and least experienced. Many of the men had been in the Mediterranean for weeks. Some for months. "It was a challenge to be an officer and to be leading people who had more experience and knew more than you did," he said.

Although Randy expected a field hospital or frontline assignment, the army attached him to the Seventh Medical Depot Company, a unit with a record of service in Africa, Sicily, and Italy. The men around him expected they would soon be thrown into combat. "When we realized we would not be on the front lines, we were relieved," Randy said. "Still, we would be serving at a battalion aid station, so we thought we would be in the thick of things."

Whether attributable to timing, luck, or simply the normal confusion of a theater of operation, they weren't assigned to the front lines. No one had time to think about the assignment or question what they were being asked to do or whether or not they could do more. "We were too busy to worry about our roles," Randy remembered.

Originally, the Allies had planned a two-pronged attack into France, simultaneously invading Normandy on the northwest coast and sending the Seventh Army to the Riviera on the southeastern coast. But Patch's Seventh Army encountered stronger-than-expected resistance in Italy and had to delay its shift to southern France.

Fortunately, when the Normandy invasion began, Germany transferred troops from the south of France to reinforce its defenses in the north. And when Patch freed himself from his entanglement in Italy and came ashore on the Mediterranean, his troops faced less opposition and far better weather. Thus, the invasion of the southern coast was, in Randy's words, "less eventful" and far less costly in terms of men and matériel than in Normandy. The landing, however, was not without its dangers with the Wehrmacht fighting from fortifications above and behind the beaches. Amid a barrage of artillery flying overhead between the Germans in their bunkers and the American ships offshore, the Allied troops landed and secured the beaches within thirty-six hours.[3]

Fleets of amphibious Ford jeeps, known as "Seeps," soon ferried crates of supplies from the ships to the shore. Once they reached the shore, the beach master directed the Seeps to where they could unload and stack their crates. After disgorging their supplies, the Seeps turned, drove into the surf, and motored back to the ships to reload.

Next, Randy and his men filed through the mountains of crates stacked along the beach, locating the medical supplies by the crates' maroon-colored corners. After loading the crates onto a fleet of waiting trucks, they drove the supplies to the army's nearest encampment. During the first few days after the invasion, the men worked around the clock, sleeping between supply runs or going without. The process was crowded and chaotic with convoys from ammunition, food, and clothing supply groups working side by side with the medical group, all coming and going at once. "The whole operation looked like a column of marching ants," Randy said.

Once their depots were established, the men of the Seventh Medical Depot Company went about their assigned mission, furnishing medical supplies to US and Allied camps. What sounds like a simple, straightforward task was anything but. The twelve officers and one hundred enlisted men in the company juggled nearly five thousand different items—everything from aspirin tablets to plasma to dental gold. Their duties included picking up medical supplies, transporting, and delivering the right supplies to the right place at the right time—whether to storage warehouses, field hospitals, aid stations, or medics on the battlefields.

The mission was made all the more complicated by having to keep up with an advancing army. In less than a month, the Allies liberated southern and eastern France and pushed the Wehrmacht into full retreat. With the Seventh Army close to Dijon, four hundred miles inland along the Rhone Valley and well north of the Mediterranean and its beaches, the supply groups faced a new set of problems.[4] The Seventh Medical Depot Company had to break down the depots, load their equipment onto trucks, and scramble forward. "We learned to leapfrog our operations rather than move the entire camp at once," Randy said. "When orders to move came, we took half the supplies, advanced, and set up a new depot. When the army moved again, we'd go back for the half we'd left behind and move it forward." The men grew more proficient with each move. "They never needed much more than to hear the words 'We're moving' before jumping into action."

In all, his unit moved dozens of times before their final push into Germany. "We weren't in many places very long," Randy said. One town, however, stands out in his memory: Sarrebourg, France, where they spent the winter of 1944. "I can't remember how to spell the name of the town, but I remember the cold. We had taken over a house in the town, so we were indoors, but the house had no heat. I wore everything I had to keep warm."

The depot rarely ran short of supplies, but if it did, the men improvised. "We had two guys from the Ozarks who had been farmers before the war and could repair just about anything. Back then, that's what people did." During one spate of cold weather, Randy remembered, the two former farmers mounted metal rods onto a jeep, welded them together, and stretched canvas across them as a shield against the wind and cold. "It worked too," he said, but they had to be careful. If they drove the altered vehicle anywhere near General Patton's headquarters, the military police would order the contraption disassembled, claiming it a hazard. With their heads and sides covered, the police argued the men could not spot enemy aircraft or other dangers.

Another of Randy's men fashioned duodenal tubes from spare latex tubing, carving the end of the tubing into the shape needed to drain a wound. And as disposable hypodermics were not yet in use, one man sharpened hypodermic needles with a bicycle wheel–driven grinder. "The patients may not have liked the primitive substitutes, but we made do," Randy said. Then there was the time a field hospital's anesthesia machine malfunctioned during surgery. Randy reports that a patient opened his eyes and asked, "How are things going, doc?" Randy's men fixed that machine too.

As the war progressed, the Allies gained the upper hand. Resupplying the troops became a simpler exercise and supplies were plentiful, so bartering became a favorite activity among the troops. They traded their cigarettes, chocolate bars, and soluble—ten-to-one packs of coffee (designed to serve one cup for ten men or ten cups for one man)—with citizens from nearby towns for eggs and chickens. But whiskey was the most popular commodity for bartering, and Randy and the medical supply unit were a prime source of the precious liquid, particularly after his company stumbled onto a large cache of Benedictine. They had enough of the fine French liqueur to line the walls of their supply closet, so much so his men eventually tired of the taste. Rumors of the stash spread, and soon the commanding officer made a surprise visit to the depot. He opened the closet door, took one look, and ordered half the stash transferred to the group's headquarters on the next truck.

Without their private stash to use for bartering, the men fell back on their cartons of "medicinal" whiskey. Once when Randy went to the quartermaster to request bread-baking and other supplies for his men, the quartermaster said, "If someone came in here with a bottle of bourbon, they could have anything they wanted." Randy left, returned later with a bottle under his arm, and exited with all the supplies he needed and more.

All things considered, Randy enjoyed serving in the Seventh Medical Depot Company. He'd become good friends with some men in the group, not unlike his experience back in 1941 on the small Westminster campus. The army, however, had not forgotten Randy's training as an assistant battalion surgeon and, from time to time, requested his reassignment. With Randy excelling in his role, his commanding officer, a colonel, was not about to let him transfer. He found excuses to keep Randy in the medical supply unit. While gratifying to learn the colonel appreciated him, Randy said, in fact, the colonel was much more interested in his own advancement. "He insisted no one in his unit could receive an award higher than his own." The next time a request came for Randy's reassignment, the colonel stepped in to say what a fine job Randy was doing where he was. "He embellished the story so much, the Seventh Army surgeon said it sounded like I was a candidate for the Legion of Merit." On realizing his plans had backfired, the astonished colonel replied, "He's not interested in any awards; he just wants to do his job."

Despite the constraints the colonel had placed on his career, Randy was eventually promoted to first lieutenant. When he heard the news, Randy celebrated with a round of beer for his men—beer kept cool deep in a well they'd found in their camp.

Being an officer had its downsides, however, including pulling duty to censor mail. Officers read and examined each letter the troops wrote home, checking for sensitive information such as where the men were or what they were doing. Officers clipped any offending words from the pages with a razor and certified the correspondence by signing their names to the envelopes. Reading his men's letters was Randy's least favorite duty, he said, likening it to peering over the transom into someone's room. "These were guys you lived with. It was not good duty."

He remembered how some of his men tried to pass messages in clumsily coded words. "Be sure to say hello to Aunt Nancy," one soldier wrote when camped outside Nancy, France. Randy took a razor and cut out the passage, leaving the soldier with what appeared more a slice of Swiss cheese than a piece of paper.

Incoming mail was an altogether different experience and an occasion the men treasured. The mail often came in batches—sometimes weeks or months of letters arriving at a time. In Darmstadt, Germany, Randy received six weeks' worth of mail. He put the letters in order and read them chronologically, finding out in one he had lost his grandmother and, a few letters later, that his grandfather had died.

Finally, in 1945, when reports of the German surrender reached the camp, a man in his command reminded Randy of a promise he had made. "You said I could tie one on when Hitler surrendered," the soldier said. "I'm here." Randy cracked open a box of whiskey, and the soldier indulged, tying one on with a hangover that lasted for three days. Unfortunately, Randy did not have as much to celebrate. He was not eligible to return home immediately.

In the summer of 1945 the Allied leaders—Truman, Stalin, and Churchill—met in Potsdam, Germany, to discuss borders, reparations, disarmament, and demilitarization. The agreements reached at the conference included provisions for handling the mountains of supplies captured or abandoned across Europe as the armies had withdrawn.[5]

There was much to do both in Europe and in the Pacific. The US Army Air Forces alone expected to handle disposal for 400,000 tons of bombs and ammunition, more than 200,000 tons of technical supplies, 24,000 aircraft engines, and 12,000 vehicles. By the end of 1946, the United States War Assets Corporation would dispose of over $500 million worth of the excess supplies, equivalent to more than $6 trillion today.[6]

In one instance in the Pacific, rather than return equipment to the United States, the military dumped millions of dollars' worth of equipment into the ocean. Jeeps, trucks, bulldozers, semitrailers, forklifts, tractors, bound sheets of corrugated iron, unopened boxes of clothing, and cases of Coca-Cola tumbled into the ocean, settling on the sea bottom off the coast of Espírito Santo, an island in the Vanuatu archipelago. If nothing else, many years later the waste created a deep-sea diving paradise.[7]

The army kept Randy, one of the more talented men in the group, in Germany until 1946 to help dispose of materials captured from the Germans or left behind by the Allies and to aid the millions of displaced persons. For each cache of material discovered, Randy's men inventoried and then secured the materials in military depots scattered across the area. Besides the jeeps, trucks, bombs, and ammunition encountered in his line of duty, Randy handled an odd assortment of other items, including a load of mercury and platinum—enough, he guessed, to supply thermometers for Germany and the world.

There were other oddities as well. Once Randy saw a Russian demand for the return of a film production company, complete with actors, allegedly moved from the sector destined for Russian control. And another time, when he set off to inspect a stockpile of material, he met opposition from an officer standing guard at the gated storage facility. Randy kept demanding entry. The officer kept denying him. Finally, the officer revealed the facility contained "heavy water," a product used in the production of nuclear weapons. For once, Randy became derelict in his duties, deciding he did not need to inspect the material firsthand.

In his role helping displaced persons, Randy worked briefly for the United Nations Relief and Rehabilitation Administration assisting the victims of war in areas under control of the United Nations. In Randy's case, this included the millions of refugees in camps in Germany, Italy, and Austria. The refugees, many of whom the Germans forced into labor camps, had suffered hunger and other depravations. "They were little more than walking skeletons," Randy remembered.[8]

No manuals existed to explain how to handle those who needed aid. Once again, the soldiers improvised. Randy remembered the day an attractive young woman came into his tent in the Seventh Medical Depot headquarters. Crying and nearly hysterical, the woman tried to explain in broken English that villagers in her town threatened to hang her father for serving as the Nazis' *Burgermeister*. Randy grabbed a few men and hopped into a jeep and followed the woman on her bicycle back to her village. There, they found a group of men, one with a rope in his hands, marching the young woman's father into a field. Wherever they went after the war, Randy said, the Americans became a distraction. Displaced people grabbed their hands and thanked them for liberating their country. This time was no exception. After some quick thinking, Randy asked if the men had ever had the chance to ride in a jeep. Heads shook. In moments, the group climbed aboard the jeep and Randy headed back to camp and straight to the military police. The woman and her father escaped unharmed.

Later, when the chief of medical supply, a colonel, returned home, Randy was promoted to captain. He assumed the colonel's responsibilities, even moving into his apartment in Heidelberg and acquiring his Lincoln zephyr. The added comforts aside, Randy's role was much larger; he feared he lacked the business experience to carry it out, but he improvised and persevered. As he described his contribution, Randy said it was a small role in helping to restart the German pharmaceutical manufacturing capabilities. In late 1946, after twenty-two months in Europe, Randy returned home carrying an American Campaign Medal, a European-African-Middle Eastern Campaign Medal with five Bronze Stars, a World War II Victory Medal, and a Meritorious Service Unit Plaque. He also brought with him a lifetime of experience, expertise in business management, a sense of accomplishment, and twenty hours of college credit. He returned to Westminster to finish college. There, he met his future wife, Jane.

After graduating, Randy went to work for his father, but as he had discovered earlier with medicine, insurance was not for him either. While considering his options, the army called Randy back to active duty in 1950 for Korea. This time, he served with the recently combined army, navy, and air force Armed Services Medical Procurement Agency (ASMPA) stateside—in Brooklyn, New York, near the navy yards. Randy's experience in managing supplies had prepared him well for his new responsibilities in the traffic department, overseeing shipping from the ASMPA's storage facility to military depots around the country and from there to depots abroad, including Korea.

Finally, in 1952, with two wars behind him, Randy took a job with the A&P company in Pittsburgh. He started at the bottom but rose to director of operations, using many of the supply, personnel, and administrative management skills he acquired while in the army. His responsibilities included distribution, store design, trucking, and labor relations. Later, he transferred to the New York headquarters as president and then chairman of the A&P subsidiary for supermarket services and as an A&P corporate vice president.

One evening in the early 1970s, Randy sat with his wife and three children at the dinner table long after the dishes should have been cleared. They talked about women in the workforce and the difficulty women had in finding full-time work. He took the discussion to heart and created an innovative, all-female A&P operation, handling inventory and shipping for A&P stores across the country. The division encouraged part-time work and provided daycare for children. On the day it opened in Fort Wayne, Indiana, six hundred people applied for work.

During a rare serious moment, Randy said, "It was a privilege to be involved. I saw civilization at its low ebb and human nature at its highest. I wish I could get a handful of that now."

Randy Bostwick retired in 1990 to travel and spend time with his family. "It was," he said, "a time to be close. A time to enjoy each other more than ever." And he did. Despite having lost his lifelong companion and wife of nearly sixty-nine years in 2017, he maintains a positive outlook on life, laughs at every opportunity, and enjoys time with his three children, five grandchildren, and five great-grandchildren.

CHAPTER NINETEEN

An Engineer among the Headstones

Francis D. Peterson

✯ ✯ ✯

*"Where's Joe?" one soldier asked. "The SOB went
and got himself killed," a second soldier replied.
I realized then that death is a normal state of being.*

Francis D. Peterson,
Lieutenant Colonel, US Army

One of the most poignant stories Francis Peterson told in his 1992 memoir occurred one afternoon when he was still a young boy. The scene unfolded in a cemetery in Illinois where he grew up. There, Francis and his mother stepped carefully behind a long neat row of headstones. They found a shaded bench and sat together for a short time, speaking in low tones. After several minutes had passed, Francis asked if they could go. His mother said, "Not yet." The sheriff, she explained, had not had time to reach their home and arrest his father.[1]

Francis expressed little emotion in telling this story or any other in his memoir—stories of lean times during the Great Depression—stories of his father taking a series of low-paying jobs, his mother making ends meet, his days in school often sleeping through class but earning good grades, and his own failed first marriage. Somehow, Francis managed to wall off these dark moments and those of his service in World War II to fill the rest of his days with much joy. This ability to compartmentalize unpleasantness helped him survive a horrific and unsung but all-important duty in the army's Forty-Eighth Quartermaster Graves Registration Company.

In the spring of 1941, "Pete," as Francis was better known, was drafted into the army. He completed basic training in Cheyenne, Wyoming, at the Fort Warren training center for the US Army Quartermaster Corps (QMC). The QMC's role was to supply the country's armed forces with food, clothing, and equipment and to handle special services for troops in the field. Special services included operating laundry and sanitation facilities, managing a bakery, and performing burials.[2]

Pete had worked part-time in a bakery during high school, an experience that might explain his assignment to the QMC. But rather than exploit his bakery skills, the QMC taught him to drive an army supply truck and then to train other men to drive the trucks.

Most of Pete's work took place outdoors, regardless of the season. And, despite the warm Chinook winds that stream down the eastern slope of the Rockies, winters in Cheyenne are long and cold, with an average annual snowfall of five feet. Pete persevered, but as soon as he acquired a bit of seniority he lobbied for an indoor job. He succeeded, was made a company clerk, and later was promoted to corporal but, to his dismay, discovered an indoor job was only marginally better than working outdoors. Snow seeped through the gaps of Fort Warren's unheated, uninsulated wooden structures, dusting the men working at their desks or asleep in their cots. And Pete still drilled and trained with the other soldiers outdoors.[3]

Pete's start was humble, but the army recognized the young man's leadership qualities. In April 1942 he applied for and was accepted to Officer Candidate School at Camp Lee in Virginia. After ninety days of intensive training, albeit in a milder climate, Pete became a second lieutenant. Then he transferred to Camp Swift, near Austin, Texas, where, besides undergoing yet more training, he met, courted, and married Mae Beth Thompson, a secretary at the camp. Shortly, for reasons unknown to him, the army assigned Pete to the Graves Registration Services Company, a unit whose responsibilities he could barely imagine while at home, far from the front.

On April 12, 1943, the day he left for service overseas, Mae Beth gave Pete a note bidding him farewell while reminding him she would wait in Texas for his return. "You know that I am giving up my most treasured possession and trying to be as brave as possible," she wrote. Countless other spouses and sweethearts shared similar sentiments on parting and none knew how long they would be apart. Having shared three very happy but brief months together, Pete and Mae Beth would not see each other for twenty-seven months.

After an uneventful voyage across the Atlantic in a convoy, Pete watched from the deck as his troopship entered the Mediterranean, noting they arrived "on a moonlit night through the straits of Gibraltar." The ship docked at Oran, Algeria, on the north coast of Africa, and Pete found his staging area fifteen miles outside the town. Pete described the staging area as nothing more than a barren plain filled with one-man tents for sleeping and sheltering their belongings, but he didn't say which was worse, his snow-covered bunk in Cheyenne or sleeping on the ground in Oran.[4]

Shortly after arriving, while standing in line for an ice cream cone at the Red Cross service center, Pete overheard a conversation that he said changed his perception of the war. "Where's Joe?" a soldier just back from the front lines asked. "The SOB went and got himself killed," a second soldier replied. It was a prescient conversation. "I realized then," Pete said, "that death is a normal state of being." In no time, death surrounded him.[5]

The Forty-Eighth was ordered to Bizerte, Tunisia, and from there across the Mediterranean to support the invasion of Sicily. On July 10, 1943, Pete watched the naval bombardment of the island from the deck of his ship. With the island beaches only lightly defended by the Germans, Pete soon spotted the blinking flashlights of ground troops who had swum ashore to stake out the landing areas. When Pete's ship came within a mile of shore, his group boarded amphibious trucks and headed to the beach thinking all was well. An hour and a half after landing, however, a German fighter plane strafed the men on the coast. "A trail of bullets, just like you see in the movies, passed about ten feet away," Pete said years later. Undeterred, Pete began work, creating his first cemetery at Licata, Sicily. With the help of Italian prisoner of war labor, they were burying soldiers by noon.[6]

In a speech he gave to his local Rotary Club long after the war, Pete described the mission of the Graves Registration Service (GRS) as collection of the dead, identification, preparation, burial, and disposition of personal effects. It was far more than that. During or shortly after a battle, as soon as conditions allowed, soldiers in the field faced the task of burying their dead. Often, with no time to dig proper graves, they used trenches or shell craters or dug shallow graves and covered the corpses with a light layer of earth. To mark the graves, the soldiers used whatever they could find: rocks, sticks, or the fallen soldiers' helmets.[7]

Then, as soon as practical, GRS units followed behind and exhumed the hastily buried fallen soldiers. Depending on the nature of the battle just concluded, the GRS troops might have to spend hours scouring the countryside for bodies scattered across fields, hedgerows, and villages. Once they retrieved the corpses, the GRS troops identified the remains and performed proper burials, marking the grave sites with temporary wooden markers.[8]

Pete glossed over the gruesome nature of the tasks he and his troops performed. In fact, identifying a soldier's remains often required hours of examining a body or body parts in every stage of decomposition and recording minute observations on the army's Form 1 GRS. The form documented details of the deceased, including height, weight, dental charts, fingerprints, shoe size, clothing sizes, vaccination marks, hair color, and marks on the soldier's clothing.[9]

The GRS men also inventoried personal effects found on the bodies, including money, wallets, bracelets, and watches, returning to loved ones only those items in good condition. Battle-damaged items and letters to and from war zone girlfriends were removed and destroyed.

As a platoon leader, Pete also oversaw and took part in selecting the sites and constructing dozens of temporary cemeteries. Site selection, he explained, was a complex effort. He had to keep up with and even anticipate troop movements, finding sites with good road access but shielded from public view, particularly from soldiers going to and from combat. On finding a site, Pete acquired—or, more accurately, appropriated—the land for the army's use, often from reluctant landowners. Next, Pete designed a layout for the graves, including a plot for the American dead and separate plots for fallen Allied soldiers, enemy soldiers, and prisoners of war.

Some of the earliest graves registration units to arrive in Europe operated with little or no guidelines for their mission. But by 1943, the GRS troops followed precise, documented standards and could make use of the tens of thousands of wooden sticks the army provided for grave markers and a similar number of white cotton mattress covers for shrouds. The army had not, however, foreseen needing proper tools for constructing the cemeteries.[10] Pete improvised, falling back on what he had learned in geometry—his favorite high school class—to create ninety-degree angles for cemetery perimeters and long, arrow-straight rows to align the grave markers, all in respect for the fallen.

Although Pete did not leave any words to describe the magnitude of the job he faced, Capt. Mersin. J. DeKorp, commanding officer of the Forty-Sixth Quartermaster GRS, did. DeKorp's wartime journal notes a daily average of eighty American and forty enemy soldier burials during a one-month period in 1944.[11]

Sympathetic to the difficulties of the duty, the army approved GRS whiskey and cigarette requisitions without question. Pete took his responsibility to his men seriously and kept them well supplied.

In Sicily, he crossed paths with Gen. George Patton twice. Once, Pete ran afoul of the general for establishing a cemetery in view of his men. Although another graves registration unit had selected the site in question, Pete's unit dutifully moved the cemetery, including "existing graves and all to a site in an olive grove five miles away," as requested, or more accurately as commanded.

The second encounter with Patton involved a stash of cognac. Pete had found what he thought was a reliable source of locally made spirits for his platoon's enjoyment. On one of his frequent trips to resupply his men from the cache, he discovered the door barred and a soldier standing guard. General Patton had claimed the trove.

The general bore Pete no ill will. After the fighting in Sicily, Patton wrote a letter of commendation for him. In the letter, Patton expressed his appreciation for the "superior and loyal manner in which Peterson performed his duties" and for the condition of the American cemeteries.[12]

Pete, like many other soldiers, carried a camera with him to war. He photographed both the cemeteries he helped establish as well as important historic and tourist sites across Europe. As he traveled, he worked sightseeing into his company's route, snapping and saving photos of what he called his "tour."

Pete saw parts of Italy, France, Belgium, the Netherlands, and Luxembourg. In southern Germany he stopped at Berchtesgaden, Hitler's Eagle's Nest resort. The building had been ransacked and cleared of its furnishings, but Pete was able to admire the view, eye level with the distant peaks of the Bavarian Alps. From there, he continued on to Czechoslovakia, Austria, Lichtenstein, and Switzerland. On occasion, as he crossed and recrossed borders, authorities grew suspicious. When stopped and questioned, Pete recited his prepared and well-rehearsed response—his travels were necessary to search for American dead. With a bit of dry humor, he notes in his memoir, "We never found any isolated burials on the tour."[13]

While operating at a distance from the fighting, Pete's work was not without peril. When he and his men came under fire, they scrambled for shelter, often in half-dug or empty graves. They also learned to watch where they stepped when collecting the dead. While constructing his second cemetery in Sicily, between Palermo and Messina, on a hillside overlooking the Mediterranean, one of the Italian laborers stepped on an explosive. "Unknown to us, the area from the bottom of the hill to the shore had been mined. . . . The lucky ones carried the wounded to the hilltop. I saw one, whose leg had been blown away, die in front of me. None of our men went into the area." As Pete and his men learned, the German Army made widespread use of booby traps, including laying trip wires to hidden explosives on the battlefield and concealing live grenades beneath fallen Allied and Axis soldiers.[14]

The most notable incident of Pete's tour of duty occurred in Bari on Italy's east coast. In December 1943 the Fifteenth Air Force was busy setting up head-quarters in Bari, from where they could oversee operations of the airfields in nearby provinces. Absorbed in their task and with the Germans falling back and believed to be stretched thin, the Allies grew complacent. They did not foresee an attack on Bari and considered the German reconnaissance flights over the area nothing more than a nuisance.[15]

On December 2, thirty ships crowded the Bari harbor. Ignoring wartime blackout regulations, ships' crews unloaded tons of supplies from cargo holds under bright lights. The Liberty ship SS *John Harvey* was one of the ships in the harbor. Unbeknownst to all but a handful of the ship's officers, the *John Harvey* carried more than a load of conventional war matériel. One hundred tons of mustard gas bombs lay secreted in its hull.

Earlier in 1943, President Roosevelt had reaffirmed the country's policy on chemical weapons, saying, "I state categorically that we shall under no circumstances resort to the use of such weapons unless they are first used by our enemies." The mustard gas was intended, as revealed later, as a reserve if the situation Roosevelt contemplated occurred. British prime minister Churchill was much less reticent. He viewed the use of chemical weapons as an evolution in warfare. "It is simply a question of fashion changing as she does between long and short skirts for women," he said. Churchill, nonetheless, yielded to pressure from his military advisers about their fears of German retaliation and held Britain's chemical weapons in reserve.[16]

After German reconnaissance flights reported finding light to nonexistent defenses at Bari, the Luftwaffe launched an airstrike on the harbor. It sank seventeen ships and damaged another eight. Fire erupted aboard the still-intact *John Harvey,* and the chemical weapons exploded, sending a mushroom-shaped fireball over the harbor. Smoke and toxic gas filled the air. Everyone on board the *John Harvey* was killed. Scores of other soldiers and civilians working in the harbor suffered chemical burns or inhaled poisonous fumes and later died.

While accounts of the disaster spread, British and American governments tried to conceal the presence of the mustard gas. Roosevelt did not want to appear duplicitous after making his statement condemning the use of chemical weapons. For his part, Churchill wanted to avoid the embarrassment and potential adverse publicity the incident afforded the Germans—the Bari port had been under British jurisdiction. Nevertheless, the heavy toll from the raid and the release of the poisonous gas could not be concealed. With a thousand troops lost, the attack at Bari was the second deadliest attack of the war and earned the name "Little Pearl Harbor."[17]

Pete's graves registration company attended to those who died in the raid, but, characteristically, he skipped mention in his memoir of the particular horrors he witnessed. For his and his platoon's work over the months they served in Europe, Pete received several commendations and was awarded the Legion of Merit, one of America's highest military decorations. The award citation mentions "exceptionally meritorious conduct in the performance of outstanding services," and states:

> He displayed outstanding ability and resourcefulness in investigating the smallest clues, conducting research work through all available records and making personal contact with local civilians for the purpose of recovering bodies of missing US Army Air Forces crews from isolated graves throughout the area. With limited means and extraordinary forethought, Lt. Peterson planned and established with appropriate simplicity a US military cemetery.

The citation also mentions the incident in Bari where Pete "exhibited untiring efforts and remarkable zeal in assisting in the identification of casualties resulting from the enemy air raid."[18]

If asked, now decades after the war, few people could name more than one or two cemeteries where America's military veterans lie buried: Arlington and Gettysburg on American soil and perhaps Normandy and Meuse-Argonne in France. But at the height of the Second World War, over 350 temporary military cemeteries and untold numbers of individual grave sites dotted the European landscape.[19]

In 1947 families of 171,000 American soldiers requested repatriation of their fallen family members' remains from those hundreds of cemeteries to the United States.[20] The military could not have fulfilled their wishes without the GRS's meticulous record keeping during and following the fighting. The remains of the ninety-three thousand others were exhumed and transferred to one of thirteen sites the United States selected as permanent cemeteries across Europe: Ardennes and Henri-Chapelle in Belgium; Brittany, Epinal, Lorraine, Normandy, Rhone, and Suresnes in France; Cambridge in the United Kingdom; Florence and Sicily-Rome in Italy; Luxembourg; and the Netherlands. Two additional cemeteries are located, one each, in North Africa and the Philippines. All remaining sites were deconstructed and the land returned to the original owners. The American Battle Monuments Commission, in existence since 1923, maintains the sacred sites on land the host countries donated. The sites honor not only those buried there but also the troops missing in action, lost, or buried at sea (seventy-nine thousand in World War II).[21]

In September 1945 Pete left Le Havre, France, aboard a former French luxury liner, the *Marechal Joffre*. Now serving as a troopship and carrying 2,700 troops, the *Joffre* was towed to open waters to avoid a ship loaded with a cargo of unexploded dynamite that the Germans had sunk to block the harbor. Once clear of the obstruction, the ship headed for America. "October 1, 1945, we arrived at New York. Our ship was alive with flags and all troops were on deck for a first glimpse of the U.S.A.," Pete wrote in his unpublished memoir. Bands played and signs welcoming the troops home flew from ships, piers, and buildings lining the harbor. "Each ship we met greeted us by a three-blast whistle, our pilot answered each one with three blasts also." After the men disembarked, the army treated them to a steak dinner. It was the day Pete and his companions had waited years to see.[22]

Pete returned home to Mae Beth. He had been absent for over two years, seen much of Europe, and some of the worst scenes and the aftermath of war, but he picked up where he left off. Relying on his prewar experience, Pete worked for a while in a bakery. Then he took advantage of the GI Bill and went back to school. Pete enrolled at the University of Texas in Austin to stay close to home and earned a degree in electrical engineering in 1950.

While at one time he worked at IBM, one of the country's largest employers, Pete did so as far from big cities as he could, preferring simpler places with small-town values. He moved from Austin; to Enid, Oklahoma; to Plano, Texas; and then back to Enid, where he became active in his church and spent his last days enjoying woodworking and photography.

No one can say whether the memory of spending time in a cemetery with his mother or the family strife of his early years haunted Pete. But in his memoir, Pete wrote that despite the family tensions, he respected both his parents. They remained together for much of his youth, and they instilled in him the desire to seek something better—which he did, for the men in his company, for the soldiers he served, and for his daughters.

Pete Peterson and Mae Beth had three daughters who asked many times what he had done in the war. Like other veterans, Pete was a man of few words on the war. But finally, in 1992, with continued nudging from his daughters, he compiled his memoir—written, as he noted, "from memories still there." He died in 1995 at the age of ninety-seven and is survived by his daughters, their husbands, eleven grandchildren, and nine great-grandchildren.

Epilogue

Sixteen million American men and women served in the major theaters of World War II (Europe, North Africa, the Pacific, and China-Burma-India) as well as in the other lesser-known areas of the conflagration. In 2019, as the seventy-fifth anniversary of the war's end approached, the great majority of those men and women had passed on. No one has an accurate account, although the US Department of Veterans Affairs estimated fewer than four hundred thousand World War II veterans were alive in mid-2019. Relatively speaking, only a handful of their stories have been documented. By the mid-2030s, except for the hardiest or luckiest few thousand, they will have disappeared, and the remaining untold stories will be gone forever.[1]

Thanks to the efforts of projects across the country, such as the Library of Congress's Veterans History Project and the Georgia-based Witness to War organization, thousands of veterans have taken a seat in front of a video camera to tell their stories and to have those tales recorded for generations to come. Some of the most inspiring stories have found their way to theaters, television documentaries, and best-selling books celebrating the veterans' bravery and self-sacrificing deeds.

Millions of veterans, however, will never tell their stories. Not the veterans who went to war, fought, came home, and then put the war behind them, choosing not to speak of it again. And particularly not the veterans who did not see combat—who performed no acts they considered brave or heroic, who took no hill or village, who shot down no enemy. If asked, these veterans would say they "just did their job." They believed they had nothing to tell. These veterans—noncombat veterans—were the veterans I set out to find and whose stories I wanted to uncover, if for no other reason than so few stories have surfaced from noncombat veterans who accounted for more than half the men and women who served. Mostly, however, even before hearing their stories, I was convinced they had something to say.

But, why, I wondered at the outset, had this group of veterans been ignored? The obvious answer is that given the choice, people prefer to read (or watch, in the case of films) stories honoring the bravery and heroism of men and women who accomplished things the reader did not do and cannot imagine doing. They prefer the entertainment and inspiration derived from watching a soldier claw his way up a cliff, outlast a barrage of bullets, or find the inner strength to survive the hardship and horror of war.

In contrast, noncombat veterans' experiences are presumed to be uninteresting and unworthy. We are supposed to think of them as desk jockeys, grease monkeys, number crunchers, or pencil pushers—people who worked in comfort far from the battle lines, people who, overcome with fear, shirked their duty to their country and their fellow soldiers. These men and women were supposed to harbor guilt or remorse that kept them silent.

I believed, however, if someone took the time to listen to a noncombat veteran's story, to probe beyond the surface, they would find stories worthy of being told. The nineteen veterans whose stories I heard ran the gamut of experiences. Some of the men were drafted and expected to confront the enemy face-to-face as infantrymen, but the army sent them behind the front lines. Some volunteered and hoped to go into battle but were also sent to the rear echelon. Some volunteered only when they knew they would be drafted. And some, to avoid being sent into the infantry, volunteered for anything but the army, primarily the army air forces, hoping to fly but being held back to serve as instructors or reassigned for health reasons.

In fact, in their first days and weeks in uniform, noncombat veterans stood as much in harm's way as their counterparts in combat units. German U-boats and enemy aircraft did not distinguish between the cook, the mechanic, the nurse, or the supply officer and the rifleman crossing the ocean to his duty station. Once on the ground, the men and women in noncombat positions worked beneath skies filled with aircraft going to or coming back from the front, were subject to enemy strafing or artillery fire, and felt the impact of enemy bombs.

Jack Coyle, one of the nineteen veterans featured in this book, lived in China behind the lines with the threat of discovery, imprisonment, and death every day. Randy Bostwick loaded and unloaded medical supplies from beaches, artillery flying overhead from the ships offshore and the enemy emplacements behind the beaches. And a third, Frank Cone, was captured and died in a prisoner of war camp.

All nineteen did their part and served as proudly as any combat soldier or sailor.

To be sure, there were also other men who refused to fight and who served as noncombatants or who refused military service altogether and went to prison.

Early on, at the urging of one veteran, I learned to draw the distinction between noncombat and noncombatant. I leave the task of telling the noncombatants' stories, many of which may be equally intriguing, to another author or another day.

In writing this book, I hoped to bring to light stories from all branches of the military and from all theaters of war and to cover a cross section of non-combat roles as defined by the military occupation service (MOS) codes. I set no quotas or limits and turned away no veteran willing and able to talk. I also wanted to complete the project by the seventy-fifth anniversary of the end of the war, knowing full well with each passing day fewer veterans would be available or able to tell their stories. Even so, seven of the nineteen stories were told by a veteran's sons or daughters, brought to life with photo albums, memoirs, diaries, letters to and from home, letters of commendation, and medals. The medals the nineteen veterans received include: a French Legion of Honor Medal (Chevalier), a Sino-American Cooperative Organization Medal, eight Bronze Stars, a Silver Service Star, four Distinguished Flying Crosses, five Air Medals, a Congressional Gold Medal, and one Legion of Merit Medal.

To appreciate the veterans' comments, readers must imagine the United States in the 1940s, a country and time far different from today. Eleanor Millican Frye said, "I can't really explain to anyone living today why I joined. It was a different time back then. People had a different mind-set. Everyone did anything they could to support the country." Everyone included civilians. Bobbie Schneidewind added to her husband Bill Schneidewind's story in describing the competition between her young girlfriends to create the largest ball of tinfoil, even stripping the shiny metal from inside cigarette packets. When done, the girls donated the accumulated foil to their hometown fire department. In fact, as Winston Groom points out in his book, *1942,* much of the metal gathered from well-meaning citizens proved unsuitable for manufacturing aircraft and so it was turned back again into appliances and pots and pans.[2] But for the families on the home front, whether the tinfoil, automobile bumpers, tires, or nylon stockings were recycled into war matériel was beside the point. They were patriots and believed they had done their small part in the war effort.

To my surprise, many similarities emerged from the stories the veterans told. All the veterans were eager to serve and defend their country, even if not excited about joining the army. Some, to be sure, enlisted in the army air forces or navy to avoid an infantry position and what they feared was certain death. Marie Stepp, a nurse, enlisted because she feared President Roosevelt would be true to his word and drag her into the army as a buck private at half her pay. Still, once they had joined, all were willing to do whatever job the military needed. When the military held back the most qualified teacher, the most skilled mechanic, and the best pilot to teach others, they swallowed their disappointment and set about making their students the best soldiers, sailors, and airmen they could be.

They were willing to go wherever the military sent them. Most had no idea at the outset how far from home they would travel, what strange sights they would see, or under what conditions they would serve. George Keating from the state of Washington served in Europe, five thousand miles from his home, while Louis Thompson from outside Washington, DC, served in the Philippines, nine thousand miles away.

I learned others things, too, as I listened to the veterans: the things that sustained them through their duty, including friends, family, faith, and humor.

We carry a popular image in our minds of soldiers becoming lifelong friends with their brothers in arms, forging bonds stronger than any others of their lives, whether in World War II or any other war in the modern era. Stephen Ambrose wrote in *Band of Brothers,* "Within Easy Company, they had made the best friends they had ever had, or would have. They were prepared to die for each other, more important, they were prepared to kill for each other."[3] Except in the case of Josephine Sanner Davis's group of four nurses, Randy Buffington's pilots, and Frank Cone's fellow prison camp surgeons, this strong connection among the noncombat veterans was largely missing.

This is not to say the veterans did not make good friends or look out for each other; in some cases they did. Most, however, held more tightly to their bonds from home—their families, sweethearts, and childhood friends. And as they hurried back to their homes and families, most allowed the new friendships they had made, like their memories, to recede into the background in favor of moving forward. Much later in life, a few wished they had kept in touch with their fellow soldiers, and they sought out squadron, battalion, group, or division reunions. There, despite feeling they might not have anything in common with complete strangers, if not men they had known during the war, the shared experience of a bygone era allayed their fears.

Letters from their families at home brought small moments of joy to all. The men, for the most part, wrote letters, too—even if not as religiously. Fortunately, mothers, wives, sons, and daughters saved stacks of these letters, stained, creased, and faded but full of insight into the circumstances and the veteran's state of mind.

With mothers, sweethearts, or young wives at home, the men could think of little else. Between the first "my dearest darling" and the last "I love you," they wrote their most intimate thoughts, repeating over and over again how much they longed for their reunions. Bud Surprenant, ever the athlete, wrote how much he missed home and football. He told his mother of his experiences at sea and signed each letter, "your loving son."

They bought souvenirs for their family: sweaters, handmade leather shoes, a pair of wooden shoes, a set of teacups, plates hewn from exotic woods. They kept chits from poker games and menus from restaurants. More than one of the storytellers rose from their chairs to pull an ornate figurine, a handmade flask, or a medal from a display cabinet—their treasured artifacts, symbols of their pride.

And at one time or another during the war, the nineteen men and women most certainly prayed for their families and friends and for their safe return home. They were less outwardly religious than I expected, with the exception of Howard King and James Neyland. Howard became a deacon at his church after the war and never once doubted God had a hand in setting the course of his life. James, the soldier who celebrated the end of the war in the bars in France and remembered little of his trip home, found religion later in life, attended the Southwestern Baptist Theological Seminary, and later became active with his church. For the rest, their deeply ingrained values were sufficient to keep their outlook positive and their focus on the future.

More than once, I heard that being asked so long after the war about their experience brought back memories and details that the veterans had forgotten. All were good memories and brought smiles to their faces. Perhaps what unites this group of disparate souls is a unique sense of humor, one only a ninety-year-old has. With each of those who shared their tales, I've smiled, chuckled, laughed out loud, and occasionally doubled over and laughed till I cried.

One or two remembered feeling a twinge of guilt or frustration that they did not see combat, although, wiser with perspective of years, they are thankful they did not. Not one ever heard during or after the war their noncombat role was something less worthy. With his inherited sense of humor, Roland Surprenant described his father, Bud Surprenant, and his rough-and-tumble reputation as a merchant marine: "He had no regrets, and no one ever gave him a hard time about his choice of service in World War II, at least to his face. And if they did, I don't think they would have kept that opinion for long!"

Since completing the interviews and writing the veterans' stories, I have had the delightful opportunity to watch veteran Louis Thompson lead thousands of spectators in the pledge of allegiance and to attend veteran Eleanor Frye's hundred and first birthday celebration. Unfortunately, I have also had to mourn the passing of five of the veterans I interviewed. Thankfully, the others go forward, taking one day at a time, some buoyed by the knowledge their stories are worth telling and that they will not be forgotten. I consider it an honor and great privilege to tell their stories and to call all of them friends.

Acknowledgments

First and foremost, I wish to thank the nineteen veterans whose stories appear on these pages for their service during World War II and for the legacy they leave members of my generation and those to come. The book could not have been completed without them agreeing to sit and talk, even though at the outset more than one was puzzled by my interest. Often, after our first meeting, a veteran would call or write to say they'd found something else I might be interested to see. My answer never varied. Yes, I was interested. And I went to see whatever they had discovered, whether it was another photo, letter, magazine article, yearbook, or medal.

The collaboration extended well beyond the veteran to include a wife, son, daughter, or friend. In almost every instance, to fill in the details time had worn thin, a friend or family member had to dig through an attic or basement for photographs and diaries and wrack their own memory for tales still untold. And for their invaluable help, I want to thank them as well.

They include Bobbie Schneidewind (William B. Schneidewind); Michael Kennedy (Joseph A. Kennedy); Letia Henson and Bo Soulé (Robert Gara Soulé); Roland Surprenant (Francis Rae "Bud" Surprenant); Donna and David Darracott (Ike Minkovitz); Patrick Keating (George H. Keating); Rhonda Withrow and Patricia Jackson (Orin Fred "Randy" Buffington); M. Alexis Scott (William A. Scott III); Jackson W. Coyle (Jack T. Coyle); Linda Smith and Peggy Harker (Louis C. Thompson); Kent Davis, Jane McDonald, Mary Grace Schaap, and Joseph Neidinger (Josephine Sanner Davis); Rita Van Fleet (Marie Touart Stepp); Ray Lunsford (Joyce Maddox Lunsford Kellam); Knox Glass (Frank Cone); and Jill Lyons (Francis "Pete" Peterson).

Finding the veterans and convincing them to sit down had its challenges. For that I thank my own network of friends and acquaintances, the numerous social media groups I approached, and the members of veterans' organizations, two of which deserve special mention. They are the Atlanta World War II Roundtable and the North Georgia Veterans Organization, who with a combined membership of nearly four hundred people share a passion for preserving the history of the war and who sponsor lectures, exhibits, presentations, and regional armed forces events. The Roundtable graciously allowed me to solicit stories from the membership and introduced me to Jack Coyle, Howard King, and Bill Schneidewind, while the North Georgia group practically kidnapped every noncombat World War II veteran within fifty miles of their meeting place and brought me Frank Cone, Marie Touart Stepp, and Louis Thompson.

My advisers, readers, reviewers, and editors deserve my thanks as well, particularly for balancing their criticism of early drafts with optimism for the final product. I wish to thank Jonathan Jordan in particular for his early faith in my endeavor and his advice in helping to structure the book, to say nothing of his close read and suggestions drawing on his extraordinary knowledge and expertise on the events and historical figures that define World War II. Thanks goes to the Kent State University Press as well for recognizing the potential for the book and for bringing it to market. I am also indebted to the countless volumes of works on World War II that provided both education and entertainment over the many long days and nights of reading and research. Two sources in particular demand mention—the United States Center of Military History and the Office of Air Force History. I cannot imagine having tackled this project without the former's seemingly endless list of studies on the war, whether about the draft, troop training and transport, or logistics, and the latter's exhaustive study of the development of the country's air force both leading up to and during the war.

Finally, I owe much gratitude to two veterans in my family, my husband and my father. To my husband who heard many times over, "Yes, it is eight o'clock, and no, I haven't started dinner," or "Yes, it is two in the morning, but I just need another minute or two." And to my father, for giving me an appreciation of the war and every soldier who served and every patriot who lives. Every work I write on World War II begins and ends with him.

Appendix

Interviews

With one exception, the author conducted interviews with the nineteen veterans, their sons and daughters, and close friends over a period of a year and one half from July 2017 through January 2019. The author's interview with Josephine Sanner Davis took place in August 2012. When possible, the interviews were conducted in person; otherwise, interviews occurred by video conference, phone, and email. Key interview participants, dates, places, and formats are listed below.

Chapter 1: William H. Schneidewind and Barbara Schneidewind in person in Atlanta, Georgia, on October 27, 2017, and by phone November 9, 2017; Barbara Schneidewind by email on October 12, 2018.

Chapter 2: Joseph A. Kennedy in person in Oshkosh, Wisconsin, July 28, 2017; Joseph Kennedy, Michael Kennedy, and Tom Loveless by video conference on January 29 and April 4, 2018; Michael Kennedy and Tom Kennedy by email on January 30, March 10, and March 13, 2018.

Chapter 3: Letia Soulé Henson, Bo Soulé, and Helen Soulé in person in Atlanta, Georgia, on July 18, 2018; by email on August 1, 2018.

Chapter 4: Eleanor Millican Frye by phone on October 24, 2017; in person in Lookout Mountain, Tennessee, on November 14, 2017; by mail on December 11, 2017, and February 21 and April 6, 2018.

Chapter 5: Roland Surprenant by phone on October 20, 2017; by email on January 7 and September 9, 2018.

Chapter 6: Donna Minkovitz Darracott and David Darracott in person in Cumming, Georgia, on January 14 and October 1, 2018.

Chapter 7: Louis C. Thompson and Peggy Thompson Harker in person in Cumming, Georgia, on August 21, 2018; Louis Thompson and Linda Thompson Scott in person in Jasper, Georgia, on October 18, 2018.

Chapter 8: George H. Keating and Patrick Keating by video conference on August 23, 2017; Patrick Keating by email on September 8, September 30, and October 2, 2017.

Chapter 9: James K. Neyland in person in Atlanta, Georgia, on March 22, 2018; by phone on April 10, 2018.

Chapter 10: Patricia Buffington Jackson by email on July 31, 2018; Rhonda Buffington Withrow and Patricia Buffington Jackson in person in Ellijay, Georgia, on August 11, 2018.

Chapter 11: M. Alexis Scott by phone on December 12, 2018.

Chapter 12: Jackson T. Coyle in person in Atlanta, Georgia, on February 6, 2018; by email on February 21 and April 26, 2018.

Chapter 13: Howard O. King Sr. in person in Atlanta, Georgia, on June 5 and August 10, 2018; by phone on July 6 and July 15, 2018.

Chapter 14: Joyce Maddox Lunsford Kellam with Ray Lunsford in person in Buford, Georgia, on January 29 and February 27, 2018; Ray Lunsford by phone March 8, 2018.

Chapter 15: Knox (Jamie Cone) Glass and Lillian Glass in person in Jasper, Georgia, on October 2, 2018.

Chapter 16: Josephine Sanner Davis in person in Alpharetta, Georgia, on August 20, 2012; Kent Davis in person in Alpharetta, Georgia, on September 30, 9017; Joseph Neidinger by phone November 17, 2017; Jane McDonald by email on November 11, 2017; Mary Grace Schaap by email on January 18, 2018.

Chapter 17: Marie Touart Stepp and Rita Van Fleet in person in Jasper, Georgia, on April 18 and July 11, 2018; Rita Van Fleet by email on August 8, 2018.

Chapter 18: Randell A. Bostwick by phone on February 13 and March 14, 2018.

Chapter 19: Jill Peterson Lyons in person in Milton, Georgia, on July 1, 2017 and March 30 and August 24, 2018; by email on March 17, 2018.

Notes

PART I. THE ARMY KNOWS BEST

1. Wardlow, *Responsibilities, Organization, and Operations,* 10.
2. Wagner and Osborne, *Library of Congress World War II Companion,* 156, 257.
3. Kamarck, *Selective Service System and Draft Registration,* 4–5.
4. Flynn, *The Draft,* 16–22.
5. Palmer, *Procurement of Enlisted Personnel,* 5.
6. Lee, *Employment of Negro Troops,* 48–50, 414.
7. Wagner and Osborne, *Library of Congress World War II Companion,* 167–68.
8. Flynn, *The Draft,* 31–32.
9. Palmer, *Procurement of Enlisted Personnel,* 10.
10. Keim, *The CPS Story,* 8–10.
11. Palmer, *Procurement of Enlisted Personnel,* 11–13.

1. A PLATOON OF STUDENTS

1. McCormick, "Rutgers in World War II."
2. Palmer, *Procurement of Enlisted Personnel,* 28–39.
3. Palmer, *Procurement of Enlisted Personnel,* 28–39.
4. Keefer, *Scholars in Foxholes,* 56, 99, 123; Adams, *Snow & Steel,* 318–19.
5. Palmer, *Procurement of Enlisted Personnel,* 28–39.
6. Craf, "The Facts about the A.S.T.P. Reserve."
7. D'Este, *Patton,* 375; Jordan, *Brothers, Rivals, Victors,* 28, 39; Smith, *Eisenhower in War and Peace,* 50.
8. Nelson, *MacArthur in Japan,* 205.
9. Benjamin Fine, "'Information' Hour in Army Gives None," *New York Times,* May 15, 1951.

2. THE MAN WHO WANTED TO FLY

1. Jacobs, "Hurrah for the Red, White, and Blue," 38–48.
2. Greer, "Individual Training," 6:568.
3. Greer, "Individual Training," 6:566–71.

4. Fredriksen, *Warbirds,* 301.

5. Fredriksen, *Warbirds,* 324.

6. Fredriksen, *Warbirds,* 240.

7. Greer, "Individual Training," 6:569–71.

8. Greer, "Individual Training," 6:577–78.

9. Fredriksen, *Warbirds,* 86; *Curtiss P-40 Warhawk,* 61.

10. B. W. Armstrong to 2nd Lt. J. A. Kennedy, Aug. 22, 1945, private collection.

11. Armstrong to Kennedy.

12. Letter of Commendation to 1st Lt. Joseph A. Kennedy, n.d., private collection.

PART II. ACROSS THE SEA AND OVER THE HUMP

1. Wardlow, *Movements, Training, and Supply,* 325–70.

2. Lidell-Hart, *Rommel Papers,* 328.

3. Wardlow, *Movements, Training, and Supply,* 210.

4. Wagner and Osborne, *Library of Congress World War II Companion,* 308–14.

5. Wilmot, *Struggle for Europe,* 472–73.

6. Wardlow, *Movements, Training, and Supply,* 311.

7. Wardlow, *Movements, Training, and Supply,* 295–305; Periscope Film, "Troop Train," filmed 1943, YouTube video, 10:51, posted Sept. 2014, https://www.you tube.com/watch?v=IIrSwQr4A3c.

8. Periscope Film, "Troop Train."

9. Periscope Film, "Troop Train."

10. Wardlow, *Movements, Training, and Supply,* 84–85.

11. Groom, *1942,* 162.

12. "Family Is Reunited after Torpedoing of Ship," *Times-Picayune,* May 25, 1942.

13. Wagner and Osborne, *Library of Congress World War II Companion,* 177.

14. "U.S. Merchant Ships Sunk or Damaged in World War II," *US Merchant Marine,* accessed Feb. 2018, http://www.usmm.org/shipsunkdamaged.html; King, *U.S. Navy at War,* 287–305.

15. Geroux, *Mathews Men,* 48–49.

16. Dimbleby, *Battle of the Atlantic,* 133, 258–64.

17. Carter, "Early Development of Air Transport and Ferrying," 1:313–14.

18. Carter, "Air Transport Command," 7:6–7; "North Atlantic Route," 7:93; Heck, "Northwest Air Route to Alaska," 7:152–53.

19. Christie, *Ocean Bridge,* 36.

20. Carter, "Air Transport Command," 7:7–8, 7:29–30.

21. Heck, "Airline to China," 7:114–16.

22. Carter, "Air Transport Command," 7:30–31.

23. Carter, "Air Transport Command," 7:30–31; Cole, *Women Pilots of World War II,* xvii, 1–5.

24. Goldberg, "Allocation and Distribution of Aircraft," 6:415–16.

3. JACK OF ALL TRADES

1. "Soulé Steam Feed Works, Company History," Mississippi Industrial Heritage Museum, accessed July 25, 2018, http://www.soulelivesteam.com/home.html.

2. Joyner, *James Hamilton Keeton,* 4–9.

3. Joyner, *James Hamilton Keeton,* 13.

4. Joyner, *James Hamilton Keeton,* 19.

5. "Our Congressional Gold Medal Journey," Civil Air Patrol, accessed July 24, 2018, http://www.capgoldmedal.com.

6. Wiggins, *Torpedoes in the Gulf,* 238.

7. Steve Cox, "Civil Air Patrol: A Story of Unique Service and Selfless Sacrifice," Maxwell Air Force Base, Dec. 8, 2016, https://www.maxwell.af.mil/News /Features/Display/Article/1024853/civil-air-patrol-a-story-of-unique-service -and-selfless-sacrifice/.

8. Dimbleby, *Battle of the Atlantic,* 258–64.

9. "History of Civil Air Patrol," Civil Air Patrol, accessed Aug. 17, 2018, https://www. gocivilairpatrol.com/about/history-of-civil-air-patrol.

10. Awarding Congressional Gold Medal to World War II Members of the Civil Air Patrol Act of 2014, S. 309, 113th Cong., 2nd Sess., May 19, 2014.

11. Mingos, *Aircraft Yearbook for 1944,* 144.

12. *Sixth Ferrying Group,* 40.

13. Carter, "Early Development of Air Transport and Ferrying," 1:319.

14. "History of Civil Air Patrol."

4. DRESSED IN MAINBOCHER

1. "Lt. (jg) Millican Is a Ship Router at Charleston Base," unidentified newspaper, Charleston, SC, n.d.

2. Treadwell, *Women's Army Corps,* 254–55.

3. "Requirements for Joining," Women's Reserve of the US Naval Reserve, accessed Oct. 22, 2017, http://www.blitzkriegbaby.de/waves/waves2.htm.

4. Bureau of the Census, Department of Commerce, Historical Census of the United States, Colonial Times to 1970 (Washington, DC: Government Printing Office, 1975).

5. Scrivener, "US Military Women in World War II," 361–66.

6. Ebbert and Hall, *Crossed Currents,* 51–55.

7. The Hotel Northampton History, Hotel Northampton, accessed Oct. 2, 2017, http:// www.hotelnorthampton.com/history.

8. Ebbert and Hall, *Crossed Currents,* 54.

9. "Lt. (jg) Millican Is a Ship Router."

10. "WAACS and WAVES," 74.

11. "Homefront Heroines: The WAVES of WWII," Homefront Heroines, accessed Oct. 23, 2017, http://www.wordpress.homefrontheroinescom/?page_id=1409.

12. Scrivener, "US Military Women in World War II," 361–66.

13. "Eleanor Millican of Georgia Weds Dr. Augustus Frye, Jr. at Camden," *Portland Sunday Telegram and Sunday Press Herald,* July 23, 1950.

5. AN ATHLETE ON THE HIGH SEAS

1. "President's Statement on Maritime Day," *247.*
2. "US Maritime Service: The Forgotten Service," US Merchant Marine, accessed Jan. 2, 2017, http://www.usmm.org/usms.html.
3. Williams, *Liberty Ships of World War II,* 19–20.
4. Geroux, *Mathews Men,* 135–36; "Liberty Ships," Jacksonville Historical Society, accessed Jan. 7, 2018, http://www.jaxhistory.org/liberty-ships/.
5. "Liberty Ships and Victory Ships, America's Lifeline in War," *National Park Service,* accessed Jan. 7, 2018, https://www.nps.gov/nr/twhp/wwwlps /lessons/116liberty_victory_ships/116liberty_victory_ships.htm.
6. "Address in Celebration of Liberty Fleet Day," *397–99.*
7. "US Maritime Service: The Forgotten Service."
8. Bud Surprenant to Mr. and Mrs. Surprenant, July 17, 1944, private collection.
9. Bud Surprenant to Mr. and Mrs. Surprenant, Sept. 25, 1944, private collection; Bud Surprenant to Mr. and Mrs. Surprenant and Oct. 29, 1944, private collection.
10. "Merchant Seamen Are D-Day Heroes," editorial, *New York Times,* June 10, 1944; Geroux, *Mathews Men,* 270.
11. "Merchant Seamen Are D-Day Heroes."
12. Bud Surprenant to Mr. and Mrs. Surprenant, July 16, 1944, private collection.
13. Bud Surprenant to Mr. and Mrs. Surprenant, Aug. 13, 1944, private collection.
14. Frank Garcin, "Nazi Planes Bomb Surprenant's Ship," *Glens Falls Post Star,* 1944.
15. Garcin, "Nazi Planes Bomb Surprenant's Ship."
16. Harry S. Truman to Francis Surprenant, n.d., private collection.
17. Tom Stanfield to Bud Surprenant, Feb. 10, 1946, private collection.
18. Andrew J. Waber, "Popular Perceptions of the American Merchant Marine during World War II" (master's thesis, Florida State University, 2008), 26, http://diginole.lib.fsu .edu/islandora/object/fsu:175956/datastream/PDF/view.
19. Waber, "Popular Perceptions," 10.

6. TALKING LOGISTICS

1. Ashton, "Expanding Jewish Life in America, 1826–1901," 54–55.
2. Ike Minkovitz to Alfred (surname unknown), n.d., private collection.
3. Stout, *Fortress Ploesti,* 91–97.
4. Goldberg, "AAF's Logistical Organization," 6:378.
5. Stout, *Fortress Ploesti,* 91–92.
6. Stout, *Fortress Ploesti,* 91–97.
7. Stout, *Fortress Ploesti,* 96.
8. Ike Minkovitz to Elizabeth Minkovitz, May 23, 1944, private collection.
9. Ike Minkovitz to Elizabeth Minkovitz, Jan. 5, 1944, private collection.

10. Ike Minkovitz to Elizabeth Minkovitz, Aug. 19, 1944, private collection.

11. Stout, *Fortress Ploesti,* 91–98.

12. Goldberg, "The AAF's Logistical Organization," 6:366–72.

13. Ike Minkovitz to Elizabeth Minkovitz, June 29, 1944, and July 4, 1944, private collection.

14. Raymond and Crawford, *Three Crawford Brothers,* 353–54.

15. Alter, *From Campus to Combat,* 182.

16. A. Stang, "Statesboro Man is Congratulated," *Bulloch Times, Statesboro Eagle,* n.d.

17. H. R. Alexander to soldiers, sailors, and airmen of the Allied Forces in the Mediterranean Theatre, n.d.

18. Ike Minkovitz to Elizabeth Minkovitz, Aug. 3, 1944, private collection.

7. AROUND THE WORLD

1. Bykofsky and Larson, *Operations Overseas,* 581–85.

2. Hogan Jr., *US Army Campaigns of World War II,* 17–20.

3. "Flying Quartermasters Bundles for Burma Boys," *Quartermaster Training Service Journal* 5, no. 21 (Nov. 24, 1944), *https://www.qmfound.com/article/flying-quartermasters-bundles-for-burma-boys/.*

4. "Flying Quartermasters."

5. Bykofsky and Larson, *Operations Overseas,* 581–85.

6. Bykofsky and Larson, *Operations Overseas,* 589–603.

7. Hogan Jr., *US Army Campaigns of World War II,* 24–26.

PART III. KEEP 'EM ROLLING AND FLYING

1. Greer, "Training of Ground Technicians," 6:629.

2. Kooker, "Foundations of a War Training Program," 6:486.

3. Greer, "Training of Ground Technicians," 6:629–30.

4. Greer, "Training of Ground Technicians," 6:629–30.

5. Hutter, "Cutting the Cord," 18–19.

6. Bureau of Ships, "Structural Repairs in Forward Areas During World War II," Naval History and Heritage Command, Dec. 1949, 1, https://www.history.navy.mil/research/library/online-reading-room/title-list-alphabetically/s/structural-repairs-forward-areas-wwii.html.

7. "Individual Training in Aircraft Maintenance in the AAF," *Army Air Forces Historical Studies,* no. 26 (Historical Division, 1944), 1, https://www.scribd.com/document/106636940/WWII-Aircraft-Mechanics-Training.

8. THE MAN WITH A PERFECT RECORD

1. George Keating, interview by Martin Madert, July 23, 2013, compact disc, Witness to War Foundation, Norcross, GA.

2. Greer, "Training of Ground Technicians," 6:629–31.

3. Bykofsky and Larson, *Operations Overseas,* 73–74.

4. Hinrichs, *Missing Planes,* xii.

5. Hinrichs, *Missing Planes,* 24.

6. N. B. Harbold to 3rd Bombardment Division, Nov. 16, 1944, private collection.

7. Colman, *Rosie the Riveter,* 16.

9. WITH A WELDER'S TORCH FOR A WEAPON

1. "World War I and the Legacy of Chemical Weapons," Stratfor Worldview, Apr. 22, 2015, https://worldview.stratfor.com/article/world-war-i-and-legacy-chemical-weapons.

2. "Ship Sightings in the Port of New York—50 Years Ago," World Ship Society Port of New York Branch, accessed Mar. 25, 2018, http://www.worldshipny.com/pony1952.shtml.

3. "Ship Sightings in the Port of New York—50 Years Ago."

4. Bykofsky and Larson, *Operations Overseas,* 73–74.

5. Garth, *St. Lô,* 1–6, 127.

10. ONE OF FIVE

1. Goldberg, "AAF Aircraft of World War II," 6:216–17.

2. Anderson, *Army Air Forces Stations,* 5.

3. Miller, *365th Fighter Squadron,* 10–13.

4. Jones and Dorr, "Cold Front."

5. Miller, *365th Fighter Squadron,* 8–9.

6. Howard Gurley to Patricia Buffington Jackson, Apr. 19, 2003, private collection.

7. Leslie Boze to Patricia Buffington Jackson, Oct. 6, 2003, private collection.

8. Leslie Boze to Patricia Buffington Jackson, Oct. 6, 2003, private collection.

9. Miller, *365th Fighter Squadron,* 18–24.

10. Miller, *365th Fighter Squadron,* 26.

11. Miller, *365th Fighter Squadron,* 28–44.

12. Miller, *365th Fighter Squadron,* 84–85.

13. Howard Gurley to Patricia Buffington Jackson, Apr. 19, 2003, private collection.

11. BEARING WITNESS

1. Lee, *Employment of Negro Troops,* 72.

2. Lee, *Employment of Negro Troops,* 111–12.

3. "Leon Bass, Educator and Witness to the Holocaust, Passes Away at 90," Georgia Commission on the Holocaust, Mar. 31, 2015, https://holocaust.georgia.gov/blog/2015-04-01/leon-bass-educator-and-witness-holocaust-passes-away-90.

4. Lee, *Employment of Negro Troops,* 68, 441–50.

5. Samuels, "Uncovering Lost Voices," 126–27.

6. M. Alexis Scott, "William A. Scott, III" (PowerPoint presentation, Association for the Study of African American Life and History, African Americans in Times of War, Atlanta, GA, Sept. 12, 2018).

7. Cole, *Ardennes,* 673–74.

8. Stewart, "A Reel Story of World War II."

9. William A. Scott III, interview by Cathy Solomon, United States Holocaust Memorial Museum, Oct. 1981, https://collections.ushmm.org/search/catalog/irn513324.

10. M. Alexis Scott, "William A. Scott, III."

11. M. Alexis Scott, "William A. Scott, III."

12. William A. Scott III, "WWII Veteran Remembers the Horror of the Holocaust," *Atlanta Daily World,* May 13, 2011, Politics, https://atlantadailyworld.com/2011/05/13/wwii-veteran-remembers-the-horror-of-the-holocaust-holocaust-commemoration/.

13. Scott, "WWII Veteran Remembers."

14. Murray, "Blacks and the Draft."

15. Scott, "WWII Veteran Remembers."

16. Delmont, "African-American Soldiers."

17. "Honoring American Liberators," United States Holocaust Memorial Museum, https://www.ushmm.org/m/pdfs/20040514-infantry-83.pdf.

18. Asa Gordon, "William A. Scott, III and the Holocaust: The Encounter of African American Liberators and Jewish Survivors at Buchenwald," accessed Jan. 22, 2019, http://asagordon.byethost10.com/LIBERATORS/ENCOUNTR.HTM.

19. Spielberg and Cesarani, *Last Days,* 222.

20. Scott, "William A. Scott, III."

21. Scott, "WWII Veteran Remembers."

22. Scott, "William A. Scott, III."

23. Scott III, interview by Cathy Solomon, United States Holocaust Memorial Museum.

12. ON FOOT, ON HORSEBACK, OR IN A SAMPAN

1. Jack Coyle, recording by the USO, Jan. 1944, private collection.

2. Jack Coyle to Ida Coyle, Mar. 18, 1943, private collection.

3. Jack Coyle to Ida Coyle, Sept. 8, 1943, private collection.

4. Jack Coyle to Ida Coyle, Nov. 3, 1943, private collection.

5. "A Look Back . . . The Office of Strategic Services: Training in the Forest," Central Intelligence Agency, May 21, 2009, https://www.cia.gov/news-information/featured-story-archive/office-of-strategic-services-training.html.

6. Jack Coyle to Ida Coyle, Nov. 17, 1943, private collection.

7. Jack Coyle to Ida Coyle, Mar. 9, 1944, private collection.

8. *Rice Paddy Navy: The Reminiscence,* 205–6.

9. Kleiner, *Flying Tigers,* 200–201.

10. Pike, *Hirohito's War,* 345–47.

11. Pike, *Hirohito's War,* 350.

12. Guy Tressler, interview and videography by Dan Cocks, *Veteran Voices of Pittsburgh Oral History Initiative Archive (Farkas Collection) and the Veterans Breakfast Club (VBC),* Nov. 30, 2013, http://veteranvoicesofpittsburgh.com/guy-tressler-navy/.

13. Stratton, *SACO,* 1–8; Yu, *Oss in China,* 31.

14. Allen, *My Name's Not Johnny!,* 52.

15. Morison, "U.S. Naval Group," 289–93.

16. Miles, *A Different Kind of War,* 3–4, 277.

17. Stratton, *SACO*, 66.

18. Jack Coyle to Ida Coyle, July 16, 1944, private collection.

19. *Rice Paddy Navy: The Reminiscence*, 198–200.

20. Mishler, *Sampan Sailor*, xii.

21. Allen, *My Name's Not Johnny!*, 48.

22. Miles, *A Different Kind of War*, 59.

23. Allen, *My Name's Not Johnny!*, 45–46.

24. Stratton, *SACO*, 195.

25. Miles, *A Different Kind of War*, 237.

26. Stratton, *SACO*, 30–33.

27. Stratton, *SACO*, 291–92.

28. *Rice Paddy Navy: The Reminiscence*, 128–31.

29. *Rice Paddy Navy: The Reminiscence*, 145.

30. US Navy Department, "SACO in China During World War II," Naval History and Heritage Command, Sept. 13, 1945, https://www.history.navy.mil/research/library/online-reading-room/title-list-alphabetically/s/saco.html.

31. Mishler, *Sampan Sailor*, xiii.

32. Allen, *My Name's Not Johnny!*, 46.

33. Mishler, *Sampan Sailor*, xiii.

34. Miles, *A Different Kind of War*, 537.

35. Chief of Naval Operations to Jack Coyle, 1959, private collection.

13. DEFYING THE ODDS

1. King, *In Spite of All Odds*, ix.

2. Dickson and Allen, *Bonus Army*, 1–5, 38.

3. Bureau of Naval Personnel, "The Negro in the Navy: United States Naval Administration History of World War II #84," Naval History and Heritage Command, 1947, https://www.history.navy.mil/research/library/online-reading-room/title-list-alphabetically/n/negro-navy-1947-adminhist84.html.

4. Brian Walsh, "RTC Command Celebrates Black History Month," Gosport, Feb. 22, 2013, 4, https://issuu.com/ballingerpublishing/docs/gosport-02-22-2013.

5. Wagner and Osborne, *Library of Congress World War II Companion*, 294–95.

6. Jordan, *American Warlords*, 54–58.

7. Nelson, *MacArthur in Japan*, 1:235–36.

8. Castillo, *Seabees of World War II*, 38.

9. Elly Farelly, "Bringing Home the 8 Million Boys after World War II; Operation Magic Carpet," War History Online, June 29, 2016, https://www.warhistoryonline.com/world-war-ii/brining-home-8-million-boys-wwii-operation-magic-carpet.html.

PART IV. GOING HOME

1. Sanders, "Redeployment and Demobilization," 7:545.

2. Sanders, "Redeployment and Demobilization," 7:554–58.

3. Farelly, "Bringing Home the 8 Million Boys after World War II."

14. INSIDE THE SECRET CITY

1. Donald G. McNeil Jr., "Plastic Bags to Keep Premature Babies Warm," *New York Times,* June 3, 2013, Global Health, http://www.nytimes.com/2013/06/04/health/plastic-bags-to-keep-premature-babies-warm.html.

2. William Head, "A Brief History of WR-ALC and Warner Robins AFB," Office of History, accessed Mar. 2, 2018, https://www.robins.af.mil/About-Us/History/.

3. Kay Grant, "Oak Ridge, the Town the Atomic Bomb Built," HistoryNet, June 1, 2010, http://www.historynet.com/oak-ridge-the-town-the-atomic-bomb-built.htm.

4. Kiernan, *Girls of Atomic City,* 101.

5. Kiernan, *Girls of Atomic City,* 68–69.

6. Robinson Jr., *Oak Ridge Story,* 93–96.

7. "Fire Warning," *Knoxville Journal Cavalcade,* July 30, 1950.

8. Robinson Jr., *Oak Ridge Story,* 93–96; Charles W. Johnson, "Oak Ridge," Tennessee Encyclopedia of History and Culture, Oct. 8, 2017, http://tennesseeencyclopedia.net/entries/oak-ridge/.

9. Johnson, "Oak Ridge."

15. HELPING, HELPING, HELPING

1. D. W. Robinson to Maxwell Cone, Apr. 26, 1963, private collection.

2. Frank Cone, "Lament of a Medical Officer Isolated by a Typhoon," in Frank Cone to Marian Cone, Nov. 17, 1941, private collection.

3. Bailey, *US Army Campaigns,* 4–7.

4. Bailey, *US Army Campaigns,* 4–7.

5. Frank Cone to Marian Cone, Nov. 17, 1941, private collection.

6. Morton, *Fall of the Philippines,* 84–88.

7. Morton, *Fall of the Philippines,* 161.

8. Frank Cone to Marian Cone, Dec. 30, 1941, private collection.

9. Frank Cone to Bess Cone, Mar. 2, 1942, private collection.

10. Frank Cone to Marian Cone, Dec. 30, 1941, private collection.

11. Frank Cone to Bess Cone, Mar. 2, 1942, private collection.

12. Whitman, "Last U.S. Horse Cavalry Charge," 38–45.

13. Young, *Battle of Bataan,* 7.

14. Bailey, *US Army Campaigns,* 20.

15. Blanton, "Just to Remember," 4–5.

16. Wade Robinson to Maxwell Cone, Apr. 26, 1963, private collection.

17. Wade Robinson to Maxwell Cone, Apr. 26, 1963, private collection.

18. Wade Robinson to Maxwell Cone, Apr. 26, 1963, private collection.

19. Wade Robinson to Marian Cone, Nov. 10, 1945, private collection.

20. Sides, *Ghost Soldiers,* 25, 65–71, 247–50.

21. LeMoyne Bleich to Marian Cone, Nov. 5, 1945, private collection.

22. Burfeind, "Memorial Shows Horror," 5.

23. *Manila American Cemetery and Memorial* (Arlington, VA: American Battle Monuments Commission, n.d.).

16. TO SEE THE WORLD

1. Blood, *Kindred Spirits,* 1.
2. Bellafaire, *Army Nurse Corps,* 4.
3. Blood, *Kindred Spirits,* 8.
4. Blood, *Kindred Spirits,* 21.
5. Blood, *Kindred Spirits,* 68–96.
6. Massman, *Hospital Ships of World War II,* 2–5, 48–50.
7. Blood, *Kindred Spirits,* 76–77.
8. Garcia, "German POWs on the American Homefront."
9. Blood, *Kindred Spirits,* 90.
10. Blood, *Kindred Spirits,* 95–96.
11. Emily Yellin, "Lining Up for Wartime Weddings," *New York Times,* Feb. 2, 2017, https://www.nytimes.com/interactive/projects/cp/weddings/165-years-of-wedding-announcements/world-war-two-weddings.
12. Blood, *Kindred Spirits,* 101, 132.

17. A SOUTHERN LADY IN THE RANKS

1. "Radio Address Summarizing the State of the Union Message," *The American Presidency Project,* accessed Mar. 26, 2018, https://www.presidency.ucsb.edu/node/210108.
2. "Radio Address Summarizing the State of the Union Message."
3. "Radio Address Summarizing the State of the Union Message."
4. Debbie M. Lord, "*Mobile Press Register* 200th Anniversary: Mobile Plays Larger Role in War Effort; Racial Tensions Rise (1940–1949)," *Mobile Press Register,* June 25, 2013, http://blog.al.com/live/2013/06/mobile_press-register_annivers.html.
5. Taylor, *United States Army in World War II,* 128.
6. Taylor, *United States Army in World War II,* 129.
7. Taylor, *United States Army in World War II,* 131.
8. Richard Stradling, "Come Celebrate Camp Butner's 75th Anniversary on Saturday," *News and Observer,* Sept. 21, 2017, http://www.newsobserver.com/news/local/article174559286.html.

18. INNOVATING AND IMPROVISING

1. James M. Myers, "Camp Barkeley," Handbook of Texas Online, Texas State Historical Association, accessed Feb. 24, 2018, http://www.tshaonline.org/handbook/online/articles/qbc02.
2. Dan Sebby, "Dewitt General Hospital," California Military Department, accessed Feb. 24, 2018, http://www.militarymuseum.org/DewittGenHosp.html.
3. Wiltse, *Medical Service,* 367–75.
4. Wiltse, *Medical Service,* 375–77.
5. "The Potsdam Conference, 1945," Office of the Historian, US Department of State, accessed Feb. 25, 2018, https://history.state.gov/milestones/1937-1945/potsdam-conf.

6. Sanders, "Redeployment and Demobilization," 7:570–72.

7. Sasha Archibald, "Million Dollar Point," *Cabinet* 10 (Spring 2003), http://www.cab inetmagazine.org/issues/10/million_point.php.

8. "Summary of AG-018 United Nations Relief and Rehabilitation Administration (UNRRA) (1943–1946)," United Nations, https://search.archives.un.org/downloads/united -nations-relief-and-rehabilitation-administration-unrra-1943-1946.pdf.

19. AN ENGINEER AMONG THE HEADSTONES

1. Francis D. Peterson, "In Response to a Daughter's Request" (unpublished memoir, 1992), 2.

2. "46th Quartermaster Graves Registration Company," WWII US Medical Research Center, Unit Histories, accessed Mar. 31, 2018, https://www.med-dept.com/unit-histories /46th-quartermaster-graves-registration-company/.

3. "History of F. E. Warren Air Force Base," US Air Force, Feb. 27, 2018, http://www .warren.af.mil/About-Us/Fact-Sheets/Display/Article/331280/.

4. Peterson, "In Response to a Daughter's Request," 8–9.

5. Peterson, "In Response to a Daughter's Request," 8–9.

6. Peterson, "In Response to a Daughter's Request," 9.

7. "46th Quartermaster Graves Registration Company."

8. Steere, "Graves Registration Service in World War II," 73–74, 140–41.

9. "46th Quartermaster Graves Registration Company."

10. "46th Quartermaster Graves Registration Company."

11. "46th Quartermaster Graves Registration Company."

12. Lt. Gen. George S. Patton Jr. to First Lt. Francis D. Peterson, Dec. 13, 1943, private collection.

13. Peterson, "In Response to a Daughter's Request," 13.

14. Peterson, "In Response to a Daughter's Request," 10; Rottman, *World War II Axis Booby Traps,* 10–12.

15. Eric Niderost, "World War II: German Raid on Bari," HistoryNet, June 12, 2006, http://www.historynet.com/world-war-ii-german-raid-on-bari.htm.

16. Barton J. Bernstein, "Why We Didn't Use Poison Gas in World War II," *American Heritage* 36, no. 5 (Aug./Sept. 1985), https://www.americanheritage.com/content/why-we -didn't-use-poison-gas-world-war-ii.

17. Niderost, "World War II."

18. E. C. Helms, Captain, QMC, Dec. 1, 1944, private collection.

19. Mason B. Webb, "Burying the Dead in WWII: The Quartermaster Graves Registration Service," Warfare History Network, Dec. 24, 2018, http://warfarehistorynetwork.com/daily /wwii/burying-the-dead-in-wwii-the-quartermaster-graves-registration-service/.

20. Webb, Warfare History Network.

21. Commemorative Sites Booklet (Washington, DC: American Battle Monuments Commission, 2018), 2.

22. Peterson, "In Response to a Daughter's Request," 26.

EPILOGUE

1. America's Wars Fact Sheet, US Department of Veterans Affairs, May 2019.

2. Groom, *1942*, 255.

3. Ambrose, *Band of Brothers*, 61.

Selected Bibliography

Adams, Peter Caddick. *Snow & Steel: The Battle of the Bulge, 1944–1945.* Oxford: Oxford Univ. Press, 2014.

"Address in Celebration of Liberty Fleet Day. September 26, 1941." *Public Papers of the Presidents of the United States, Franklin D. Roosevelt, 1941 Volume.* New York: Harper Brothers Publishers, 1950.

Allen, Keith. *My Name's Not Johnny!: A Journey of Life, Love, Courage, and Faith.* N.p., 2016.

Alter, James. *From Campus to Combat: A College Boy Becomes a WWII Army Flier.* Philadelphia, PA: Garrett County Press, 2006.

Ambrose, Stephen E. *Band of Brothers, E Company, 506th Regiment, 101st Airborne, from Normandy to Hitler's Eagle's Nest.* New York: Simon and Schuster, 1992.

Anderson, Barry. *Army Air Forces Stations: A Guide to Where US Army Air Forces Personnel Served in the United Kingdom During World War II.* Maxwell Air Force Base, AL: USAF Historical Research Center, Jan. 1985.

Archibald, Sasha. "Million Dollar Point." *Cabinet* 10 (Spring 2003). http://www.cabinet magazine.org/issues/10/million_point.php.

Ashton, Diane. "Expanding Jewish Life in America, 1826–1901." In *The Columbia History of Jews and Judaism in America,* edited by Marc Lee Raphael. New York: Columbia Univ. Press, 2008.

Bailey, Jennifer L. *The US Army Campaigns of World War II: Philippine Islands.* Washington, DC: Center of Military History, United States Army, n.d.

Bellafaire, Judith A. *The Army Nurse Corps. The Campaigns of World War II: A World War II Commemorative Series.* Washington, DC: Center of Military History, US Army, 2011.

Blanton, N. H. "Just to Remember." *The Quan.* Nov. 1982.

Blood, Orpha Mae Riggle. *Kindred Spirits in the Service of Uncle Sam.* Stephenville, PA: R. and J. McDonald, 2013.

Burfeind, Barbara. "Memorial Shows Horror." *The Quan.* Mar. 1984.

Bykofsky, Joseph, and Harold Larson. *Operations Overseas. The United States Army in World War II: The Technical Services, The Transportation Corps,* edited by Kent Roberts Greenfield. Washington, DC: Center of Military History, United States Army, 1990.

Carter, John D. "The Air Transport Command." In Craven and Cate, *Services around the World,* 3–45.

———. "The Early Development of Air Transport and Ferrying." In Craven and Cate, *Plans and Early Operations,* 310–65.

————. "The North Atlantic Route." In Craven and Cate, *Services around the World,* 92–113.

Castillo, Edmund L. *The Seabees of World War II.* 2nd ed. New York: Random House, 2010.

Christie, Carl A. *Ocean Bridge: The History of RAF Ferry Command.* Toronto: Univ. of Toronto Press, 1995.

Cole, Hugh M. *The Ardennes: Battle of the Bulge. The United States Army in World War II: The European Theater of Operations,* edited by Stetson Conn. Washington, DC: Center of Military History, United States Army, 1965.

Cole, Jean Hascall. *Women Pilots of World War II.* Salt Lake City: Univ. of Utah Press, 1992.

Colman, Penny. *Rosie the Riveter: Women Working on the Homefront in World War II.* New York: Crown Publishers, 1995.

Craf, John R. "The Facts about the A.S.T.P. Reserve." *The Clearing House* 18, no. 7 (Mar. 1944). https://www.jstor.org/stable/30187137.

Craven, Wesley Frank, and James Lea Cate, eds. *Men in Planes.* Vol. 6 of *The Army Air Forces in World War II.* Washington, DC: United States Air Force, 1983.

————, eds. *Plans and Early Operations.* Vol. 1 of *The Army Air Forces in World War II.* Washington, DC: United States Air Force, 1983.

————, eds. *Services around the World.* Vol. 7 of *The Army Air Forces in World War II.* Washington, DC: United States Air Force, 1983.

Curtiss P-40 Warhawk: Pilot Training Manual for the P-40. Washington, DC: United States Army Air Force, n.d.

Delmont, Matthew. "Why African-American Soldiers Saw World War II as a Two-Front Battle." *Smithsonian Magazine,* Aug. 24, 2017. https://www.smithsonianmag.com/history/why-african-american-soldiers-saw-world-war-ii-two-front-battle-180964616/.

D'Este, Carlo. *Patton: A Genius for War.* New York: Harper Perennial, 1996.

Dickson, Paul, and Thomas B. Allen. *The Bonus Army: An American Epic.* New York: Walker, 2004.

Dimbleby, Jonathan. *The Battle of the Atlantic: How the Allies Won the War.* Oxford: Oxford Univ. Press, 2016.

Ebbert, Jean, and Marie-Beth Hall. *Crossed Currents: Navy Women from WWI to Tailhook.* Washington, DC: Brasseys, 1993.

Flynn, George Q. *The Draft: 1940–1973.* Lawrence: Univ. Press of Kansas, 1993.

Fredriksen, John C. *Warbirds: An Illustrated Guide to U.S. Military Aircraft, 1915–2000.* Santa Barbara, CA: ABC-CLIO, 1999.

Garcia, J. Malcolm. "German POWs on the American Homefront." *Smithsonian,* Sept. 15, 2009. http://www.smithsonianmag.com/history/german-pows-on-the-american-homefront-141009996/.

Garth, David. *St. Lô.* American Forces in Action Series. Washington, DC: Center of Military History, United States Army, 1946.

Geroux, William. *The Mathews Men: Seven Brothers and the War Against Hitler's U-Boats.* New York: Penguin, 2016.

Goldberg, Alfred. "AAF Aircraft of World War II." In Craven and Cate, *Men and Planes,* 193–227.

————. "The AAF's Logistical Organization." In Craven and Cate, *Men and Planes,* 362–97.

————. "Allocation and Distribution of Aircraft." In Craven and Cate, *Men and Planes*, 398–424.

Greer, Thomas H. "Individual Training of Flying Personnel." In Craven and Cate, *Men and Planes*, 557–99.

————. "Training of Ground Technicians and Service Personnel." In Craven and Cate, *Men and Planes*, 629–73.

Groom, Winston. *1942: The Year That Tried Men's Souls*. New York: Grove Press, 2005.

Heck, Frank H. "Airline to China." In Craven and Cate, *Services around the World*, 114–51.

————. "The Northwest Air Route to Alaska." In Craven and Cate, *Services around the World*, 152–72.

Hinrichs, Edward. *Missing Planes of the 452nd Bomb Group*. 3rd ed. Victoria, BC: Trafford, 1995.

Hogan, David W., Jr. *The US Army Campaigns of World War II: India Burma, 1942-1945*. Washington, DC: Center of Military History, United States Army, n.d.

Hutter, Ryan M. "Cutting the Cord: Sustaining Untethered Air Superiority Operations in the Pacific." Montgomery, AL: Air Univ., Air Command and Staff College, 2016.

Jacobs, Bruce. "Hurrah for the Red, White, and Blue." *Army Magazine*, Aug. 2000.

Jordan, Jonathan W. *American Warlords: How Roosevelt's High Command Led America to Victory in World War II*. New York: NAL Caliber, 2015.

————. *Brothers, Rivals, Victors: Eisenhower, Patton, Bradley, and the Partnership that Drove the Allied Conquest in Europe*. New York: NAL Caliber, 2012.

Joyner, Leslie M. *James Hamilton Keeton and His Planes*. Meridian, MS: Lauderdale County Department of Archives and History, 2010.

Kamarck, Kristy N. *The Selective Service System and Draft Registration: Issues for Congress*. CRS Report R44452. Washington, DC: Congressional Research Service, 2016.

Jones, Thomas D., and Robert F. Dorr. "Cold Front: Meet the Men Who Kept the Thunderbolts Flying." *Air and Space Magazine*, July 2005. https://www.airspacemag.com/military-aviation/cold-front-7359183/.

Keefer, Louis E. *Scholars in Foxholes: The Story of the Army Specialized Training Program in World War II*. Jefferson, NC: McFarland Publishing, 1988.

Keim, Albert N. *The CPS Story: An Illustrated History of Civilian Public Service*. Intercourse, PA: Good Books, 1990.

Kiernan, Denise. *The Girls of Atomic City: The Untold Story of the Women Who Helped Win World War II*. New York: Touchstone, 2013.

King, Earnest J. *U.S. Navy at War, 1941–1945: Official Reports to the Secretary of the Navy*. Washington, DC: United States Navy, 1946.

King, Howard O. *In Spite of All Odds*. Atlanta, GA: Howard O. King, 2017.

Kleiner, Sam. *The Flying Tigers: The Untold Story of the American Pilots Who Waged a Secret War against Japan*. New York: Viking, 2018.

Kooker, Arthur R. "The Foundations of a War Training Program." In Craven and Cate, *Men and Planes*, 454–87.

Lee, Ulysses. *The Employment of Negro Troops. The United States Army in World War II: Special Studies*, edited by Stetson Conn. Washington, DC: Center of Military History, United States Army, 2001.

Lidell-Hart, H., ed. *The Rommel Papers.* New York: Da Capo Press, 1953.

Massman, Emory A. *Hospital Ships of World War II: An Illustrated Reference to 39 United States Military Vessels.* Jefferson, NC: McFarland Publishing, 1999.

McCormick, Richard P. "Rutgers in World War II." *Journal of the Rutgers University Libraries* 58 (1997): 1–10. http://dx.doi.org/10.14713/jrul.v58i0.23.

Miles, Milton E. *A Different Kind of War: The Little-Known Story of the Combined Guerrilla Forces Created in China by the U.S. Navy and the Chinese during World War II.* Garden City, NY: Doubleday, 1967.

Miller, Kent. *The 365th Fighter Squadron in World War II: In Action over Europe with the P-47.* Atglen, PA: Schiffler Military History, 2006.

Mingos, Howard, ed. *The Aircraft Yearbook for 1944.* New York: Lanciar Publishers, 1944.

Mishler, Clauton. *Sampan Sailor: A Navy Man's Adventures in WWII China.* Washington, DC: Brassey's, 1994.

Morison, Samuel Eliot. "U.S. Naval Group, China." Chap. 14 in *The Liberation of the Philippines: Luzon, Mindanao, the Visayas, 1944–1945.* Vol. 13 of *The History of United States Naval Operations in World War II.* Chicago: Univ. of Illinois Press, 1959.

Morton, Louis. *The Fall of the Philippines. The United States Army in World War II: The War in the Pacific,* edited by Kent Roberts Greenfield. Washington, DC: Center of Military History, United States Army, 1953.

Murray, Paul T. "Blacks and the Draft: A History of Institutional Racism." *Journal of Black Studies* 2, no. 1 (1971): 64. http://www.jstor.org/stable/2783700.

Nelson, Harold W., ed. *MacArthur in Japan, the Occupation: Military Phase.* Vol. 1 supplement in *Reports of General MacArthur.* Washington, DC: United States Army, 1994.

Palmer, Robert R. *The Procurement of Enlisted Personnel: The Problem of Quality. The United States Army in World War II: The Army Ground Forces,* edited by Kent Roberts Greenfield. Washington, DC: Center of Military History, United States Army, 1991.

Pike, Francis. *Hirohito's War: The Pacific War, 1941–1945.* New York: Bloomsbury Publishing, 2015.

"The President's Statement on Maritime Day. May 22, 1942." *Public Papers of the Presidents of the United States, Franklin D. Roosevelt, 1942 Volume. New York: Harper Brothers Publishers, 1950.*

Raymond, George, and Fred Crawford. *Three Crawford Brothers: The WWII Memoirs of Three Pilots.* Bloomington, IN: Authorhouse, 2008.

Rice Paddy Navy: The Reminiscence of the SACO US Veterans. Chinese National Military Affairs Office, n.d.

Robinson, George O., Jr. *The Oak Ridge Story: The Saga of a People Who Share in History.* Kingsport, TN: Southern Publishers, 1950.

Rottman, Gordon L. *World War II Axis Booby Traps and Sabotage Tactics.* Oxford: Osprey Publishing, 2009.

Samuels, Gregory. "Uncovering Lost Voices: African American Involvement in the Liberation of Concentration Camps During the Holocaust." In *Mending Walls: Historical, Socio-Political, Economic, and Geographical Perspectives,* edited by Richard A. Diem and Michael J. Berson. Charlotte, NC: Information Age Publishing, 2017.

Sanders, Chauncey E. "Redeployment and Demobilization." In Craven and Cate, *Services around the World*, 545–82.

Scrivener, Laurie. "US Military Women in World War II: The SPAR, WAC, WAVES, WASP, and Women Marines in US Government Publications." *Journal of Government Information* 26, no. 4 (1999): 361–66. https://doi.org/10.1016/S1352-0237(99)00051-9.

Sides, Hampton. *Ghost Soldiers: The Forgotten Epic Story of World War II's Most Dramatic Mission*. New York: Doubleday, 2001.

Sixth Ferrying Group. Baton Rouge: Army and Navy Publishing Company of Louisiana, 1944.

Smith, Jean Edward. *Eisenhower in War and Peace*. New York: Random House, 2012.

Spielberg, Steven, and David Cesarani. *The Last Days: Steven Spielberg and Survivors of the Shoah Visual History Foundation*. New York: St. Martin's Press, 1999.

Steere, Edward. "The Graves Registration Service in World War II." In *QMC Historical Studies*. Washington, DC: Office of the Quartermaster General, 1951.

Stewart, Phillip W. "A Reel Story of World War II: The United News Collection of Newsreels Documents the Battlefield and the Home Front." *Prologue Magazine*, Fall 2015. https://www.archives.gov/publications/prologue/2015/fall/united-newsreels.html.

Stout, Jay A. *Fortress Ploesti: The Campaign to Destroy Hitler's Oil*. Havertown, PA: Casemate, 2011.

Stratton, Roy Olin. *SACO: The Rice Paddy Navy*. 2nd ed. Tucson, AZ: US Press and Graphics, 2004.

Taylor, Richard R. *The United States Army in World War II: Medical Training in WWII*, edited by William S. Mullins. Washington, DC: Medical Department, United States Army, 1974.

Treadwell, Mattie E. *The Women's Army Corps. The United States Army in World War II, Special Studies*, edited by Kent Roberts Greenfield. Washington, DC: Center of Military History, United States Army, 1991.

"WAACS and WAVES." *Life Magazine*, Mar. 15, 1943.

Wagner, Margaret E. and Linda Barrett Osborne. *The Library of Congress World War II Companion*, edited by David Kennedy. New York: Simon and Schuster, 2007.

Wardlow, Chester. *Movements, Training, and Supply. The United States Army in World War II: The Technical Services, The Transportation Corps*, edited by Kent Roberts Greenfield. Washington, DC: Center of Military History, United States Army, 1990.

———. *Responsibilities, Organization and Operations. The United States Army in World War II: The Technical Services, the Transportation Corps*, edited by Kent Roberts Greenfield. Washington, DC: Center of Military History, United States Army, 1999.

Whitman, John W. "Last U.S. Horse Cavalry Charge." *Military History* (June 1995): 38–45.

Wiggins, Melanie. *Torpedoes in the Gulf: Galveston and the U-Boats, 1942–1943*. College Station: Texas A&M Univ., 1995.

Williams, Greg H. *The Liberty Ships of World War II: A Record of the 2,710 Vessels and Their Builders, Operators and Namesakes, With a History of the Jeremiah O'Brien*. Jefferson, NC: McFarland Publishing, 2014.

Wilmot, Chester. *The Struggle for Europe*. Old Saybrook, CT: Konecky and Konecky, 1952.

Wiltse, Charles M. *Medical Service in the Mediterranean and Minor Theaters. The United*

States Army in World War II: The Technical Services, edited by Stetson Conn. Washington, DC: Center of Military History, United States Army, 1987.

Young, Donald J. *The Battle of Bataan: A Complete History.* 2nd ed. Jefferson, NC: McFarland Publishing, 2009.

Yu, Maochun. *OSS in China: Prelude to Cold War.* Annapolis, MD: Naval Institute Press, 2011.

Index